# Beyond the Pale

# QUESTIONS FOR FEMINISM

Edited by Michèle Barrett, Annette Kuhn, Anne Phillips and Ann Rosalind Jones, this socialist feminist series aims to address, in a lively way and on an international basis, the wide range of political and theoretical questions facing contemporary feminism.

THE POLITICS OF DIVERSITY Feminism, Marxism and Nationalism
*edited by Michèle Barrett & Roberta Hamilton*

UNEQUAL WORK *by Veronica Beechey*

THE WEARY SONS OF FREUD *by Cathérine Clément*

FEMALE SEXUALIZATION A Collective Work of Memory
*by Frigga Haug et al.*

SEA CHANGES Culture and Feminism *by Cora Kaplan*

WOMEN AND THE NEW GERMAN CINEMA *by Julia Knight*

CONSUMING FICTION *by Terry Lovell*

THE PIRATE'S FIANCEE Feminism, Reading, Postmodernism
*by Meaghan Morris*

ABORTION AND WOMAN'S CHOICE The State, Sexuality and Reproductive Freedom *by Rosalind Pollack Petchesky*

FEMALE SPECTATORS Looking at Film and Television
*edited by E. Deidre Pribram*

SECRETARIES TALK Sexuality, Power and Work *by Rosemary Pringle*

READING THE ROMANCE Women, Patriarchy and Popular Literature
*by Janice A. Radway*

GRAFTS Feminist Cultural Criticism *edited by Susan Sheridan*

BEYOND THE PALE White Women, Racism and History *by Vron Ware*

PLAYING THE STATE Australian Feminist Interventions
*edited by Sophie Watson*

# Beyond the Pale

## White Women, Racism and History

VRON WARE

VERSO
London · New York

First published by Verso 1992


**Verso**
UK: 6 Meard Street, London W1V 3HR
USA: 29 West 35th Street, New York, NY 10001-2291

Verso is the imprint of New Left Books

**British Library Cataloguing in Publication Data**
A catalogue record for this book is available

**Library of Congress Cataloging-in-Publication Data**
A catalogue record for this book is available

ISBN 0 86091 336 8
ISBN 0 86091 552 2 Pbk

Typeset in Garamond by York House Typographic Ltd, London
Design consultancy: Paul Elliman
Printed and bound in Great Britain by
Biddles Ltd, Guildford and King's Lynn

*For Paul (your turn now)*

*and*

*Katie Impey, who deserved more and better*

## Contents

# Sources

Illustrations are courtesy of the following:

Dak bungalow: author's collection, courtesy of Harald Lechenperg. 'Europe Supported by Africa and America': from *John Gabriel Stedman's Narrative of a Five Years Expedition Against the Revolted Negroes of Surinam*, newly transcribed from the original 1790 manuscript, edited, and with an Introduction and Notes, by Richard and Sally Price, Johns Hopkins University Press, Baltimore and London 1988 (by permission of Richard and Sally Price). Annette Ackroyd: by permission of The British Library. Josephine Butler: Mary Evans Picture Library. Women of the Ku Klux Klan: Charles Moore/Black Star/Colorific. Ida B. Wells: Department of Special Collections, the University of Chicago Library. Catherine Impey: author's collection. Jerry Hall: Ford Models Inc., and Jerry Hall.

# Acknowledgements

This book seems to have been growing with me for most of my adult life. It would be impossible even to remember everyone who has contributed or helped along the way. I am happy to have this chance to thank my parents, Tom and Elizabeth Ware, for their trust and tolerance.

My gratitude goes especially to Cora Kaplan, Kate Pullinger, Olivia Smith for their enthusiasm and encouragement all the way through, and for reading chapters and making suggestions; to Tricia Bohn, Miranda Davies, Hermione Harris for talking and listening; to Rosa Ainley, Mark Ainley, Karen Alexander, Valerie Amos, Pete Ayrton, David A. Bailey, Jos Boys, Sue Cavanagh, Max Farrar, Beryl Gilroy, Paul Hallam, Shaheen Haque, François Lack, Benita Ludmer, Angela McRobbie, Derrick Saldaan McClintock, Sarah Martin, Bridget Orr, Pratibha Parmar, Ann Phoenix, Nick Robin, Fleming Rogilds, Cynthia Rose, Joe Sim, Lynne Tillman, Caroline Ware, Val Wilmer, Patrick Wright for all kinds of support and encouragement (and sometimes babysitting); to Isaac Julien for buying me books and helping me out with some tricky bits; to friends who have died: Maurice Ludmer, who helped me find direction in 1977; Peggy Snow, whose gentleness and wit is so badly missed; Sarah Baylis, who once rightly scolded me for describing the book as 'just a . . .'

I would like to thank Barbara Taylor, Catherine Hall and Laurence Marlow for passing on valuable references and information; the Clark family archives in Street for their kind co-operation; Amana Gibson, Chris Gibson and Ruth Smith for extra special childcare; Annette Kuhn and Anne Phillips for their enthusiasm for the book in the first place and their patience in waiting for it to happen; and Stephen Morland for a new friendship.

Living in the USA gave me the time to finish the book: I will always be grateful to Hazel Carby, not just for scrutinizing the final draft, but for helping us set up temporary home there with the help of Michael Denning and Nicholas Carby-Denning. I would also like to thank Judith Aissen, Ben Clifford and Jim Clifford especially for their support in being parents, in the hope that our many interrupted discussions may continue; and my contemporaries Dana Seman and Gloria Watkins who helped to enlarge my wardrobe creatively as well as my mind.

Marcus and Cora each gave me a new purpose and a new rhythm to work in. Some of my best ideas happened in their company, probably because they always gave me good reason to stop working, or maybe because their energy and creativity occasionally rub off.

Thanks is not enough for my two collaborators and friends who really made this book begin and end, who gave me guidance and inspiration all the way through, and whose ideas were incorporated at every stage:

Mandy Rose, whose own thinking and political integrity have contributed massively to this project, who co-wrote the original outline for the book after we had jointly unearthed much of the material in Part four, and who then, amongst many other things, suggested and researched Annette Ackroyd as a case study.

Paul Gilroy, whose immense knowledge, integrity and insight has enriched my own writing and thinking beyond measure; and who, by sharing everything else from broken nights to the word processor, turned this book into a joint endeavour without ever writing a word of it.

# Introduction

> Connections can only be traced so far before they begin to be politically dangerous. For example, few white feminists have explored how our understandings of gender relations, self, and theory are partially constituted in and through the experiences of living in a culture in which asymmetric race relations are a central organizing principle of society. 
>
> Jane Flax[1]

One night, nearing the end of writing this book, I happened to catch the tail end of a Conservative Party political broadcast on television. Thinking that I was watching an unscheduled horror movie I was at first puzzled by the sight of a lone baby lying in its cot in the dark while a violent storm threatened to pull the house from its foundations. Suddenly the film cut to a woman in her nightclothes kissing a very pink and cheerful baby. Gradually I realized the connection between the two images. The mother was in her nightclothes because she had just woken up from a nightmare in which her baby was being threatened by the destruction of the environment. Against a background of dreamy New Age music and repeated shots of the besotted mother and her child, a man's voice assured listeners that the Conservative Party had placed the task of saving the environment on top of its agenda. In a crescendo of images and music (the father appeared at this point, fully dressed, to allay fears that the mother might be a single parent) the commercial ended with the reassuring message that the Conservative Party was going to stop the threat of destruction which hung over 'us' all.

What interested me first about this propaganda was the way that the relationship between the woman and her baby was being used to signify ideas about both 'nature' and nation. On one level it might seem very obvious to read the narrative as an attempt to make the ideology of the nuclear family indispensable to the survival of the 'natural' world. A great deal of environmentalism is dedicated to saving the world for 'our children', and there is not necessarily anything dubious about this. Yet on another level, the figure of the comfortably well-off mother with her blue-eyed baby, exhibiting all the right maternal instincts, was a more complex figure who was likely to have a different effect on different groups of people, and it seemed important to work out how the imagery might be interpreted.

In just a few minutes the film was able to connect her womanness with vulnerability, sensitivity, passion, security, danger, dependence, motherhood. These qualities and attributes were suggested primarily by her gender, but her 'race', her 'whiteness', was also working in less visible ways to reinforce the racist and masculinist ideology that informed the making of the commercial. How differently would the message have read if either of the parents or the baby had not been white? It would have immediately transformed the size and constituency of the world that was being threatened by destruction. As it was, the nuclear family could be read as the cornerstone of the nation, defined in a racially exclusive way. The baby represented the future – it was 'white'. The father stood for authority – he too was 'white'. The mother both symbolized 'nature' and stood as the link between the 'natural' world and man's attempts to live in harmony with it. By being 'white' her image was able to convey complex messages about race and gender which defied a simple explanation.

This book is predicated on a recognition that to be white and female is to occupy a social category that is inescapably racialized as well as gendered. It is not about *being* a white woman, it is about *being thought of* as a white woman. In other words I have concentrated on the development of ideas and ideologies of whiteness rather than analysing what it actually means to grow up white in a white supremacist society. I understand 'race' to be a socially constructed category with absolutely no basis in biology; the term 'racism' encompasses all the various relations of power that have arisen from the domination of one racial group over another. This accounts for the way I have referred to black and white people throughout without specifying the obvious diversity of either category. In the ideological framework that I discuss, what matters is that a person is either white or non-white, even though the implications of their particular kind of blackness, or non-whiteness, is fundamentally affected by their ethnic or cultural origin. At the same time I recognize that this diversity exists and creates its own politics, but that is not my concern here.

In my search to unravel the different meanings of white womanhood I was forced to become a historian, searching for significant moments in the past which would explain how this category was produced. My two central themes are, first, the need to perceive white femininity as a historically constructed concept and, second, the urgency of understanding how feminism has developed as a political movement in a racist society. Although the questions that I raise in these historical chapters are derived from nineteenth-century political life they are questions that persist into the present. For instance, I discuss how particular English women dealt with cultural difference when they encountered women in India a hundred years ago, focusing on tensions among feminists that continue to survive in the late twentieth century. I have used the word 'feminism' throughout to mean the political formation that grew out of the early nineteenth-century demands for women's rights, and which continued to oppose and redefine dominant views of what constituted 'womanhood'.

Although framed within a British context, I think that both these themes will be relevant in any country where structures of white supremacy, racism and male dominance continue to affect people's lives. The book was mainly written in England but finished in the US which not only allowed me to feel closer to some of the historical material but also gave me a more direct sense of the likely political currency of my argument in different places. I arrived in New York just in time to read about the highly publicized trial of three black teenagers accused of raping and beating an affluent young white woman who had been jogging in Central Park. The crime itself and subsequent police action had quickly become symbols of the ungovernability of New York, a city widely seen to be disrupted by violence and racial tension. Before and during the trial different voices attributed racism to different sources: to the accused young men for choosing a white victim; to the police who had arrested them and others and obtained confessions; to the media; to the people who defended the woman's right to jog alone in Central Park. Comparisons were made between this case and the police and public response to recent racist assaults on black people: particular analogies were drawn with the case of Tawana Brawley, a young black girl who claimed to have been the victim of a gross racial and sexual assault. Here the femininity of both victims was used to focus on the racism entailed in the different ways that their cases were dealt with by the authorities, but there was apparently no attempt to connect this racism with the fact that both women claimed to have been victims of male violence. The whole case of the Central Park rape showed up once again the difficulties of composing an anti-racist feminist response to the spectre of the rape of a white woman by black men and then making that voice heard above the cacophony of sexist and racist babble that arose when the crime became public.

I wrote this book in an attempt to understand the links between racism and male dominance so that being against one form of oppression involves the possibility of being against the other, with nothing taken for granted. I quickly found that while there is one set of problems involved in knowing what to say about this interconnection, there is another in knowing just how to talk about it. Throughout the book I have repeatedly had to address the difficulties involved in finding a language that would express the links between race and gender without prioritizing, without oversimplifying. Partly in response to this, and also as a way of connecting all the different strands of history, I move between a number of voices and styles throughout the book. For instance, I have used straightforward historical accounts and biography where I feel that the information is relatively unknown; turning to autobiography, both my own and others', not only to bring political dilemmas alive but also to underline the importance of recognizing different sorts of narratives within the history of feminism itself. But to suggest that this is from start to finish a book about history would be misleading: where I break off to describe and analyse images that I have run into on the train, at the dentist's, on the television, it is to remind myself as much as the reader that I am talking about ideologies that surround and influence us now. I feel what I have written is, in a sense, provisional; I cover a lot of ground but at the end I am only just ready to start talking about theoretical questions and political strategies that follow on from my initial argument.

The book takes the form of a series of interconnected essays which are best read in the order in which they appear. Parts 1 and 5 both deal with contemporary feminism and racism while the three middle sections deal with history. Each of these is based on primary sources, supplemented by background reading on women's history, black history and histories of slavery, abolition or imperialism. The notes are intended either as references or suggestions for further research, and sometimes for making points that seem tangential to the main argument.

Part 1, which was written as a series of discussions using the different voices that I have described, begins by identifying various images of white womanhood embedded in familiar racist discourses, focusing on two important political arenas: crime and education. It considers the reasons why white feminists have managed to avoid dissecting these cultural and racial components of white femininity, although they have become eager to hear what black women have to say about their racialized and gendered identities. I use autobiography here to help situate myself both as a feminist and as a woman who has been politically engaged with anti-racism. This is partly a response to the difficulties of talking about the shortcomings of feminism, an attempt to avoid over-generalizing and speaking on behalf of other women; but it is also a straightforward account of my entitlement to speak about these issues. It leads up to the point at which I began to identify the need for historical research. My argument for the reinterpretation of history begins with recent feminism in Britain and the US and then looks back over four hundred years to the beginning of racial slavery.

Part 2 suggests that the politics of anti-slavery is an appropriate starting point to examine the problematic nature of the category 'woman' in feminist historical research. Although the main part of this essay concerns abolitionism as an organized political movement, I first introduce the idea that women's literature prior to and during this period contained a fascinating discourse on the relationship between the white woman and the slave, something which needs to be taken into account when considering historical connections between race and gender. I then take two abolitionist pamphlets written by different women's groups as a basis for thinking about the inclusiveness of womanhood as a category intersected by race as well as class. In looking at the separate histories of abolitionism and of the changing relations of gender and class I found that I was moving between two subjects that continue to be intensively researched and debated by different groups of historians, but which are not normally connected to each other. I suggest here the importance of race and class and gender as tools to analyse and comprehend the overall shifting social and political dynamics of the period. This chapter also charts the effect of abolitionism on the emerging women's rights movement in Britain, which I discuss generally in terms of language and tactics and in the context of individual women's political lives.

The relationship between feminism and imperialism forms the core of the third part of the book, and concerns the extent to which feminists defined womanhood against or in line with dominant ideologies of Empire, which demanded particular roles of white women. Recognizing that feminism has never been a homogeneous political grouping, I focus on two particular English women's connections with social reform in India as a means of exploring the relationship between black and white women in the Empire, and discussing how feminism was incorporated into its project to bring civilization to the outer reaches of the globe.

Part 4 also deals with the relationship between feminism and imperialism, but from a perspective aimed at discovering connections between anti-racist and anti-imperialist politics and the different feminisms of late nineteenth-century Britain. It gives an account of the British campaign against lynching in America in the 1890s, a campaign initiated and mainly organized by women. At the centre of this grouping was Ida B. Wells, an African-American woman who toured Britain giving lectures on the political and economic dynamics of racism in her country at the invitation of Catherine Impey, editor of the anti-racist journal *Anti-Caste* and a woman whose militant contribution to the anti-imperialist movement seems to have gone unrecorded except in Ida B. Wells's autobiography, *Crusade for Justice*.

Wells's analysis of lynching as a form of racial terror centred on a critique of the ideology of white womanhood, which legitimated lynching as an apparently spontaneous response to the alleged rape of white women by black men. This Part considers the impact of her arguments on feminist groupings at that time, showing how conflicting definitions of female sexuality and thus of femininity itself were inextricably tied to ideologies of race and class. When I first encountered this episode I was enormously intrigued by the narrative of the anti-lynching campaign but quite at a loss as to how to represent it. At that time I felt that there was no context for discussing Catherine Impey's work, her friendship with Ida B. Wells and her political relationship to feminism and that there was a danger of elevating her to heroic status. This came home to me when I once gave a one-off, rather experimental talk about the history of white women and racism, and spoke, among other things, about Catherine Impey's life as reflecting a particularly female tradition of opposing racism which feminists needed to explore. I was roundly condemned at the end for having tried to prove that white women had not always been racist. This was a good lesson to learn, for although I felt misunderstood, my enthusiasm for this woman with whom I felt an almost intimate connection was overshadowing my attempts to be analytical. The effort and eventual satisfaction involved in finding out what actually happened during the course of Ida B. Wells's visit also made it harder for me to distance myself from the material in order to extract the most important questions. It was mainly through understanding more about the development of feminism in that period that I began to figure out the significance of anti-lynching politics and the impact of Wells's analysis on different groups of people in Britain.

The final essay, Part 5, links the history of Empire with contemporary feminism in two ways. First, it suggests that a significant number of white post-war feminists have indirect experience of colonialism through their families, and that this factor could become a potential resource for addressing connections between race and gender. Second, I argue that the way in which historical memory is solicited by contemporary cultural forms is an important but neglected site of struggle over the different meanings of whiteness and womanhood, which feminism badly needs to interrogate. I move on to consider basic theoretical questions about the relationship between racism and male dominance before drawing together the main themes of the book. As in Part 1, I discuss contemporary images of white femininity, this time in the context of the environmental movement. During the period in which the book was written I became increasingly involved in ecological politics, and aware of the need to incorporate issues of race, class and gender into a new understanding of the relationship between human beings and their environments.

Living in Britain and the US in the 1990s it is hard to predict what will happen to feminist politics in those parts of the world. Postmodernist philosophy has encouraged many theorists to ask basic questions about the social relations of gender, which also includes, as Jane Flax suggests, thinking about *how* we think about them as well. These inquiries are often motivated by the desire to fracture the traditional category of 'women' and to understand how male dominance is reproduced in different societies. The effect of such radical rethinking on feminist political action has yet to be seen, but there is a danger that such philosophical uncertainty will make it even harder to find a basis of political unity among women. In my conclusion I argue that blackness and whiteness are both gendered categories whose meanings are historically derived, always in relation to each other but rarely in a simple binary pattern of opposites. It is partly through disassembling these meanings that important political connections between women are able to emerge. These connections may indeed be 'politically dangerous' but they will help to ensure that feminism has a future as a radical movement that can unite women across existing divisions of class, race and culture. What we need now, as June Jordan has written so powerfully, is to move away from partnership in misery towards partnership for change.

*Finsbury Park, London / Guilford, Connecticut*
*November 1990*

## Note

1. Jane Flax. 'Postmodernism and Gender Relations in Feminist Theory'. *Signs,* vol. 12, no. 4., 1987.

Part One

# The White Woman's Burden?

## Race and Gender in Historical Memory

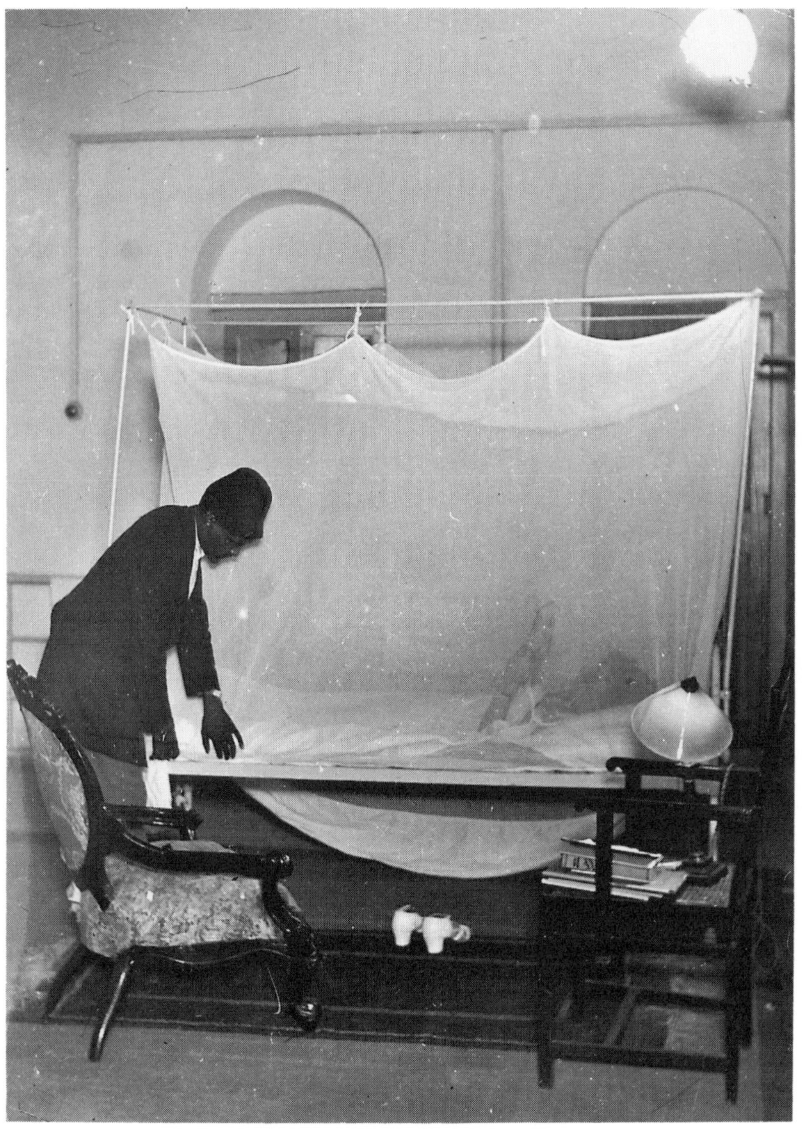

Dak bungalow, Memsahib's bed

There is a story circulating in London about a white English woman who decided to stay in New York as part of her vacation. Nervous about travelling as a single woman and alarmed at the prospect of being in a city renowned for violent crime, she booked into an expensive hotel where she thought she would be safe. One day she stepped into an empty elevator to go up to her room, and was startled when a tall black man accompanied by a large ferocious-looking dog came in and stood beside her just as the lift doors were closing. Since he was wearing shades she could not be sure whether he was looking at her, but she nearly leapt out of her skin when she heard his voice: 'Lady, lie down'. Terrified, she moved to obey him, praying that someone would call the elevator and rescue her in time. But instead of touching her the man stepped back in confusion. 'I was talking to my dog,' he explained, almost as embarrassed as she was. Fortunately, the elevator had reached her floor and she was able to scramble out without further explanation. The following day, the English woman was due to leave the city. She went to check out of her hotel and was astonished to be told not only that her bill had already been paid but there was also a huge bunch of flowers waiting for her. There must be a mistake she told them, but the hotel official assured her that they were meant for her. She took the flowers and read the card: 'Thank you for the most memorable event of my life, Lionel Ritchie.'

This is more or less the version of the story that I first heard, related by a reliable friend about a friend of a friend. The details made it sound plausible – the woman in question was a social worker in her early sixties who was travelling on her own for the first time. I was even told where she lived in London. I discussed the anecdote with another friend, who recounted it at a party, only to be told by another woman present that she had read a similar version in a book about urban myths. The name of the singer and the age of the woman varied, but the structure of the story remained basically the same, involving a white woman from England encountering a black man in New York.

Urban myths presumably circulate as long as they correspond to contemporary preoccupations and fears, allowing for different emphasis in the telling and retelling. This story turns on the white woman's racist fantasies, but in the version that I first heard the listener was invited to sympathize or even identify with her up to the moment of her humiliation. The intimidating demeanour of the innocent black man is offset by his charm and generosity, which is in turn transformed by the knowledge that he is a rich and famous singer of romantic soul ballads, thus occupying an entirely different class position from the one the woman had supposed. His dog, a Dobermann pinscher, although first encountered as an extension of his masculinity, turns out to have been tamed and feminized by him. The location is significant because while it removes the object of the racist fantasy to a foreign city associated with black crime, the protagonist carried with her fears nurtured in her own society.

What makes this story work, enough to elevate it to the status of a myth whose origins are lost in the sands of time? Why is the woman white and the man black, and what is it about the way that racism works that makes the relationship between these two figures fraught with sexual and racial tension? This essay is an attempt to address these and other related questions and to dissect the imagery brought to life in this story from a feminist perspective. I shall argue that the mythic quality of this anecdote can only be fully understood in the light of the long histories first of slavery and then of colonialism which have produced ideologies about race, gender and class that continue to affect social relations between black and white, male and female, in post-industrial societies. I hope to demonstrate that the construction of white femininity – that is, the different ideas about what it means to be a white female – can play a pivotal role in negotiating and maintaining concepts of racial and cultural difference. This particular couplet figuring the vulnerable white woman and her fantasy of the aggressive black man represents one important facet of an ideological relationship, expressed most effectively in the politics of crime and public order. In this context, particular ideas about white and black femininity work against each other in relation to black and white masculinity to legitimate different types of power and domination which affect everyone. However, in other political arenas white femininity can take on altogether different meanings which contradict those I have already described; later in this section I explore contemporary debates in education to demonstrate some of the ways in which gender and race intersect to reinforce notions of cultural difference and cultural superiority.

## White Woman as Victim

'Eight years ago in a respectable street in Wolverhampton a house was sold to a negro. Now only one white (a woman old-age pensioner) lives there.

This is her story . . .'[1] In 1968, Enoch Powell's historic 'Rivers of Blood' speech gave new power to the image of the vulnerable, elderly, white woman, victimized and bullied by an alien people. Throughout the next two decades the picture of this woman, her face distorted by fear, continued to be one of the most potent symbols of British racism – a sign that the black presence in the inner cities was an unwanted intrusion on a sacred but fragile way of life.

Nearly fifteen years after Powell's speech, a small unobtrusive-looking pamphlet was published by the Salisbury Group, which represented the so-called New Right, a political formation that emerged after the 1979 Tory election victory. Called *The Old People of Lambeth*, it was an illustration of the continuing resilience of this particular set of racist imagery.[2] Interviews with elderly white men and women on subjects such as 'crime', 'the police', 'immigration' and 'politics' returned again and again to the same lament: that since the war these people had suffered a dramatic change in the quality of life, particularly since blacks had been allowed to come and terrorize them in their own neighbourhoods: 'The native population of Lambeth feels little natural sympathy with the West Indian arrivals. Without having any arrogant or dogmatic theory of racial superiority, the old people of Lambeth can see with their own eyes that they are surrounded by people more primitive than they, who lack their respect for law and privacy.' A truly English and harmonious way of life had apparently given way to a constant state of siege. 'They are afraid all the time they are awake; and many of them cannot sleep because they are frightened.' The final paragraph of the pamphlet stressed the patriotism of the old people interviewed, their devotion to the Royal Family, their memories of not one but both world wars, and their readiness to work, raise families and to obey the law. 'And yet, without any provocation on their part, they find most of the things they value neglected or taken away. As one old man said simply, "It's our country and our Queen. Why should we be afraid to go out?"'

In both these examples of racist imagery the combination of old age and femininity works to convey the powerlessness and physical frailty of a white community threatened by the barbarism of the unwanted black 'immigrants' who neither understand nor have respect for the values of civilization. Both sets of images reinforce the idea that white people – the nation – share a consensus about a way of life which is threatened by close contact with outsiders. The language in which this type of racism is expressed is often infused with metaphors of rape, the assault of the helpless victim, the invasion of defenceless property, the ever-present threat of violence that intimidates the physically weak. In this discourse England reverts to being an island besieged by aliens and the violence begins at the point of immigration. When, for example, many families from the Indian subcontinent attempted to enter Britain before the new visa restrictions came into effect in November 1986, papers like the *Sun*, the *Star* and the *Mail* fell back on the same wartime analogies which had been evoked during previous immigration crises in the early 1960s: the situation at Heathrow airport was variously described as a siege or an invasion, with floods or hordes of immigrants trying to pour into the country on false pretences.

Where crime is concerned – particularly crimes involving violence – the racist vocabulary of the press is similarly precise. Words like 'savage', 'monster', 'beast', 'fiend', nearly always accompanied by photos, combine to evoke a particular response from the white reader. Brutal attacks on white women, old or young, which have been allegedly committed by a black man, often employ these epithets and visual images to suggest innate savagery and evil tendencies. The more horrific the incident, and the greater the violence inflicted on the woman or child, the more the reader is drawn into sharing a racist consensus about black men, and consequently black people generally. Crimes against black women or black children carried out by white men rarely receive much attention in the media, while violence allegedly inflicted on black women or children by black men is frequently relayed to the public as further proof of black deviancy. These kinds of images are further influenced by the wider political climate in which particular types of crime can become symbols of crime in general; if there is a heightened awareness of rape, child abuse or street robbery, for example, this will also affect the social meaning and implications of an individual incident. I am not disputing that such crimes take place, but emphasizing that in Britain today the race, gender and class of both the victims and the perpetrators are likely to become significant factors both in the way that crime is reported and in the manner in which it is handled throughout the legal institutions. In fact this would be true in almost every society that I can think of since the dynamics of race, class and gender are to be found everywhere. My concern here is to interrogate the significance attached to race and gender in an attempt to find the connections between racism and male dominance in the society in which I live.

Nor do I intend to suggest that ideas about women's safety are derived purely from ideology without regard to women's actual experience. It is worth looking in some detail at different interpretations of women's vulnerability in relation to men. The threat to women's safety stems from the idea that women are more likely to be victims of male aggression and less likely to be able to defend themselves. This is a complex subject which continues to provoke intense discussion among feminists. Women are told repeatedly from childhood by parents, school, the media and other influential sources that it is unsafe for them to be in certain places at certain times, unless they are accompanied by a man, despite the evidence that suggests that they are actually more at risk from violence in the home. While women deal with this threat to their safety in many different ways, often depending on their mobility, race, income, class, age, sexuality and other aspects of their personal experiences, surveys show that on the whole women are vastly more afraid than men to go out, particularly at night.[3] Women's ability to move around freely at all times is severely restricted by the knowledge that they might be risking their lives in doing so – and, if an attack does happen, be blamed for inviting it. This means that the majority of women are simply denied access to a range of activities which most men take for granted.

One of the problems in quantifying the actual threat to women's safety in public places is that fear itself cannot be measured and is a factor in its own right, whether or not it corresponds to the likelihood of being attacked. Crime statistics, particularly relating to rape and street crime, play a significant role in increasing levels of fear, and they are frequently sensationalized by the media. In fact in this case statistical calculation is a poor guide because if women do not go out because they are scared, they are therefore less at risk from certain types of attack. The images of vulnerability and defencelessness involved in many discussions about women's safety in the city often feed into racist assumptions about who are the victims and who are the perpetrators of crimes against women. Sensational and sometimes inaccurate reporting in the press has given the impression that areas where there are sizeable black populations are particularly dangerous for women, especially the elderly. That is not to say that crime does not happen there, but it is often represented in such a way that it confirms stereotypes of unruly black criminals preying on helpless white women.

One of the major connections between crime and public order is the struggle for control of public space. Throughout the 1980s racist ideology fixed the idea that the inner cities were unsafe because that was where most blacks lived, and the phrase 'the inner city' became shorthand for 'the race problem'. This was particularly evident during the election coverage of 1987 when the expression was on almost every politician's lips. Turning on the TV one night, we were treated to a wordless definition of 'inner city', expressed through images of Handsworth, an area of Birmingham associated with controversial policing practices and local resistance. Dramatic documentary footage showed buildings being set alight (blacks rioting) followed by a picture of an elderly white woman who had been beaten about the face (blacks mugging). Where the imagery of the decaying heart of the city suggests the breakdown of community life, the crime and lawlessness that appears to have taken its place demands tough action from the police to restore a sense of order. What I am interested in here is the way that certain ideas about white femininity work to legitimate that 'tough action' which can then lead to a greater repression of the population as a whole, regardless of race, gender or class.

A political broadcast for the Labour Party, made in 1986 at the height of a wave of public concern about law and order, demonstrated how an image of white female vulnerability could be used to convey a specific political agenda on crime and police protection. It provided an example of the way that racism can lurk like the proverbial mugger behind the murky shadows of political discourse without ever seeming to show its face. A young white woman – a girl, in fact, seen later (or is it earlier?) in school uniform in the bosom of her nuclear family outside their newly built home – walks hurriedly along a deserted street at night, passing under an unlit bridge. The sound of approaching footsteps, belonging unmistakably to a man, imply that she is being pursued. As the tension builds up, the girl passes a street sign which signifies that she is in southeast London. Just as you think that she is about to be attacked, she runs straight into the arms of a man. (We see his legs before we see his face.) Like her we almost cry with relief, he is a policeman, a friendly, cheery sort who will take her back to the station for a cup of tea while he rings her parents. Or perhaps he will escort her home, telling her mum and dad that she ought not to be out alone in such an area, not with the sort of things that happen to decent folk these days especially in South London.

By placing a representative of the most symbolically vulnerable section of society – a white female child – somewhere in the inner city – where the majority of black people live – the makers of this propaganda were able to conflate powerful messages of a crime rate that has got out of control, the ever-present threat of male violence against women, the dangers of being out in the inner city at night when it is dark, and the malevolent unseen forces that lurk on unpoliced streets. The explicit aim was clearly meant to be that the Labour Party would put more police in the streets which would automatically make any reasonable law-abiding person feel safer. Viewed outside its historical context there was no sense that the police represented anything other than the benign forces of law and order. However, when I first watched this statement I was horrified by what I felt was the Labour Party's capitulation to racism, even though I had no illusions about its past record. Five years earlier, riots had erupted first in Brixton, South London, and then all over the country, in protest at the racism of the police, which was acknowledged by the Scarman Report that followed. The broadcast was made only months after riots in Handsworth, Tottenham and again in Brixton, following the serious wounding of one black woman and the death of another as a result of police activity, and where both blacks and whites testified to the often brutal policing of their communities. The context in which it appeared made it almost impossible to refer to public order issues without also addressing either the documented racism of the police force or the assumption that black youth were predominantly responsible for public disorder. By choosing to ignore recent history the broadcast tried to sidestep difficult and contentious problems, but failed to do so because the images in the film were themselves replete with racist associations.

Visual images of black and white men and women can be invested with different racial, sexual or class meanings according to where they are situated in relation to one another. As the political climate constantly shifts the smallest details can become disproportionately significant. By chance I came across an interesting example of this in the promotional paper *Docklands Light Railway News* (jobs special issue).[4] The middle page spread proclaimed 'Now here's what WE want and what we can offer YOU'. Coloured drawings illustrated the range of jobs available and the tasks that applicants would be expected to perform, along with details of qualifications and salaries. One of the drawings, captioned 'Traffic supervisors will check that all is well at all of our stations' showed a kindly blue-uniformed officer (all the uniformed figures are white), equipped with radio control, assisting a young white women buying a ticket at an automatic dispenser. For good measure, a young white boy was seen walking along the pavement in the background as a sign that the area would be safe for unaccompanied children. Immediately behind the couple at the ticket machine lurked the figure of a black man wearing sunglasses, his head turned in the direction of the white woman. Both his posture and his shades combined to suggest that all would not be well if the traffic supervisor was not on the scene. In the context of popular racist conceptions about the criminal tendencies of black men, the reader was invited to share an interpretation of the scenario which accords with a kind of 'common-sense' thinking. Meanwhile, as if to demonstrate the flexibility of the different codes attached to race, class and gender, the same spread portrayed a happy equal-opportunity-style cameo of a traffic assistant inside the train sharing a joke with a black man, who is sitting in a carriage with a white woman and a man in a wheelchair, observed approvingly by a middle-class couple in the background.

Several months after collecting this particular gem I came across a later issue of the same paper where the same images were used but for quite different purposes.[5] The picture that had showed the possible hazards of buying a ticket for the railway was now used on the front cover to illustrate how easy it was to buy one. It was tempting to interpret the scenario as an indication that it was so easy that even a woman or a black person could understand the process, especially with the help of a friendly traffic supervisor. The problem was that it was still not clear what the black man was doing lurking in the background. Over the page, the equal opportunity picture had been turned into an illustration warning passengers not to fiddle the fares. Instead of sharing a joke with the black man, the traffic assistant now appeared to be checking a suspect's ticket. The fact that everyone in the picture was smiling rather invalidated the stern warning given in the accompanying article, but it was significant that the reader was again invited to identify the black man as a possible deviant.

These illustrations are interesting not because they set out to represent an explicitly racist point of view but because they allow racism to be expressed through familiar, everyday imagery. They are rarely challenged, but if they were, the publishers would surely deny that any racism was intended. The reason that these particular interpretations invited by the juxtaposition of black and white, male and female can be so readily overlooked is because they correspond to certain ideas about race, class and gender which have passed into the realm of common sense. In other words, for many people it is thought to be self-evident that women need protection from male violence and that black men are likely to harbour criminal intentions.

At the same time, the way that the social relationships of both race and gender combine to produce meanings in these images is by no means fixed;

they become altogether different if the narrative is changed. Consider, for example, a portrait of the world-famous black boxer Frank Bruno and his wife, Laura, who is white. As long as Bruno is represented as the gentle giant who combines patriotism, humility and a respect for the family, his marriage to a white woman is likely to signify his wish to become completely British. In any society, however, where there are social hierarchies based on race and gender, let alone class, there is a wide range of possible readings of images of black and white couples who are confessed lovers. White women, for example, who are seen with black men might appear to be socially or sexually deviant; while a white man with a black woman might be regarded as having a taste either for sexual adventures or for a submissive partner, depending on her ethnic or cultural origin. Similarly a black woman who has a white partner might conceivably be seen as wanting to turn her back on black men in general because of ideas about their behaviour or, alternatively, as providing a kind of sexuality that white women are unable to match.

At the beginning of this Part I explained that I wanted to track down the sources of the different meanings attached to white womanhood in an attempt to understand and so refute their ideological power. It is clear that in this project gender on its own cannot be a useful analytical tool, and neither can race; black men, black women, white women, white men are all categories that have both racial and sexual connotations which can be further transformed or complicated by class. In the next section I look at some of the ways in which race, gender and class intersect in ideologies of cultural difference.

## White Woman as Symbol of Civilization

The inner-city riots of 1981 and 1985 helped to keep issues of public order, racism and policing central to the political stage during the 1980s, but education has since become another equally important focus for racial conflict. Although debates about public order and education both centre on black youth, it is the struggle around racism in schools that has seen discussion of nakedly biological racial difference transformed into that of innate cultural difference. Before looking at the way in which different types of femininity articulate cultural diversity I shall first outline some of the background to the racial politics of education.

The attempts of the Conservative government to reform public education have led to a new agenda of racism which aims to control previous radical or liberal methods of dealing with discrimination and difference. Throughout the previous decade educationalists – in so far as they recognized there was a problem – favoured the multicultural approach which tried to raise awareness of other cultures represented in schools without actually changing the curriculum. This approach soon came under attack from the anti-racists, who felt it was ineffective in dealing with racist teaching materials, out-of-date curricula and staff who were not trained to recognize and tackle racism wherever they met it. But multiculturalism – which covers a number of ways of acknowledging the different cultural backgrounds of students – also produced waves of reaction from the traditionalists, who saw white British children as martyrs in a system which apparently preferred to recognize alien tongues and religions instead of English and Christianity. Ray Honeyford, the Bradford head teacher, for example, became notorious for his insistence that the Asian children in his school leave their own culture at the school gates.[6] Shortly afterwards parents of white children in Dewsbury staged a protest rather than send them to Headfield, the local, predominantly Asian, Church of England school. On this occasion one of the main complaints was that the children had made chappatis instead of pancakes on Shrove Tuesday. The school, however, defended Headfield's policies, pointing out that 'Christmas was observed, the Christmas story was told, cards were sent and a party was held'.[7]

The protesting parents' cause was taken up enthusiastically by the press: they were cited as claiming that their children's 'cultural upbringing' would be at risk if they were so outnumbered. It is worth noting here that white women have been at the forefront of parents' attempts to intervene in debates on race and culture in education. In this instance one mother was quoted as saying: 'There is a strong chance that my son will grow up learning Urdu – confusing him. I am sure it will affect his education.'[8] Although the headlines invariably carried the word 'race' in large letters, the parents appeared to be unanimous that their concern to redirect their children's education did not spring from racism; indeed several were adamant that their protest was not against Asian people themselves. The main issue was establishing the right to choose which school their children went to.

While the 1980 and 1988 Education Acts allow parents a choice of schools providing it does not interfere with the authority's 'efficient use of resources', race relations law forbids a local education authority from carrying out any act which constitutes racial discrimination. Shortly after the Dewsbury incident, Cleveland Council agreed to transfer a white child from one school to another when her mother complained that she was 'learning Pakistani'. After an investigation by the Commission for Racial Equality had found that the Council had behaved unlawfully, the secretary of state for education decreed that a parent's right to choose should override race relations law. The decision was welcomed by the Parental Alliance for Choice in Education, the body which provided legal advice for the Dewsbury parents and backs parents in similar disputes with local authorities. Their spokesperson was able to repeat the familiar litany: 'It has nothing to do with race but with culture', and, as if by way of proof, 'In Dewsbury muslim parents supported the right of white parents to remove their children from school'.[9] The movement for separate Muslim schools is also inevitably cited as evidence that cultural segregation is desired on both sides – a fact which is somehow supposed to prove that there is no question of racism. However, the cultural separatism expressed in the demand for Muslim schools also underlines the complexity of the issue: there seems to be a problem when Asian children are in the majority in British schools, but there is also an explicit concern that black children educated outside the national system will not be exposed to the social and cultural values of their adopted country.

In order to make sense of these localized debates about the cultural content of children's education, it is essential to ask what motivates those who claim their non-racist desire to keep their cultures separate. I believe that ideas about the relative status of women in different communities feed their anxiety, although this is not always expressed directly and it cannot be reduced to a simple problem of parents not wanting their own children to be influenced by gender relations of which they disapprove. Of course there are varying structures of male dominance operating within different communities whether they are formed around ethnicity or class, and it is perfectly understandable that many people are opposed to laws and social practices that they associate with societies other than their own. However, the conflict produced by the wearing of the *hajib,* or headscarf, in schools by Muslim girls, which is discussed in more detail in Part 5, is one example of how modes of femininity are made to speak for wider cultural values. Now, however, I want to examine ways in which representations of white femininity articulate powerful, if subtle, racist messages that confirm not only cultural difference but also cultural superiority.

The case of the two Birmingham schoolgirls whose father sold them into marriage while on holiday in his native North Yemen provided an opportunity for commentators to lament the fate of Muslim women compared with that of their European counterparts. Many people in Britain were understandably outraged to learn that girls who had been born and educated in England could be forced to marry boys hardly older than themselves, bear their children and live in exile in remote mountain villages. The mother's campaign to rescue her daughters was taken up as a crusade by journalists, one of whom apparently risked her life by travelling to North Yemen to interview them secretly. In her book, published after one of the young women had returned to Birmingham, she contrasted her own situation with that of women in the Yemen, often implicitly, often through casual observations of the life she saw around her:

> I also wore a long-sleeved blouse, buttoned to the neck, and had sunglasses on. Pretty safe, I would have thought. I was only to learn from the British Ambassador's wife at the end of the week that my problem was I tucked the blouse into my trousers. I should have been wearing it outside. I got very fed up with being touched, stared at and shouted at by men. The women, I noticed, would turn away with a sort of scandalised sneer.[10]

The reader is invited to share her evident distaste for a society in which women appear to be simply bought and sold by their elders, and to view its inhabitants with a rather more derisory sort of scandalized sneer. In this way, the image of the Western 'liberated' woman, who enjoys equality with men that is enshrined in law, together with the freedom to dress, behave and work as she likes, is thrown into sharp relief by that of the Muslim woman, forced into submission from girlhood and deprived of any social, economic or political rights to independence. While the act of comparing social and sexual relations in two different societies may seem like pertinent journalism, the way it is done in this example conforms to a broader ideologically charged survey in which the position of women in a society indicates the level of civilization it has achieved. This is an idea that appears through history in various permutations, and which I shall be interrogating throughout this book. It has meant that the story of the young Arab women's passage from civilization's inner city to its outer margins and back again can never be contained as a simple tale of patriarchal duplicity and bureaucratic nightmare.

The Royal Family has provided useful vehicles for reinforcing the image of the civilized white woman who is distinguishable from her non-white and non-Christian sisters by her clearly marked social and sexual freedom. Media descriptions of Princess Diana visiting the Middle East in 1986 were a typical example of this process. The *Sunday Express* writer Jean Rook said it all where many others left it to innuendo: 'The culture shock to a Briton's system didn't really bite until we bit this dust where women are treated like less than it. . . . But if the Arabs are a culture shock to Diana, she is a healthy smack in the yashmak to them.' Diana's clothes, her figure, her conversation, her marriage, even the rims of her sunglasses became symbols of the cool, sophisticated and, above all, liberated womanhood that marks Britain out as a more civilized country. In contrast, Arab women were portrayed as being literally fettered with gold chains, smothered in clothing and deprived of conjugal rights, in a society where 'even second class princesses . . . are expected to sit down, sit still, shut up and put up.'

Throughout these descriptions of the English princess, a rose to 'make this dusty, dry desert bloom',[11] different styles of femininity were being compared directly with each other. But other versions of aggressive, powerful or merely active femininity can also be suggested in the absence of other women. In a feature in the fashion journal *Vogue* on the film *White Mischief*, set in the so-called Happy Valley in Kenya in the 1930s, images of unsubmissive white femininity were constructed through reference to black men and wild animals.[12] Greta Scacchi, for example, who played the female lead, appeared on a double page spread flanked by two black actors dressed as Masai warriors. Staring straight into the camera, and wearing a bright red suit and hat, with bare arms and legs, she rested her hand on the arm of one of the men as if to prove her power and their submission. The unnamed 'warriors', who, the reader was told, were played by Sumburu in the film, were also dressed in red, covered with jewellery and holding full-length spears. They had become a symbol of the white people's rule over the country, and formed an exotic, but tamed, backdrop to the domestic dramas of the colonizers. In another image that symbolized the taming of the savage, Geraldine Chaplin, who also played a leading role in the film, was photographed sitting in a haughty, nervous pose with a docile leopard on a leash and chain. Smaller pictures, which did not show famous film stars in period costume, were captioned with a minimum of detail in the best ethnographical tradition: 'Scenes from the Kenyan landscape: native with zebroid (half zebra, half horse), and bougainvillaea'. The whole feature ended with a section called 'Travel Notes' which explained how to get there, where to stay, which tour operators to contact – as though the Africa of the film still existed unchanged.

Fashion pictures often situate models against a background of ethnic, primitive, or even 'savage' femininity or masculinity in order to achieve a range of impressions, from strength to vulnerability. The recent spate of high budget films set in the context of Empire, of which *White Mischief* was just one example, is often directly connected to nostalgic fashion imagery which expresses particular aspects of colonial memory. In this way codes of femininity help to reconstruct a historic past through images which are both made and interpreted in the light of contemporary ideologies. In a fashion series in the *Observer* colour magazine which coincided with the release of *Out of Africa* in 1986, the model and her crew were flown to the Ivory Coast courtesy of British Caledonian to capture the spirit of the moment.[13] In one full-page shot the model adopted a virginal pose, with hands clasped and eyes lowered, wearing a completely white outfit down to her shoes and stockings. In the background, walking behind her, was the blurred image of an African woman in brightly coloured 'native costume', with child on her hip and basket of fruit on her head. Another page showed the same model, again clothed in a long white dress, but with a dark jacket, matching shoes and hair ribbon, holding a large straw hat. In complete contrast to the cool unperturbed Englishwoman in the first picture, this time she appeared to be hurrying, her head, with hair dishevelled, turned back over her shoulder as if she were aware of danger. In the background and on a level with her eyes, the very blurred figure of a black man could be seen emerging from the bushes at the side of the road.

Black children are sometimes employed to highlight a particular aspect of a fashion 'look'. In a clothes advertisement in another fashion magazine several young black boys wearing outsize men's shirts appeared alongside a white model similarly dressed.[14] The backdrop of sandy desert combined with the image of a lone white women to produce an effect of independence and androgyny. During the same summer, a trend appeared in the shops for clothes patterned with dancing black figures, symbols of the exotic, the ethnic and the cosmopolitan. I was struck by a more up-market version in an expensive department store window: fabric printed with photographic images of a veiled 'oriental' mother and child in tasteful grey and white adorned an otherwise naked plaster model.

Black women are increasingly visible as fashion models in their own right, which indicates how ideas about what it can mean to be a black or white woman shift in the perpetual search for images of femininity that are linked to patterns of pleasure and consumption. The *Observer* colour magazine ran a spread featuring purple fabric and vases to coincide with the opening of the film of Alice Walker's novel *The Colour Purple.* In one shot a black woman was shown naked from the waist up, in profile, appearing to drink from a rectangular glass vase. In another, titled 'African violet', a black woman's silhouette, her head in profile and glass bowl resting on her shoulder, conjured up images of enslavement. In 1989 the international clothes company Benetton ran a major European campaign promoting 'United Colors of Benetton' which featured a naked white baby held against a naked black woman's breasts. A television commercial for a deluxe Citroën model cut repeatedly between different angles of a black woman in African dress striding in bare feet and the car gliding along the road, both in the same barren landscape.

I select these images because I want to emphasize that we are surrounded by complicated and contradictory messages about many different aspects of human identity. I am focusing on images of white women primarily in order to analyse the components of a specifically white femininity, but this only makes sense in the context of ideas about black women as well. Yet there is a significant difference in the way that black and white feminists have so far approached the whole subject of femininity. Black feminists have mainly dealt with the deconstruction of imagery of black women through an understanding of race, class and gender relations, recognizing that in a racist society it would be totally inadequate to discuss images of non-white people without considering ideas about race. Pratibha Parmar, for example, has argued that the representation of Asian women in Britain cannot be divorced from the social and political relations that sustain racism:

> Depending on the political motivation and climate, specific images of Asian women are mobilised for particular arguments. The common sense ideas about Asian female sexuality and femininity are based within, and determined by, a racist patriarchal ideology. Women are defined differently according to their race.[15]

While this statement might seem perfectly acceptable when applied to images of black women, the ways in which race figures in the interpretation of images of white people is rarely discussed. Feminism, for example, has tended to deal with the representation of white women in terms of gender, class and sexuality without also acknowledging the dynamics of race. Why is it that there have been so few studies by white feminists of white femininity? In a predominantly white society it is hard to get away from the assumption that to be white is to be normal, while to be not-white is to occupy a racial category with all its attendant meanings. Moving beyond images and questions of representation to broader issues of political theory and action, it is time to consider the awkward question of the white feminist response to racism.

## Feminism and Racism

> Unchallenged, racism ultimately will be the death of the women's movement in England, just as it threatens to become the death of any women's movement in those developed countries where it is not addressed.
>
> Audre Lorde[16]

In the recent history of feminism, that is, from the identifiable days of the 'Women's Movement' in the late sixties and early seventies, racism has proved to be an inescapable problem for white women: of all the different factors that have divided feminists over the last twenty years, few have caused so much bitterness and resentment. To begin with, there was almost an assumption among many women that as feminism was a progressive, even revolutionary force, it contained within it an automatic anti-racist position, which was often expressed through solidarity with national liberation struggles. The absence of black women in any large numbers and the increasing preoccupation of many women with political splits and tensions within feminism meant that race and racism were low on the agenda in the first decade. In 1978, however, groups of feminists all over Britain began to organize specifically against racism, in conjunction with various other local and national radical and liberal forces, in response to the greater visibility of fascist groups such as the National Front and British Movement. This Women Against Racism and Fascism (WARF) network did not survive as a national alliance, but some local groups contributed to new ways of thinking about gender and race. One such group, in Manchester, wrote a paper for a pamphlet called *Taking Racism Personally* which was produced by a mixed collective. The aim of the pamphlet was to argue that white people – especially professed anti-racists – should take responsiblity for their own racism and anti-Semitism, and it advocated consciousness-raising in groups as a way of 'dealing with' what it called personal racism. The WARF paper described how one group of women set about 'looking at racism within ourselves'. By the end of the exercise they concluded:

> What we did is really only a beginning in confronting our own racism. We have to go on, making use of what we've learnt. The fight against racism has to go on in ourselves, in our work and in our communities, and at the level of institutionalised racism – discrimination in housing, education, the immigration laws. We see all levels as equally important. They're all part of the same thing – what we do in one area should help us in another.[17]

The technique of sharing personal problems and working out feelings seemed an appropriately feminist way of approaching questions of race since it appeared to extend the interpretation of personal politics that separated feminist practice from that of most left groups. In other words, for many people it confirmed the importance of changing consciousness from within, rather than concentrating on external structures of power. When the Manchester document first came out many white women welcomed the fact that it pointed towards something different they could actually do about racism as feminists – as opposed to going on demonstrations or organizing petitions. It was to be a significant contribution towards anti-racist practice over the next few years, although the insistence of the Manchester group that the racism of individuals was inseparable from other more public forms went largely unheeded, and the quest to uncover personal racism was frequently elevated to a supposedly political end in itself.

Meanwhile, changes within feminism produced other ways of thinking about racism, and in particular the relationship between black and white women. By the early eighties the women's movement had acquired a far more respectable public face with developments such as the founding of women's publishing companies and the greater visibility of women officers and feminist issues within local government. During this same period, groups of women within the movement who felt marginalized on account of their class, race or sexuality began to organize autonomously and to challenge the authority of the white middle-class women who they felt had dominated feminism up to that point. These changes, combined with a greater awareness of racism that resulted partly from the 1981 riots, contributed to a new agenda in women's politics which stressed the differences between women within a far more uneasy framework of mutual support. Breaking down women's experiences according to race, age, disability, class, sexuality or any other basis of identity, either chosen or imposed from outside, meant that a very fractured and far more complex network of women-identified politics emerged. One of the problems that emerged out of this fragmentation was that new and rigid dogmas were developed in an attempt to mediate between the different facets of women's experiences. For example, there was often great hostility towards any woman who tried to speak about a condition or identity of which she did not have direct experience. There was a confusion between claiming knowledge of another woman's life and speaking on her behalf on the one hand, and addressing the social relations that produced the oppression or discrimination on the other.

It is hard to go beyond these generalizations about how and why racism has been dealt with by feminism in this country, especially since it has affected so many women's lives so deeply. It is also the case that racism has deeply affected many other aspects of British social and political life, of which feminism is just a part. This book is not an attack on feminism, although it was born out of a deep frustration with it. However, it is one thing to be able to agree that racism has always been a difficult issue for British feminism, and quite another to analyse why this is so. Rather than go on trying to compress what I think is a history of the race question in recent feminism, I want to ask myself a few questions: Why do I care, what do I know about it, what exactly *is* the problem?

## The Political and the Personal

> I believe that white feminists today, raised white in a racist society, are often ridden with white solipsism – not the consciously held belief that one race is inherently superior to all others, but a tunnel-vision which simply does not see nonwhite experience or existence as precious or significant, unless in

> spasmodic, impotent guilt-reflexes, which have little or no long-term, continuing momentum or political usefulness.
>
> Adrienne Rich[18]

I was born into a family that enjoyed a fairly typical mixture of middle-class, mid-twentieth-century colonial connections. On one side we were supported by money raised in the imperial trade between Britain and India; on the other we felt a more immediate connection to the old Empire through my father's experiences in the Indian Army. We lived in a small village, but well before I was sent off to boarding school at the age of eleven I had gained a sense of my family having lived in or been part of worlds far beyond the one I knew. My father rarely talked of India, which we knew was something to do with the horrors of The War, but whenever he did it always seemed remote and unreal – like, for example, when he talked about his prowess on the saxophone in a jazz band in the officers' mess – something we found as hard to imagine as the idea of being encamped on a hill station in charge of a battalion of Indian soldiers. When I was ten he provided me with more tangible evidence of the world that lay waiting to be explored: he went out to Iran to take part in an archaeological expedition with an uncle and was away for six weeks. I do not remember his absence so much as getting up early to drive to the airport to meet his plane. He appeared suddenly through the crowd, looking sunburned and slightly unfamiliar. It was the presents he brought that intrigued me: old metal bracelets, a length of printed cloth, two metal stirrups that looked as if they could have belonged to Ghenghis Khan, and odds and ends he had bought in bazaars. I appropriated his *Teach Yourself Persian* and duly taught myself to write the first ten or twelve characters of the alphabet.

Growing up in a landscape full of privately educated, publicly conservative families, the seeds of contrariness blowing in the wind of 1968 found fertile ground in our house. My mother has often told me that she was criticized for not being stricter with us, although I suspect this would not have made much difference. We were not much in contact with rebellious ideas and subversive organizations, although we were certainly taught at home to question authority and to have a firm sense of justice. I would rather have died than got into trouble at school, until my mid-teens at least, and I could not have had a more sheltered life if I had tried: living in the country, attending an all-girls convent school throughout adolescence, with no access either to the town on the other side of the walls or the TV, radio or any other forms of popular culture within them. I suffered the humilation of being the second to last girl in my class to be kissed, as well as moderate but what felt like never-ending acne, and my self-respect only survived because I was thought to be clever. Escaping into books and studying provided a place in my mind where I could shut out all the unpleasantness of the reality around me. I emerged with a sense of myself as being 'different', of being able to go where no other girls like myself would dream of going and where I would be able to prove my difference from them. I realized this would mean I would be likely never to have the things they would have, like a husband, and children; but at the time it never occurred to me that I would ever actually want them. For a while Latin and Greek were the only outlet for my urge to know how other people lived and spoke. French hardly counted as it was taught so woodenly. One vivid memory stands out from my last year at school, indicating that I had already formed opinions of what was going on in the outside world: one of the students in my Greek class came in one day full of admiration for a speech made the day before by Enoch Powell. 'He is right, ' she claimed, 'He is the Cassandra of our times, and he will be proved right just as she was.' For all my ignorance about the politics of race at that time I was deeply disturbed, both by the 'Rivers of Blood' speech and by this support it had received around me.

Later, when I left school and began to live more independently, I could never, unlike my elder sister, engage with any kind of organized politics, preferring to dream about exile in more exotic and remote parts of the world. The first stage of my plan was to give up studying the so-called classics and change to 'oriental languages'. This led to a trip with a schoolfriend to Iran in 1971, as I had chosen Persian, with Arabic, as my main subject. At that time, there was scarcely anywhere else in the world so obscured by exotic mumbo-jumbo as Iran. Behind the screen of ignorance in the West, which at that time associated 'Persia' with carpets, walled gardens and Omar Khayyám, it was ruled by a dynasty of military dictators, who were intent on frog-marching the country from a rural peasant economy to an industrialized and polluted police state. The education I received during my first visit was of little use to me back in the classroom at Cambridge. Almost all my teachers, in both Persian and Arabic, were hostile to the idea of relating our studies in Middle Eastern language and literature to the living cultures which had produced them. We were expected to trudge through the old medieval set books, perfect our written grammar and emerge at the other end as satisfied scholars of orientalism. The only prospect I could see for myself in this was to become a professor, stay single and childless, and spend every vacation riding around in the desert. I already had a model in the professor who had written our grammar books, who reputedly did just that.

After an agonizing existential crisis I moved on again, this time to anthropology, which was presented to me in a crash course along with the rudiments of sociology. My motives this time were clear: I remember saying that I wanted to know how other people lived and organized themselves. The first book I bought myself for the new course was *Other Cultures* by John Beattie. Disillusionment with academic study set in fast this time as I failed to find any anthropologists who actually seemed to have been affected, in any way, by their experiences of living in another culture and that was really part of what I was curious about. It was at this point that I first encountered feminism, in a women and anthropology group, definitely the most rewarding moment of my college days. It seemed to me at that time that the project of finding out how other women lived, particularly in relation to men, in other parts of the world, was extremely worthwhile. The questions that were being asked in the group related largely to how we built up this knowledge of women's experiences and what we said about it. Was it right to impose value judgements on social systems that seemed to oppress women, or even privilege them? I cannot remember what the consensus was, but looking back it was one of those crucial questions that were asked a lot in the early days of feminism and then forgotten as other issues closer to home eclipsed them.

My education thankfully over, I set off for the East again, this time for India where I hoped to find my mission in some kind of development work. Within days of arriving I realized that the whole idea of travelling out to 'help' people in an underdeveloped country with no useful skills to offer was highly suspect, a feeling which was certainly confirmed by the friends I made while I was there. Back in England again, I accepted a friend's invitation to live in Birmingham, a sprawling industrial city, hoping to find some work with 'immigrants' who I felt needed as much support as they could get in fighting off racism. Besides, I was fed up with racist bigots I met hitch-hiking around the country who always brought every conversation round to 'Them' and who denied anyone who had not lived near 'Them' to have alternative opinions. Within a few months I was filling in as education officer for Birmingham Community Relations Council, which was not what I had in mind, and I felt distinctly uncomfortable organizing multicultural exhibitions, especially as something always went wrong or the children did not appear to be interested for the right reasons. One of the questions I was always asked – which I was warned about by those who had gone before me – was why Hindu gods had more than one pair of hands. I managed to extricate myself fairly gracefully from the job, and returned to unemployment and disillusion once more.

By then it was 1977, the year when the emergence of fascist groups first really came to my notice. After a few months of floundering about I decided I had to 'do something' and settled on the idea of working for an anti-racist paper, as I wanted to combine writing with my growing obsession with race issues. Someone told me about *Searchlight*, at that time a small but pioneering anti-fascist publication based in Birmingham. For six years I worked with the magazine, graduating from office girl to editor. It was in many ways and for all kinds of reasons a thankless, depressing and frustrating job. But it also provided a base from which to meet and work with people I respected enormously and to gain an understanding of the scale and dimensions of racism from the late 1970s onwards. It was at this time that the support for the tiny fascist parties that was expressed both during elections and on the street shifted towards the right wing of the Conservative Party, encouraged by the populist racism being voiced in 'respectable' circles. Working with *Searchlight* gave me the feeling that I was able to challenge directly certain expressions of that racism, and see some results in doing so. Whether it was hiding behind pillars taking clandestine shots of real fascists meeting closet ones, or endlessly trying to sort out muddles in the subscription lists, I was working as part of a movement at a crucial time.

Partly because of the nature of the investigative work, which was often dangerous and potentially violent, and partly because of the distinctive camaraderie that developed among male anti-fascists, I found myself quite isolated as a woman working in this field. I was forced to develop my own set of priorities, both to deal with everyday working conditions, and to respond to the information I was receiving through the research. Feminism provided a very unreliable form of support. I could not find a way of combining my commitment to anti-racist politics with the priorities and perspectives of the local and national women's movement. It was literally like having a foot in two camps. Of course it wasn't just my problem, and the splits and arguments that took place during those years left countless women feeling disillusioned and marginal to the whole idea of a 'women's movement'. But I needed support from other women in the work I was doing, in which I was very isolated, as well as some sense that the different things that I cared about connected up with each other.

The early days of the Women Against Racism and Fascism groups did provide both the support and the connections. In Birmingham we wrote leaflets, held jumble sales, film shows, public meetings, street stalls and graffiti paint-outs, and commissioned a spectacular multi-racial women's banner. When I was asked by Maurice Ludmer, the editor of *Searchlight*, to write a pamphlet on women and the National Front, several of us worked together on the ideas and first drafts before it was published. Without claiming them to be the happiest days of my life, I certainly remember a feeling of optimism and collaboration that made my life and work a great deal more enjoyable. However, the tensions and frustrations were quickly apparent. We never could quite answer the question, What exactly has racism got to do with white women? Fascism, on the other hand, provided fairly easy ground for making connections. It threatened to remove any independence that women might have gained, returning them to the kitchen and making them into breeders for the white race. Another question that was constantly asked was: How do we actually meet and work together with black women?

As time went on and neither of these questions ever got nearer to being answered, apathy set in. The Tory election victory in 1979 was the kiss of death. A contingent of socialist feminists turned up to the last big meeting to argue that the Tories had in mind precisely what the fascists had been calling for: forcing women back into the home, restricting rights to abortion and closing nurseries. Nothing about racism, nothing about the immigration laws and the promised nationality bill. This was a reaction common throughout the left at this period; the National Front had been defeated and racism was evidently no longer a priority. Our local WARF group staggered on for another year; racism had become a special interest for individuals who chose to make it that. Several rather depressing incidents brought home to me the futility of expecting anti-racism to be an active component of feminism.

One was an abortive WARF meeting on immigration for which we mailed over thirty women and not one turned up – even though, as we explained in our letter, white women were among those who stood to lose out under the new regulations. Another was trying to find other women to come and carry the by now crumpled and cat-smelling banner at what promised to be a historic national demonstration by black people against state harassment. We finally had just two WARF representatives on several coach-loads from Birmingham. It was very clear that the constituency of women who had previously been active in the anti-fascist campaigns of the late seventies – where I lived at least – felt that they had to prioritize other issues which they felt to be more directly relevant to their lives.

Another incident was the last national socialist feminist conference, which was held in London on the theme of imperialism. There were many problems and conflicts over that weekend, not least the arrest and detention of two Irish women who had been travelling over to attend the conference. During the one workshop I attended some women discussed the difficulties of supporting peoples or struggles which seemed to oppress women. I remember one woman saying she had read a book about a South American Indian tribe which was being slowly destroyed. Her feelings of outrage and concern were, she said, greatly undermined when she read elsewhere of their 'barbaric' treatment of women. The logical conclusion of what she was saying – that selective genocide might be acceptable – appeared to have escaped her. The conversation inevitably touched on 'arranged marriages', a topic which has consistently raised problems in feminist discussion. During the same workshop, another women expressed anger that we were discussing imperialism at all, asking what it had to do with women anyway.

It was around that time that a local women's magazine was started in Birmingham. A few of us went to early meetings to make sure that the paper took an anti-racist position from the beginning and included news and contributions from black women. This was welcomed although we were asked to organize it ourselves. Since I was working as a journalist I was able to supply several stories. One was about a strike by Asian women in a factory in Handsworth where the workers were trying to set up a union. I wrote the piece and finished by saying that a victory for these women would encourage black women all over the country to fight for their rights as workers. For some reason, which was later freely admitted to be ignorance, the word 'black' was altered to 'coloured' which changed the tone from being supportive to patronizing. The first issue of the paper, which carried this item, did not show any other sign of interest in or commitment to the lives of black women in Birmingham. It was totally exasperating. However, the stresses and strains between the various factions of feminism were becoming so vitriolic and divisive that it was almost impossible to talk about anything. The radical feminists seemed to have more fun as they had their own disco and pub scene, where women let their hair down to predominantly black women's music, but I was retreating from women's politics. Around this time the Reclaim the Night march was organized in protest at the failure of the police to track down a rapist operating locally. The march was a feminist tactic that had previously provoked a lot of discussion and criticism since it usually involved a torchlit procession by mainly white women through inner city areas. This was thought to be intimidating to the black people who lived there and open to racist interpretations, and many women were divided about the ethics of such ambiguous activity. In this instance, however, the urgency of the rape problem meant that there was no room to talk about race, and it was quite impossible to raise the implications of the rapist being a black man without being made to feel very uncomfortable and divisive. But I took the easy way out and kept away from these meetings as I had no energy left for confrontation. I had become identified as a 'race' person, and I felt this invalidated everything I might say.

Shortly after this I became the official editor of *Searchlight*, which had by then moved to London. After Birmingham, I found it much harder to become involved in local campaigns, and there was no network of friends and feminists like the one I was used to there. For several months I was part of a small group who met to write about and discuss the subject of white women and racism, but it was difficult to engage with any form of wider dialogue. However, as in Birmingham, it had become very hard to talk publicly about racism and feminism, for a variety of reasons. I realized this when, in 1982, I was commissioned to write an article for Spare Rib, which at that time had just employed its first black member of the collective in an attempt to redress the imbalance of an all-white staff. The subject was to be the racism of the Metropolitan Police, which had presented its annual crime statistics with certain offences broken down along racial lines in order to demonstrate the disproportionate involvement of black youth in street robbery, or mugging, as it had come to be known. I wanted to make two points which I felt were relevant to feminism at that time and which I had discussed at great length with other interested and concerned women. First, I wanted to show that the racist stereotype of the black 'mugger' was almost always seen as a threat to white females, and that as a result of the police action this image was indeed being projected by the media. In my article, I showed that this racist fantasy had a history, providing examples from both nineteenth-century America and Britain. Second, I argued that for this reason feminists campaigning against male violence should make it very clear that they were not colluding in this racist stereotype. I even suggested that it was an opportunity for women to take an anti-racist position as feminists.

The final version of the article would not have earned me a prize for tact, as the second paragraph launched into a criticism of *Spare Rib*'s reporting of the police statistics incident, using it as an example of the problem I was about to discuss. I wrote: 'To speak of sex, race and crime in one breath, without making or seeing any connection, betrays the white women's movement's failure to bring an anti-racist perspective to our struggles against male violence.' Unluckily for me, although I doubt I would have changed it had I known, the piece in *Spare Rib* had been written by a black woman, who responded with an angry telephone call and two letters castigating me for my 'politics of nothingness'. The correspondence was deeply depressing at the time, but as it turned out, also instructive in the way that it helped me to clarify my own position on race and racism within feminist politics.

The fact that it was a black woman who took it upon herself to respond to my article was almost irrelevant, for she was apparently supported by the collective – I was told, however, that it was racist of me to assume that the comment had been written by a white woman. My main error had been the way I criticized other women for their failure to deal with racism without making any attempt to confess ritualistically my own personal racism, which had become by then the only legitimate way for white women to speak about the subject. I was also sent an article written by two American white lesbian feminists who had initiated a consciousness-raising group in an attempt to deal with their own racism as an example of white women 'who were really trying'. I had compounded my offence by addressing my argument to white women, and by not discussing ways in which black women were affected by male violence. It seemed that it was invalid to address race as a political problem for white women, as though 'race' somehow belonged to black people. I was found guilty of other faults too: arrogance, impatience, being anti-women, playing black women off against one another, failing to say anything constructive. In fact I had it all completely wrong.

In the end I met up with two other women from the collective in an attempt to sort out some of the misunderstandings. There were so few places to write and argue controversial points as a feminist in London that it felt quite dispiriting to have been attacked for trying. I was amazed by the rigidity of the guidelines that were apparently involved in producing a feminist argument. There was a strong fear of getting things wrong, or at least not proceeding in a collectively agreed direction. At one point, I was told on a more kindly note that the white women in the collective had not yet worked out their anti-racist practice so they could not risk printing an article that might turn out to be controversial. I believe that the incident happened at a time when *Spare Rib* was buckling under the impossible weight of being a mouthpiece for the women's movement as a whole, which no single journal could possibly bear. But it also represented to me at the time the rigidity and dogmatic tendencies of mainstream feminism as a political movement.

Over the next few months I joined a new campaign looking at the question of women and policing, but it became dominated by one particular group and so I gave up. However, my life changed completely at this point because I became pregnant, and shortly before the baby arrived, I was told that I could not have my job back as editor of *Searchlight*. Being a new mother and unemployed at once gave me a very different perspective on feminism. I joined a group of friends in founding our own disreputable journal which enabled me to write a more considered version of my earlier article, which benefited from a little more research.[19] In particular, I had begun to think about the historical connections between white women and black people, looking for patterns in the way women had responded to racism in the past. This process had started when I was introduced to the idea that American feminism had first emerged out of the campaign to end slavery, and was then reborn in the 1960s out of the civil rights movement. This discovery led me to ask about the connections in Britain between feminist and black struggles. If feminism here in the late sixties was largely inspired by what was happening in the USA, then what was the impact of African-American politics on the women's liberation movement in Britain? And to what extent was feminism made possible in the first place by the struggles of black slaves for emancipation? It was these questions that propelled me to find out more about the historical connections between race, gender and class.

## Connecting Histories

> I have a feeling that even if it weren't for all those movements of the 1960s, eventually there would have been a Women's Liberation Movement. There are certain material objective conditions that women would have gotten more and more upset about, and it would have exploded at some point. But the fact of the Civil Rights Movement, and the Black Power Movement and the Anti-War Movement and the New Left, all made that happen much faster and helped shape the way it happened. It is hard to say for sure, but my own guess is that the Civil Rights Movement probably had the most profound impact on us. It began to crack the myth of the American Dream and the promise of equality all round. Whether directly or not, it had a tremendous effect on the early consciousness of the Women's Movement.
>
> Leslie Cagan[20]

In an interview on her memories of being an activist in the sixties, American feminist, Leslie Cagan, summed up her feelings about the relevance of that time for her politics today:

> There is a social and political history to who we are. We need to share that history and those experiences with other people who were either too young to be involved at the time or, for whatever reasons, were just not touched by those movements. There are things buried in that past that will help us better understand the present, to say nothing of possibly shedding some light on the future. There is a tremendous amount that we have yet to know about the links that have existed between different struggles.[21]

The process of tracing the origins of different political movements is not merely one of academic interest. Knowing where you have come from is as important as knowing where you are going, when it comes to identifying political goals and strategies. In many ways it is irrelevant to suggest, as Leslie Cagan does, that a women's movement would have happened anyway because the conditions that gave rise to the actual expression of discontent and militancy among women – either in the 1830s or in the 1960s – cannot be disconnected from the political climate that produced the movement to end slavery or the movement for civil rights. Similarly, political ideas and strategies cannot be confined to national or geographical boundaries, and this is as true of feminism as it is of struggles against racism and imperialism. British feminism, in both the nineteenth and twentieth centuries, was inspired and informed by women's efforts in other parts of the world, particularly America and Europe, and in turn contributed to debates and developments outside Britain. American feminism has always had a very contemporary relevance for women in Britain, although the history of that dialogue has often been forgotten or obscured.

In terms of race, the connections between Britain and the USA and the lessons to be learnt on both sides have a particularly long and painful history. Black and white abolitionists, male and female, traditionally visited Britain to campaign for support and to raise funds for abolitionist or independent black projects. Debates about every aspect of race, equality, emancipation and human rights were held across the Atlantic by means of personal correspondence, journals, newspapers and pamphlets. Many of the early British feminists were influenced by the ideas and language of abolitionism, which had radical implications for their own politics.

Over a hundred years later, the way in which American feminists were inspired by the civil rights movement has been recognized, albeit unevenly, as a crucial element in determining the direction and tactics of the women's movement. As many women have since testified, feminism owed its analysis of oppression, its reliance on autonomy and separatism, its understanding of equality, to the emergence of black politics throughout the sixties. Juliet Mitchell touched on this in her history of women's politics:

> Black Power, Student, Youth and Peace Movements all embodied values that, in one way or another, easily found expression in Women's Liberation. In the United States, black women found themselves the most oppressed within and without their race: their political movement would only recognise their position if they did. But of greatest importance to Women's Liberation, Black Power focused on general oppression rather than on economic exploitation alone, and it validated separatist politics.[22]

Just as political movements throughout America and Europe reverberated among different sections of those populations, producing dialogues among blacks, students, youth, workers and women across several different countries, so feminism in Britain developed out of these same cross-currents. It acquired a flavour that was specific to those conditions and to the activists who took the first steps towards working collectively in the interests of women, but it was a movement that took its cue from a women's politics that was being worked out simultaneously in the USA.

The impetus behind the early American feminist groupings of the mid and late sixties came largely from southern white women who were active within the civil rights movement and who had been inspired by the revolt of black people in the areas where they lived and worked. For many of these women it was their experiences inside the church that propelled them into direct action alongside their black new-found brothers and sisters. In a remarkable book that documents this history, Sara Evans records interviews with women who either grew up or studied at college in a society that practised segregation between black and white. She describes how many of these women moved from an awareness of injustice against black people to a sense of their own struggle for equality:

> Twice in the history of the United States the struggle for racial equality has been midwife to a feminist movement. In the abolition movement of the 1830s and 1840s, and again in the civil rights movement of the 1960s, women experiencing the contradictory expectations and stresses of changing roles began to move from individual discontents to a social movement in their own behalf. Working for racial justice, they gained experience in organising and in collective action, an ideology that described and condemned oppression analogous to their own, and a belief in human 'rights' that could justify them in claiming equality for themselves. In each case, moreover, the complex web of racial and sexual oppression embedded in southern culture projected a handful of white southern women into the forefront of those who connected one cause with the other.[23]

As the decade progressed and other movements among the new left, students and youth began to gather momentum, black and white women working within male-dominated structures began to express their frustration with their own situation of powerlessness. Many white women experienced this as a discovery of a cause with which they could identify completely: instead of supporting someone else's struggle against oppression they could fight for themselves. Sara Evans stresses that the rebellion by mainly young white women against racism had powerful implications:

> Within southern society, 'white womanhood' provided a potent cultural symbol that also implied little practical power for women. The necessity of policing the boundaries between black and white heightened the symbolic importance of traditional domestic arrangements: white women in their proper place guaranteed the sanctity of the home and the purity of the white

> race. As long as they remained 'ladies', they represented the domination of white men.[24]

For many of the women active in the early days of the women's movement, both in the USA and in Britain, maintaining a connection between different kinds of politics was crucial to their feminism, however difficult it proved. Several have written or spoken about how hard it was to decide what their priorities were. By 1968 two camps had emerged in the US women's movement, one for the 'politicos' – those who came from the new left and who believed that capitalism was the main enemy – and one for the 'feminists', some of whom later called themselves 'radical feminists'. Ellen Willis recalls how she sided with the 'feminists', arguing that male supremacy was a systematic form of domination, requiring a revolutionary movement of women to challenge it. 'Our model of course was black power – a number of the early radical feminists had been civil rights activists.' Although the women who identified with this kind of feminism were accused by the left of being bourgeois and anti-left, the majority certainly allied themselves with various leftist causes. Ellen Willis writes that 'with few exceptions, those of us who first defined radical feminism took for granted that 'radical' implied anti-racist, anti-capitalist and anti-imperialist. We saw ourselves as expanding the definition of radical to include feminism.'[25]

Leslie Cagan remembers that she felt 'torn apart' by the distinction between 'politicos' and 'feminists'. Although she was quickly caught up in the early women's groups and was committed to the idea of feminism, her involvement in other political struggles made it hard for her to jump one way or the other:

> At the same time, deep in my heart of hearts I felt that we couldn't separate ourselves totally. We had to deal with the fact that Panthers were being shot down, we couldn't ignore the war in Vietnam. I didn't know how to do it, how to pull it all together. So I felt and acted as if I were several different people all at once; I was an anti-war activist; I was a Panther support person; I was a feminist and my women's group probably had the biggest impact on me.

For her the problem in 1968 was to remain in both camps without feeling rejected by either one. Active involvement with other liberation movements in the following months taught her the importance of combining a feminist perspective with an internationalist and leftist one and being able to offer something as well as to take from others. She describes a particular incident which for her illustrated the importance of 'organic' connections between movements. In 1970 she was one of a group of white women who campaigned to raise bail money for Joan Bird, a nineteen-year-old student nurse who was arrested with twenty other members of the Black Panther Party on a trumped up charge of conspiracy. For the women in the campaign, the issue was both that she was a woman and that she was an activist with the Black Panthers fighting racism, and they wanted to stress that in the campaign literature. At that time it was not necessarily accepted by men that women's consciousness was a valid part of any struggle and they were apprehensive that their support for Bird would not be accepted by the Panthers. Instead they met with 'a beginning of what seemed to be some mutual respect. We weren't just coming as some sort of guilty white people who wanted to help the poor Panthers. We were saying that we had a struggle too and we thought there was some way to connect the two.'[26]

In Britain the first feminist meetings and campaigns took place within the context of the left – that is, actively socialist and trade union organizing. Sheila Rowbotham, who was active within socialist and student politics in the late sixties, describes how in the early years there was a strong socialist influence in the women's movement:

> We would go on marches against Cambodia and then later on in solidarity with Portugal after the revolution there. People now have a very clear idea of the difference between the women's movement and 'the left', but we didn't really at the time. Both then and now I would regard myself as part of the left. This does not mean I'm not a feminist.[27]

Elsewhere she writes that women were optimistic at first in assuming that feminist consciousness would automatically lead to seeing connections with other people. She admits that although many feminists did see the connections, this did not always happen. In 1981, looking back at the development of the women's movement over the previous ten years, she speaks about an 'erosion of memory' which has obscured the 'experimenting and struggle about organising' that took place in the early days of the movement.

It is perhaps easy to romanticize or over-simplify periods of history when everything seemed clearer, more dynamic and creative. But it is also useful to keep track of those moments when new politics seem to be being born, because there is often a more self-conscious attempt to bring together disparate strands, to make connections across previously unconnected experiences. Those connections can so easily be taken for granted as the political context changes and new converts are drawn in. Different political constituencies do not necessarily have consistent bases for alliance or even dialogue. There can be no guarantee that apparently progressive movements will not work against each other, sometimes unconsciously and sometimes knowing fully that each harms the other's cause. Being aware of our own history, as white women trying to work out a politics which is concerned with all these issues – gender, race, class, ecology, peace – which in fact wants justice for all those who are exploited and powerless – gives us more chance to renew those alliances. Continuing Leslie Cagan's thoughts on those things that are buried in the past:

> There is a tremendous amount that we have yet to know about the links that have existed between different struggles. It is going to take the pooling of many people's different experiences and insights to see what those links are and can be. And part of that process is writing our own history. We know that 'they' are never going to write our history the way it really happened. We have to do that one ourselves.[28]

## Legacies of Empire

> Doubtless there are native women who set the highest value on their chastity, but they are the exception and the rape of an ordinary native woman does not present any element of comparison with the rape of a respectable white woman, even where the offence upon the latter is committed by one of her own race and colour.
>
> Hubert Murray, Lieutenant-Governor of Port Moresby, New Guinea, 1925[29]

> By instruction leading to the improvement of the individual we shall aid in preserving women for their supreme purpose, the procreation and preservation of the race, and at the same time promote that race to a better standard, mentally and physically.
>
> J. E. Gemmell, *Journal of Obstetrics and Gynaecology of the British Empire,* 1903[30]

> In many Oriental lands, in many parts of Africa, in the islands of the Pacific, the wife of a missionary was the first white woman ever seen by the native peoples. We cannot easily exaggerate the importance of this fact or the influence which these Christian white women exerted over primitive peoples whose own women were at best the burden bearers whose lot was to work and obey, and who were often treated with active or passive cruelty.
>
> Winifred Mathews, 1947[31]

> Now I aren't no 'and with the ladies,
> For, taking 'em all along,
> You can never say till you've tried 'em,
> An' then you are like to be wrong.
> There's times when you'll think that you mightn't,
> There's times when you'll know that you might;
> But the things you will learn from the Yellow an' Brown,
> They'll 'elp you a lot with the White.
>
> Rudyard Kipling[32]

The attempt to write history 'the way it really happened' necessarily presents insurmountable problems. It implies the possibility of there being one version of events, shared by many diverse participants. Yet how can we begin to synthesize different versions of history that exist in separate and often unrelated forms? For myself, deciding to learn more about the historical connections between white women and black people, this question became more and more important as I searched for clues in what was available. I began to read more feminist history, that is, history rewritten by feminists in pursuit of the conditions that have shaped women's lives and their resistance in the face of economic, social and political subordination. I tried to match this up with what little has been published about black British history. Inevitably the first area was limited to white women and the second mainly to black men, since there were far fewer black women than men living in Britain until recent immigration began in the 1950s. Another source of information was the wealth of written material on slavery, abolition, colonialism and racism itself, some of which included a perspective on gender but most of which did not.

The insularity of British women's history convinced me further that this was a key to understanding the way that racism had been separated from gender relations in contemporary analysis. It is still rare, for example, to find any white feminist history of the nineteenth century that relates to the

British Empire, except as a force that touched women's lives in Britain or as a possible escape route for women who failed to make a satisfying life at home. Overlooking the existence of imperialist ideologies suggests that the question of race has no relevance to the history of white women. This is despite the fact that black people have lived in Britain for four hundred years as part of the African and Asian diasporas, fighting for their own liberation as well as playing a part in working-class politics. Apart from this, British rule extended until relatively recently right round the world; English people did not exist in a vacuum on their precious island within this Empire, oblivious of what was going on in their name. Nor were women, white or black, excluded from the colonizing process.

Kipling's phrase 'the White Man's Burden' is often interpreted as referring to the great weight of uncivilized, non-Christian people throughout the world who needed colonial rule to save them from themselves.[33] Reading the poem of the same name I wonder whether it was not intended as an ironic comment on the obsession of Europeans to justify their commercial exploitation of colonies by claiming that their rule was spreading civilization and rescuing savages from themselves. But however you want to take it, there is still the question of whether Kipling's White Man could exist without White Woman somewhere at his side. We are entitled to ask what her Burden was, and what she has done with it since.

Gender played a crucial role in organizing ideas of 'race' and 'civilization', and women were involved in many different ways in the expansion and maintenance of the Empire. The presence of white women, for example, demanded that relations between the 'races' be highly regulated. The increasing number of white women who travelled out to join husbands and families in the colonies, or to work in their own right as missionaries, nurses and teachers, often had far-reaching effects on the social lives of male settlers, and consequently on the status and sexual exploitation of black women. This was particularly true where the military were concerned, since prostitution was often viewed by the colonial authorities as a necessary evil to service the working-class troops who were not permitted to bring their British wives. During the late Victorian period when theories of race and eugenics were being used to bolster the concept of the innate superiority of the white race above all others, English women were seen as the 'conduits of the essence of the race'.[34] They not only symbolized the guardians of the race in their reproductive capacity, but they also provided – as long as they were of the right class and breeding – a guarantee that British morals and principles were adhered to in the settler community, as well as being transmitted to the next generation. In the debates and discussions on the volatile situation in South Africa in the early twentieth century, it was thought to be particularly important that British women made their presence felt there.

> It is women of high moral character possessed of common sense and a sound constitution who can help build up our Empire. . . . [They can]. . . .exalt the tone of social life, bring a softening, elevating, intellectual influence.[35]

Inevitably, the colonial situation varied from place to place, and from one continent to another. The significance of white women's position within the ruling elite was not fixed either in time or geography, but varied according to the state of relations between those being colonized and those exercising power. One of the recurring themes in the history of colonial repression is the way in which the threat of real or imagined violence towards white women became a symbol of the most dangerous form of insubordination. In any colony, the degree to which white women were protected from the fear of sexual assault was a good indication of the level of security felt by the colonial authorities. In a study of European women in colonial Nigeria, Helen Callaway writes that 'the question of European women's "sexual fear" appears to arise in special circumstances of unequal power structures at times of particular political pressure, when the dominant group perceives itself threatened and vulnerable'.[36] Protecting the virtue of white women was the pretext for instituting draconian measures against indigenous populations in several parts of the Empire. In Papua, New Guinea, a law was passed – called the White Women's Protection Ordinance – which made any 'native' convicted of rape or even attempted rape of a European female liable to the death penalty. The law was passed during a frenzy of racist passions following reports of two unconnected assaults on white females in a short space of time. Contemporary records reveal that this was happening in a period of social and political uncertainty in the colony, and that the actual level of rape and sexual assault bore no relation to the hysteria that the subject aroused. White women provided a symbol of the most valuable property known to white man and it was to be protected from the ever-encroaching and disrespectful black man at all costs.[37]

The history of this particular discourse on race and gender cannot be appreciated fully without reference to earlier landmarks in the history of colonialism. Two major rebellions in the mid nineteenth century brought about intense public debates concerning the safety of white women in the Empire; both marked significant points in the development of imperialist ideology, and both influenced subsequent governmental policy as well as social relations in the colonies. So far, there has been little exploration of either event from the point of view of contemporary feminist politics in Britain, yet even these brief accounts that follow will give an indication of their important place in the history of race, class and gender.[38]

The year 1857 saw the first national uprising in India, known to the British as 'The Mutiny'. Although there had been local resistance to British rule in India before this date, there had never been widespread armed rebellion on such a scale before. Soon after the initial uprising by the Sepoys at Meerut, reports of gruesome atrocities against British soldiers and civilians began flooding back to England, and for several months the press regurgitated a diet of eyewitness accounts, military bulletins, stories and rumours to the British public who became ever more eager for revenge. Tales of vengeance provoked great public rejoicing and Bernard Semmel quotes an eyewitness report that 'the very sight of a dark man stimulated our national enthusiasm almost to frenzy'. According to Semmel:

> Day after day, the newspapers told stories of massacres of British women and children, of gruesome oriental tortures and mutilations, of assaults on the virtue and honour of English women. Reports were received of aristocratic English ladies dragged naked through the streets of Delhi and exhibited to the lecherous gaze of its senile king.[39]

It has been said that 'no episode in British imperial history raised public excitement to a higher pitch'.[40] In 1897, a woman writing in *Blackwood's Magazine* claimed that 'of all the great events of this century, as they are reflected in fiction, the Indian Mutiny has taken the firmest hold on the popular imagination'.[41] As in all wars, there were tales of heroism, bravery, deceit and betrayal, but at the centre of the 1857 uprising was the spectre of the most awful atrocity that could be imagined: the rape of English women. This was a crime that was rarely described in any detail, but alluded to in countless reports of attacks on civilians. The *Englishwoman's Review and Home Newspaper*, the only women's newspaper published at that time, provides a fascinating narrative of the way in which the

'Mutiny' was reported across the country. Since it was compiled by women, the tone of its editorial content reads differently from that of the conventional press. Relying on reports from other papers, letters, reconstructed stories, the paper adopted the tone of the aggrieved victim, giving full encouragement to the brave men who survived to avenge their sex. Accounts of dead children, of rooms filled with blood, matted hair, mangled toys, rotting clothes, would all have had a particular impact in the pages of a women's paper which aimed to reinforce the conventional female role in the domestic sphere. To speak directly of lust and sexual assault would hardly have been thinkable in such a refined context. One report, published five months after the start of the uprising in May, lingered not on actual rape so much as violence of a more representable nature:

> Every day brings news of further atrocities. The fiends of Islam actually mince the Christians – oblige poor ladies and children to lie over the dead bodies of their husbands, brothers, and fathers, there to be chopped up limb by limb! They often force down the throats of the living victims the flesh of the mangled Christians, whose fate they well know they themselves are to share immediately after![42]

One month later, under the heading, 'An Oath for Vengeance', the paper recounted the heroic story of one detachment of troops. On finding the remains of one of General Wheeler's daughters, the men divided up every hair of her head between them and took a solemn oath to kill as many 'natives' as each strand of hair in revenge for her unspeakable fate.

This anecdote illustrates the dynamics of colonial repression in which the Englishwoman symbolized all that was held most dear in British civilization. The colonized people were to be punished and made to pay for their revolt against colonial rule, but the severity of the punishment was given the appearance of legality by being carried out in the name of avenging the womenfolk. A graphic account written almost fifty years later proved that there was still an audience eager to hear the details. The fate of the women provided much of the drama:

> The fugitives who escaped from the Cashmere Gate had some very tragical experiences. Sinking from fatigue and hunger, scorched by the flame-like heat of the sun, wading rivers, toiling through jungles, hunted by villagers, they struggled on. . . . Of that much-enduring company . . . it is recorded

> that the women often showed the highest degree of fortitude and patience. Yet more than one mother had to lay her child . . . in a nameless jungle grave; more than one wife had to see her husband die, of bullet or swordstroke, at her feet.

The fortitude of the British women was frequently contrasted with their treatment by the rebels. However, in this particular account, written by W.H.Fitchett, BA, LLD, 'author of *Deeds that Won the Empire*, *Fights for the Flag*, *How England Saved Europe*, *Wellington's Men etc*', it was evidently more significant to stress barbaric cruelty rather than sexual assault:

> Outrage, in the ordinary sense, was not, on the whole, a marked feature of the Great Mutiny. The Sepoys, that is, were on fire with cruelty [more] than with lust. But their cruelty spared neither age nor sex. The wife of a captain, according to one story current at the time – and perhaps not true – was literally boiled alive in ghee, or melted butter. Children were tossed on bayonets, men roasted in the flames of their own bungalows; women were mutilated and dismembered.[43]

This extract is not only interesting for the way it differentiates carefully between 'ordinary' lust and inflamed cruelty, but also because it repeats an anecdote that the author himself suggests might not be true. Thus it is a good example of the continuing power of the 'Mutiny' narrative in the early twentieth century.

The second incident to precipitate a panic about the safety of white women was the Morant Bay uprising, which took place in Jamaica in 1865.[44] A protest demonstration of several hundred Jamaican peasants, led by Paul Bogle, marched to the local court-house to complain about the partiality of magistrates, and, meeting the full strength of the militia, set fire to buildings and forced local officials to flee. As a result, the governor, Edward John Eyre, declared martial law and sent in troops who killed 439 blacks, flogged about 600 others and burned over 1000 homes. The savagery with which the local revolt was put down – the troops met with no resistance – caused intense interest in England. The arrest and execution of George William Gordon, a prominent landowner and critic of Governor Eyre, provoked particular consternation. During the months that followed, debates about the character of the West Indian black man raged continuously. Those who supported Eyre warned that if black revolt were not stamped out, the situation would get completely out of hand. As fresh troops were dispatched to help Eyre quell another rumoured disturbance, the *Standard* reported that the black savages of Jamaica had no grievances, but sought only to satisfy their greed, hatred and lust for white property, white lives and white women.[45] Those who defended the black population were branded as 'nigger-worshippers', while the development of the so-called sciences of physical anthropology and evolutionism meant that there was a new language to express the old prejudices.[46] One newspaper suggested that the 'world-renowned question, once thought so convincing, of "Am I not a man and a brother?" would nowadays be answered with some hesitation by many – with a flat negative to its latter half by those who regard the blacks as an inferior race'.[47]

The historical memory of white women's presence in the Empire, shaped by events such as these, cements the image of the powerless, vulnerable female. However, an equally fruitful and revealing discourse emerges when white women chose to defy this role through what they did and said. There are many instances where English women challenged the expectations arising from their allotted place within the colonial system, preferring to live independently and inviting scandal and frequently loneliness by doing so. There are scattered examples of women who engaged in anti-slavery politics, who organized campaigns to support black women in different parts of the Empire, or who gave their energy to nationalist movements, but they remain eccentric individuals at best. Whereas feminist historians have uncovered many examples of feminists who braved convention at home to fight to improve the lives and opportunities of women of all classes and backgrounds, there has been little corresponding interest in British women who came face to face with the complexities of racism and male power. The exceptions to this usually fall in the 'intrepid explorer' category: women like Mary Kingsley who are frequently remembered or even celebrated for their 'feminism' – that is, their attitudes to the constraints of gender – rather than their role in the imperialist project and the way they dealt with racism and cultural difference.

The struggle for history is about much more than establishing what actually happened. It involves those who have so far been excluded or marginalized, recognizing themselves not as passive victims but as actors who have had an instrumental role in the past. Recognizing that there is a whole dimension of British history now demanding incorporation into accounts that were previously regarded as radical, or at least alternative, has enormous implications, not just for feminist historians but for historians of race and class as well. I am not speaking about simply bringing a history of black people or of racism alongside what is known about white women's history, nor of inserting gender into existing accounts of race and class. Applying a perspective of race, class *and* gender to historical inquiry should effectively transform interpretations based on race and class or class and gender. The anti-slavery movement, for example, coincided with a period of tumultuous social change in Britain. Studies of women's abolitionist work have so far been mainly restricted to a limited 'women's contribution' style of inquiry, but the evidence these studies offer us could also be used in conjunction with other material to speculate both on the changing dynamics of social, economic and political relations and on the politics of challenging slavery itself. To take another example which I shall be exploring later on, colonial society involved a highly complex web of social relations based on race, class and gender. Learning about what white women did to pass the time in that society would not necessarily contribute much to an analysis of how it reproduced itself, whereas prising apart the social relations which connected white women to white men as well as black men and black women is likely to shed more light on the mechanics of power and domination under colonialism.

The purpose of exploring the histories of slavery and imperialism is not to bring white women to account for past misdeeds, nor to search for heroines whose reputations can help to absolve the rest from guilt, but to find out how white women negotiated questions of race and racism – as well as class and gender. In other words what we need to do is to trace ideas that have historically constructed definitions of white womanhood and to ask how these ideas have been formed either in conjunction with or in opposition to feminist ideology.

The final stage of my argument concerns the legacies of these ideas today. There would not be much point in understanding how the category of white femininity was constructed through history if this information was not used to engage with contemporary ideologies of domination. It is largely by looking at the histories of racism and male dominance that we find keys to understanding the specific complexities of our societies, unearthing connections which might otherwise remain unclear or even unpalatable.

I would not want to suggest that this process is simple and straightforward, either practically or ideologically. There are important problems to be addressed, such as how we are to do this work on our own history and contemporary lives, in conjunction with other groups of people who may not be interested in our versions, or who may be in conflict with us. How do we then piece our interpretations and analyses together with other people's in order to make better sense of them? And perhaps most importantly, who are 'we' anyway? It is this last suspicious question that should begin any incursion into feminist history.

## Notes

1 Enoch Powell, *Freedom and Reality*, Paperfront, Kingswood 1969, p. 287.

2 Charles Moore, *The Old People of Lambeth*, The Salisbury Group, London 1982.

3 See, for example, Ruth Hall, *Ask Any Woman – A London Inquiry into Rape and Sexual Assault*, Falling Wall Press, Bristol 1985: J. Hanmer and S. Saunder, *Well-Founded Fear – A Community Study of Violence to Women*, Hutchinson, London 1984; and Liz Kelly and Jill Radford,'The Problem of Men: Feminist Perspectives on Male Violence', in P. Scraton, ed., *Law, Order and the Authoritarian State*, Open University Press, Milton Keynes 1987.

4 *Docklands Light Railway News*, no. 5, Autumn/Winter 1986.

5 Ibid., no. 6, Summer 1987.

6 Ray Honeyford. 'Multi-ethnic Intolerance'. *The Salisbury Review*. no. 4, Summer 1983.

7 *Daily Telegraph*, 4 September 1987.

8 *Daily Express*, 4 September 1987.

9 *Observer*, 22 April 1990.

10 Eileen Macdonald, *Brides For Sale: Human Trade in North Yemen*, Mainstream Publishing, Edinburgh 1988, pp. 86–7.

11 *Sunday Express*, 16 November 1986. In a report of the same trip, the *Guardian* (12 November 1986) provided a nice example of what Jim Clifford calls 'the Squanto effect'. During a re-enactment of a traditional wedding planned especially for Diana's entertainment, an Omani woman was asked what impression the English princess had made on her. She replied in English, 'Well, actually, I saw her last in Gleneagles, and she seems very much the same'. (Clifford, *The Predicament of Culture; Twentieth-Century Ethnography, Literature and Art*, Harvard University Press, Cambridge MA/London 1988, p. 17.)

12 *Vogue* (UK edn), June 1987.

13 *Observer,* 23 February 1986.

14 *Elle* (UK edn), July 1987.

15 Pratibha Parmar, 'Hateful Contraries: Media Images of Asian Women', in *Ten.8* no. 16.

16 Pratibha Parmar and Jackie Kay, 'Interview with Audre Lorde', in S. Grewal *et al.*, eds, *Charting the Journey: Writings by Black and Third World Women*, Sheba, London 1988, p. 125.

17 'Taking Racism Personally: White Anti-Racism at the Cross-Roads', *Peace News*, 1978.

18 Adrienne Rich, 'Disloyal to Civilization', in *On Lies, Secrets and Silence*, W. W. Norton, New York/London 1979, p. 306.

19 'Imperialism, Racism and Violence Against Women', *Emergency*, Winter 1983/4.

20 'Something New Emerges: The Growth of a Socialist Feminism', in Dick Cluster, ed., *They Should Have Served That Cup of Coffee: 7 Radicals Remember the 60s*, South End Press, Boston 1979, pp. 257–8.

21 Cluster, p. 258.

22 Juliet Mitchell, *Woman's Estate*, Penguin, Harmondsworth 1971, p. 175.

23 Sara Evans, *Personal Politics*, Vintage, New York 1979, p. 24.

24 Evans, p. 25.

25 Ellen Willis, 'Radical Feminism and Feminist Radicalism', in Sohnya Sayres *et al.*, eds, *The 60s Without Apology*, University of Minnesota Press, Minneapolis 1984, p. 93.

26 Cluster, pp. 244–5.

27 In Henry Abelove, *et al.*, ed., *Visions of History*, Pantheon, New York 1984, p. 58.

28 Cluster, p. 258.

29 Amirah Inglis, *The White Woman's Protection Ordinance: Sexual Anxiety and Politics in Papua*, Sussex University Press, London 1974, p. 72.

30 J. E. Gemmell, Presidential Address to the North of England Obstetrical and Gynaecological Society, published in *Journal of Obstetrics and Gynaecology of the British Empire*, December 1903, p. 590, quoted in Anna Davin, 'Imperialism and Motherhood', *History Workshop Journal*, 5, Spring 1978.

31 Winifred Mathews, *Dauntless Women*, Edinburgh House Press, London 1947, p. 5.

32 Rudyard Kipling, 'The Ladies', in *The Seven Seas*, Methuen, London 1897 p. 190.

33 Rudyard Kipling, 'White Man's Burden', in *The Five Nations*, Methuen, London 1903, p. 79.

34 Jane Mackay and Pat Thane, 'The Englishwoman', in R. Colls and P. Dodd, eds, *Englishness: Politics and Culture 1880–1920*, Croom Helm, London, p. 201.

35 The Hon. Mrs Evelyn Cecil, 'The Needs of South Africa, II. Female Emigration', *The Ninteenth Century*, April 1902, p. 683, quoted in Colls and Dodd, p. 205.

36 Helen Callaway, *Gender, Culture and Empire: European Women in Colonial Nigeria*, Macmillan, London 1987, p. 237.

37 For a detailed account of this history see Inglis.

38 Since I first wrote this I have read some very interesting and useful work on both events: see Jenny Sharpe, 'The Unspeakable Limits of Rape: Colonial Violence and Counter-Insurgency', *Genders*, no. 10, Spring 1991. On the Morant Bay uprising see Catherine Hall, 'The Economy of Intellectual Prestige: Thomas Carlyle, John Stuart Mill, and the Case of Governor Eyre', *Cultural Critique*, no. 12, Spring 1989.

39 Bernard Semmel, *Jamaican Blood and Victorian Conscience: The Governor Eyre Controversy*, Greenwood Press, Westport, CT 1962, p. 21.

40 Patrick Brantlinger, *Rule of Darkness: British Literature and Imperialism, 1830–1914*, Cornell University Press, Ithaca/London 1988, pp. 199–224.

41 Hilda Gregg, 'The Indian Mutiny in Fiction', *Blackwood's Magazine*, no. 161, February 1897, pp. 218–31, quoted in Brantlinger, p. 199.

42 *Englishwoman's Review and Home Newspaper*, 24 October 1857.

43 W. H. Fitchett, *The Tale of the Great Mutiny*, Smith, Elder & Co., London 1901, pp. 44, 69.

44 See Semmel for a fuller account of the uprising and the controversy it provoked in Britain.

45 Douglas Lorimer, *Colour, Class and the Victorians: English Attitudes to the Negro in the Mid-Nineteenth Century*, Leicester University Press, Leicester 1978, p. 182.

46 Lorimer, pp. 192–200.

47 Lorimer, pp. 198–9.

Part Two

# An Abhorrence of Slavery

## Subjection and Subjectivity in Abolitionist Politics

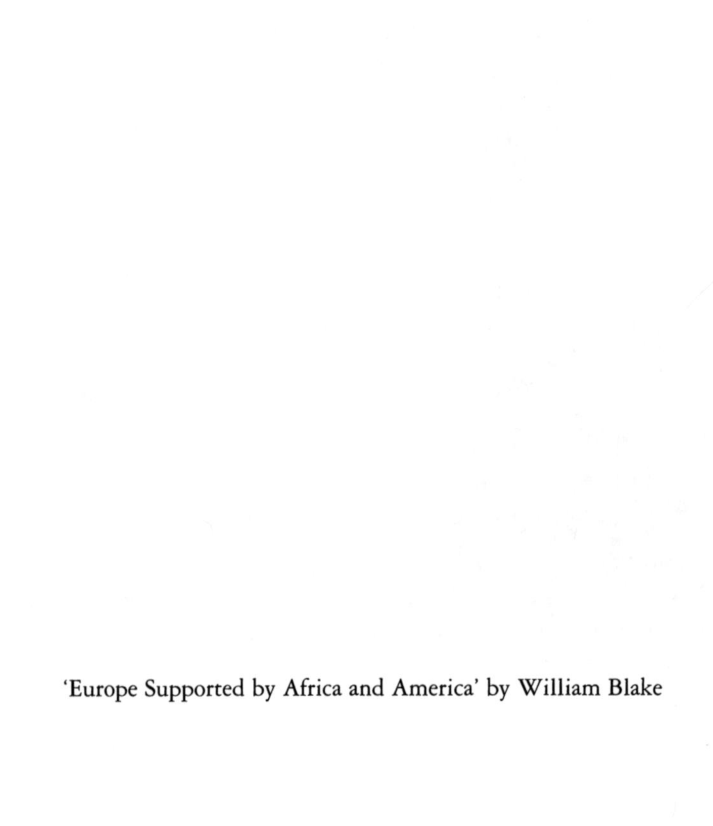

'Europe Supported by Africa and America' by William Blake

Remember them that are in bonds, as bound with them.

Hebrews xiii. 3

Can we behold, unheeding,
Life's holiest feelings crushed?
While woman's heart is bleeding,
Shall woman's voice be hushed?

Sheffield Association for the
Universal Abolition of Slavery, 1837[1]

In the last decade of the twentieth century it has become almost a ritual for works of feminist history or theory to begin by discussing the concept of 'woman' or 'women' as a tool for understanding female subordination. Writing in a collection of essays entitled *Feminism/Postmodernism*, for example, Judith Butler asks:

> Does feminist theory need to rely on a notion of what it is fundamentally or distinctively to be a 'woman'? . . . Is there a specific femininity or a specific set of values that have been written out of various histories and descriptions that can be associated with women as a group? Does the category of women maintain a meaning separate from the conditions of oppression against which it has been formulated?[2]

These kinds of questions are crucial to developing contemporary feminist theory, since in refusing any simplistic notion of homogeneity they invite a more complex and contradictory view of gender relations. At the same time, others have stressed that feminist politics require a more immediate and practical sense of connection between women if alliances across race and class are to be created and sustained, and if feminism is to make any sense as a political force. In other words, feminism needs to deal with two distinct levels of understanding 'women' as a collectivity: on the first, it would be ridiculous to say that we did not know what it means since we are continually reminded either by straightforward biology or by the social relations of gender that govern our lives, wherever we live; but on the second, there must be a recognition that the category itself is historically and culturally constructed. It follows that a historian needs to be sensitive to the ways that the category woman/women was understood during the period in question, without losing sight of the shifts in those meanings since then. The poem at the beginning of this essay is a useful illustration of this point. It was written by white, mainly middle-class women about black slave women, published in a passionate diatribe against 'foreign' slavery wherever it took place. Without seeing the context in which it appeared, there are no clues as to the social relations between the women being addressed and the women who are in trouble. Yet behind the sentimentality of the cry from woman to woman lies a fascinating history of opposition to slavery and an emerging feminist consciousness.

The project of tracing connections between race and gender starts most usefully during the years of Atlantic slavery, when the social relations of race, class and gender in Europe and America were being formed by specific economic, political and ideological forces. This is not to suggest that interlocking systems of race and gender subordination did not exist before this time, but that exploring the particular relationships between black peoples and white women throughout slavery – and the movement for its abolition – provides great insights for understanding subsequent histories. This is an enormous area of study, and in Britain at the time of writing this essay there has been very little published on British women and slavery.[3] I focus on the role of women in the anti-slavery movement as a way of tracing connections that women themselves made between the social relations of race, class and gender.

## From Oroonoko to Uncle Tom

As I set out to research this chapter I was astonished to discover that the first novel ever written by a woman dealt with the ethics of slavery, long before the abolitionist movement was formed. In 1678, the poet and playwright Aphra Behn wrote her first prose work, a book which was remarkable for two reasons. *Oroonoko – or the Royal Slave* was, some would argue, the first novel to be published in the English language – a fitting achievement for the first woman to support herself by her writing. But less well known is the impact the book had on representations of black slaves within British culture. Behn's novel was dramatized by Thomas Southerne soon after publication and was shown in London every season for almost a century. Despite substantial changes in the plot and characterization, *Oroonoko* became 'one of the most internationally popular stories of the eighteenth century . . . a prototype for a vast literature depicting noble African slaves'.[4]

The novelty of Behn's book lay in its portrayal of the leading black characters. The hero, the African Prince Oroonoko, is handsome, noble, brave and deeply hostile to Christianity. He is also capable of intense romantic love and of feeling a range of passions recognizable to his white audience. In the course of the plot he is captured and brought over to Surinam as a slave, where he leads his fellow slaves in a revolt but is eventually defeated and murdered by white officials. His defiance right up to his death is symbolized by the way he continues to smoke a pipe as his body is hacked to pieces while tied to a stake.

Within this main plot Oroonoko meets and is separated from Imoinda, the woman he loves. They are dramatically reunited on the slave plantation where they are allowed to marry. When Imoinda becomes pregnant, Oroonoko refuses to accept the prospect of his child being born into slavery. Rather than see her being raped by their captors he kills her and the unborn child as part of a suicide pact, but is so tormented by grief and desire for revenge that he is unable to kill himself, and is captured as he lies helplessly by her corpse.[5]

In order to appreciate Behn's role in changing the way black slaves were depicted, it must be remembered that she was writing at a time when blacks were seen as a different species – certainly not individuals who could think, feel and love. Anti-slavery protest from whites was almost unknown in England, and just beginning to make itself heard in America, but descriptions of the brutality and torture involved in maintaining slavery were almost meaningless as long as the slaves were not thought to value love and liberty. According to David Brion Davis, Europeans, who were not obliged to come face to face with the slaves, could generally only understand concepts of freedom and bondage in terms that were familiar to them: romance, betrayals, unjust punishment of a faithful servant.[6] Certainly Behn gave her hero physical characteristics that must have endeared him to her audience – she was careful to emphasize that his features were not those of a 'typical' African:

> His face was not that of that brown rusty black which most of that nation are, but a perfect ebony, or polished jett. His eyes were the most awful that cou'd be seen, and very piercing; the white of 'em being like snow, as were his teeth. His nose was rising and Roman, instead of African and flat. His mouth the finest shaped that could be seen; far from those great turn'd lips, which are so natural to the rest of the Negroes.[7]

Aphra Behn made her story more authentic by placing herself in the plot as a personal friend of Oroonoko. She had spent several years in Surinam with her family and used her experiences to draw up her undoubtedly fictional account.[8] In the book, she appears to have arrived on the plantation a little earlier than Oroonoko. As he was well versed in both English and French she could converse easily with him, and indeed, makes it clear that the prince preferred her company to that of the men, especially as he did not drink. In return for his confidences about his former life in Africa, where life was far more complex and 'civilized' than contemporary British thought must have presumed, she regaled him with stories of the Roman Empire, renaming him Caesar, and trying unsuccessfully to convert him to Christianity.

It is she, Aphra, whom Oroonoko called his 'great mistress', who first noticed the slave's frustration with his enforced stay on the plantation. Although it is not clear what authority Aphra held, she tried to speed up negotiations for his release and to allay his fears about his owners' motives in keeping him. The passage in which she first described this is interesting for what it says about mutual suspicion between the slave and the free woman:

> He made me some answers that shew'd a doubt in him, which made me ask, what advantages would it be to doubt? It would but give us a fear of him, and possibly compel us to treat him so as I should be loth to behold: that is, it might occasion his confinement . . . however, he assure'd me, that whatever resolution he should take, he would act nothing upon the white people; and as for myself, and those upon the plantation where he was, he would sooner forfeit his eternal liberty, and life itself, than lift his hand against his greatest enemy on that place. . . .[9]

As it turned out Aphra had no power to stop the treachery of the white planters, and Oroonoko was vindicated in his doubt.

This clearly drawn affinity between the white woman author and the figure of the slave provides a convenient starting point for this inquiry into female anti-slavery – that is, the particularities of women's efforts to free the slave. It is important to state here that anti-slavery politics cannot readily be equated with a challenge to ideologies of racial domination, but have to be seen through a historical perspective informed by a knowledge of the shifting patterns of racism. Almost two hundred years later, another work of fiction written by a white woman was to prove far more effective in changing attitudes towards the institution of slavery. Although *Uncle Tom's Cabin* was written by an American woman and first published in America, it is worth examining here as another, and certainly the most famous example of that affinity. Rereading my family copy as an adult, I was surprised by the intense power of the narrative despite representations of black people that seem patronizing and racist today.

Taking these two classic works together, it is interesting to compare their plots and characterization, as well as the ways in which each book was received on publication. Harriet Beecher Stowe's novel echoed many of the themes in *Oroonoko*. Instead of merely bestowing humanity on her black characters, she supplied them with a capacity for intense spirituality, portraying them as more 'natural' Christians than the whites. Uncle Tom, the main character of the book, was not necessarily the submissive lackey his name has come to signify. Like Oroonoko, he too defied slavery right up until his death, though his defiance was expressed by his readiness to forgive his oppressors. Where Oroonoko was proudly anti-Christian, Uncle Tom was a black Christ-figure, and the humility and purity shown by him and other slave characters only served to show up the hypocrisy of the white so-called Christian apologists of slavery.[10]

Like Aphra Behn's book, *Uncle Tom's Cabin* was incredibly popular and was immediately adapted for the stage. The speed at which it was sold and distributed throughout the world has been described as miraculous: the first 5,000 copies were sold in two days before any reviews were published; 300,000 copies were sold in America by the end of 1852.[11] Miners in California rented pirated editions for a quarter of a day, countless songs based on the book became overnight hits, a card game called 'Uncle Tom and Little Eva', based on the continual separation and reunion of families ran up big profits for a manufacturer of home amusement devices, and the first of endless dramatizations opened before the end of the year. Although Harriet Beecher Stowe was writing as an American this impact was not restricted to her own country but resonated in different parts of the world. In Britain, where nearly 200,000 copies were sold that first year in editions pirated by twenty different publishers, Harriet Beecher Stowe became an overnight celebrity and when she travelled to Europe she was cheered by crowds in overflowing halls.[12] An Italian translation – *Il Zio Tom* – was sold in all Italian cities and an edition of *Caban F'Ewythr Twm* appeared in Wales. The book was further translated into at least thirteen other languages, including Bengali, Persian, Japanese and Chinese, and in Russia it was recommended by leading revolutionary democrats as an aid in their struggle against serfdom. Closer to home, the former slave and leading African-American abolitionist, Frederick Douglass, wrote of her work: 'One flash from the heart-supplied intellect of Harriet Beecher Stowe could light a million camp fires in front of the embattled hosts of slavery, which not all the waters of the Mississippi, mingled as they are in blood, could extinguish.'[13] William Wells Brown, another African-American abolitionist, who was in London at the same time as Stowe, wrote: '*Uncle Tom's Cabin* has come down upon the dark abodes of slavery like a morning's sunlight, unfolding to view its enormities in a manner which has fastened all eyes upon the "peculiar institution", and awakening sympathy in hearts that never before felt for the slave.'[14]

Harriet Beecher Stowe described her motives for writing this book with simple clarity. She felt, she said, a desperate urge that she, as a woman, should do 'something' for the slave, urged by her sister-in-law to use her pen to 'make this whole nation feel what an accursed thing slavery is'.[15] Just before she began, she wrote to a friend:

> I feel now that the time is come when even a woman or a child who can speak a word for freedom and humanity is bound to speak. The Carthaginian women in the last peril of their state cut off their hair for bow-strings to give the defenders of their country, and such peril and shame as now hangs over this country is worse than Roman slavery. I hope every woman who can write will not be silent.[16]

Unlike Aphra Behn, Stowe did not place herself in the story to give her slave characters a greater proximity to her readers. But, when the authenticity of her book was challenged, she provided her critics with a factual account of slavery in a separate book, called *The Key to Uncle Tom's Cabin*, defending herself against the charge that she had let her female imagination run away with itself. This work proved to be a far more devastating account of the realities of slavery – for as Frederick Douglass pointed out, the slaveholders had only made matters worse by denying the truthfulness of the novel.[17] *The Key* not only confirmed the accuracy of every detail of the characters and the events that took place in the story, but corroborated them with letters, slave narratives and legal documents. Stowe also reiterated her main point that slavery was the responsibility of all those who called themselves Christians, and she included a brief history of each religious denomination and their attitude towards this question.

In the novel itself Stowe used every opportunity to preach directly to her readers. She drew attention to the hypocrisies of the liberals who supported slavery by colluding with the more obviously 'evil' slave traders; and she challenged her Northern readers who claimed to despise the institution of slavery but who refused to accept free blacks as their equals. By claiming that slavery was a purely moral and religious issue she was well aware that women would be more susceptible to her arguments, and she set out to speak to them directly. More specifically she addressed the 'mothers of America': through her descriptions of domestic life, death and the separation of women from their children and husbands, and the humiliation of sexual abuse, she stated quite explicitly that it was up to women to use their moral influence against the more rational and unfeeling qualities of men.

This division of emotional and ethical labour between the sexes was entirely consistent with mid-nineteenth century, middle-class views of social relations, both in America and in Britain. In the first part of the book Stowe introduced two white couples who personified the different approaches of male and female. The well-meaning but ultimately guilty Mr Shelby justifies his decision to sell both Tom, his most hard-working and trustworthy slave, and little Harry, the four-year-old son of his wife's maid Eliza, by arguing that the high price these two would fetch would stave off his inevitable bankruptcy. When his wife finds out that he has made the transaction she launches into an impassioned speech about the hypocrisy of bringing up slaves to be good Christians and then selling them 'just to save a little money'. Her husband clearly does not want to be reminded. He tells her that while he respects her feelings, he does not share them to their full extent; he cannot back out of the sale without jeopardizing his whole business. Mrs Shelby's reaction illustrates the particular situation that many white women found themselves in:

> This is God's curse on slavery! – a bitter, bitter, most accursed thing! – a curse to the master and a curse to the slave! I was a fool to think I could make anything good out of such a deadly evil. It is a sin to hold a slave under laws like ours – I always felt it was, – I always thought so when I was a girl, – I thought so still more after I joined the church; but I thought I could gild it over, – I thought, by kindness, and care, and instruction, I could make the condition of mine better than freedom, – fool that I was![18]

Harriet Beecher Stowe described Mrs Shelby in *The Key* as 'a fair type of the very best class of Southern women', and recounted meeting some 'pious ladies' while travelling in Kentucky who expressed very similar sentiments. These women do 'all they can to alleviate what they cannot prevent', she wrote, and are often surrounded by circumstances over which they have no control.

Another female character whose moral indignation also shames her husband – with more successful results – is Mrs Bird, the senator's wife. Over the tea-table, surrounded by young children, she scolds him for not opposing the fugitive slave law which forbade anyone to help or harbour runaway slaves. As their house was situated just across the river from the slave-owning South, they considered themselves friends of the slave and would have unquestioningly helped any fugitive who came to their door. When Mr Bird attempts to reason with his wife that to do so in future would be breaking the law, she rounds on him: ' I hate reasoning, John – especially reasoning on such subjects. There's a way you political folks have of coming round and round a plain right thing; and you don't believe in it yourselves, when it comes to practice.' The power of her emotional argument is soon revealed as a runaway slave presents herself at their door, and there is no question of turning her away.

It is during this episode that Harriet Beecher Stowe draws on one of her own most painful female experiences: the death of a child. Mrs Bird is so shocked and moved by Eliza and Harry's plight that she gives Harry the clothes of her dead son. Watched by her two young boys, Mrs Bird goes upstairs to fetch them:

> O, mother that reads this, has there never been in your house a drawer, or a closet, the opening of which has been to you like the opening again of a little grave? Ah! happy mother that you are, if it has not been so.[19]

When one of her sons asks her gently, 'Mamma, are you going to give away those things?' she replies: 'I could not find it in my heart to give them away to any common person, – to anybody that was happy; but I give them to a mother more heartbroken and sorrowful than I am; and I hope God will send his blessings with them!'

Of course, Stowe did not restrict her male and female characters to good or bad, or even simply pro- or anti-slavery, but in each case their gender affects their perception of slavery. Many thousands of words have been written about her skill as an author – she was an experienced novelist and shortly afterwards wrote another anti-slavery novel called *Dred, the Tale of a Dismal Swamp* – and critics still argue about the literary merits of *Uncle Tom.*[20] These debates, which often extend to include Harriet Beecher Stowe's place in American literature, her role in the anti-slavery movement, her views on feminism and race, and the impact of her work on other novelists, invariably revolve round the central theme of the author's status as a white middle-class woman dealing with race and slavery through the fictional lives of black people. In her own day many believed that her book had helped to change the course of history; Abraham Lincoln was reputed to have called her to see him at the start of the Civil War, and told her: 'So this is the little lady who made this big war'. In Britain a review in *The Times* actually accused her of sabotaging the prospects of abolition in America by demanding instant emancipation, something neither the blacks nor the whites were thought to be ready for. Regardless of her own politics – and there were certainly some who found her patronizing or insensitive[21] – the political impact of Stowe's work was unprecedented, coming at a time when women had almost no social and political rights of their own.

In the two hundred years that separated *Oroonoko* from *Uncle Tom's Cabin*, British women writers continued to demonstrate a concern for, or certainly a fascination with, the plight of the black slave. In particular the late eighteenth and early nineteenth centuries saw an increasing number of novels and poems written by British women about slavery, which approached the subject in a variety of different ways and which played a significant part in developing a popular anti-slavery sentiment.[22] While there are many problems inherent in grouping women writers together, regardless of class, geography or their attitudes towards the question of race, the proliferation of this type of literature is certainly an important subject for consideration.[23] It raises questions about what women saw in the condition of slavery that made them want to address it in their writing, which was, after all, their only legitimate means of public expression. Did these women see in the relationship between slave and master a reflection of the more familiar bondage of wife to husband? This analogy was not as far-fetched then as it may seem today. In 1772, a precedent was created in English law when Granville Sharpe successfully defended an escaped slave who was in danger of being shipped back to the West Indies by his owner. This case established the right of the individual not to be owned by any other person on English soil. Yet married women had no rights whatsoever, and in a sense became the property of their husbands on marriage – a point repeatedly stressed by Mary Wollstonecraft twenty years later in *The Vindication of the Rights of Women*, published during a period of radical anti-slavery agitation.

The whole discourse of the affinity between the white woman and the black slave in literature can be read as a useful introduction to women's more overtly political efforts to end slavery as an institution. Because of their own economic, social and political subordination, many felt constrained in their efforts to organize effectively, and found themselves contesting the boundaries of what was acceptable activity for women. Others, however, were not only able to accept these parameters readily, but were also able to frame their commitment to abolition as a task particularly suited to women.

## 'A Decidedly *Religious* Question'

British abolitionism emerged as a mass movement at the end of the 1780s and reached several peaks before the end of the 1860s. Several distinct campaigns were waged during this time: for abolition of the slave trade (1788, 1792 and 1814); for emancipation (1823, 1830 and 1833) and for the end of Negro apprenticeship (1838). The movement first took organizational form in 1787 when the mainly Quaker Abolition Society was founded, and over the next seventy or so years it became a permanent feature of extra-parliamentary politics. By 1830 the level of public support and involvement in the movement had given it a momentum that was to continue long after slavery was officially abolished in the British West Indies. The 1833 Act ensured that vast sums of money were handed out in compensation to slave owners and the vast majority of slaves became enforced apprentices, with scarcely any change in their daily lives, and it was not until 1838 that this system was abolished. The movement then fragmented, with a final revival during and immediately after the American Civil War.

Any discussion of how abolition was achieved has to take into account several different factors: changing world economies and developing markets; pro- and anti-slavery forces within Britain; and obviously the resistance of the slaves themselves throughout the Caribbean. Some scholars have argued that the Caribbean plantation system was becoming less economically viable by the turn of the eighteenth century, particularly with the end of the slave trade in 1807, and that the humanitarian movement of abolitionists in England was relatively ineffective in forcing the government to end slavery. Others give more weight to this movement, but disagree as to whether it was a middle-class philanthropic concern untouched by the more radical elements of society, or a genuinely popular and potentially radical alliance. These debates sometimes obscure the significance of movements of slaves in the Caribbean, most notably the successful revolution in Haiti and the declaration of the Republic of St Domingue in 1804.[24]

It is essential to refer to these debates in order to understand the varied class composition of the British anti-slavery movement and to appreciate the significance of women's involvement in it. Yet although there continues to be avid discussion on class and race in relation to the abolition of slavery, there is still relatively little study of the way that gender also figured in this history. At the same time there has been a great deal of feminist investigation into the dynamics of gender and class in the nineteenth century, most of which pays scant attention to questions of race. My focus on women abolitionists is not to provide an account of 'women's contribution' to the abolition of slavery, but to try to discover how race, class and gender intersected in a period that saw the emergence of a feminist politics. Despite significant differences (and extraordinary similarities) in the domestic and colonial policies of North America and Britain, black and white feminist research in the United States has provided a useful resource which helps to focus on gender, class and race in the British context.

In the *Album* of the Female Society for Birmingham for the Relief of British Negro Slaves, a record of one of the earliest women's organizations, compiled in 1828, I have identified some of the themes which I think are consistently found in women's anti-slavery documents, organizational reports, pamphlets and other propaganda:

> Should any Lady become interested for her fellow-subjects, the British Slaves, and be inclined to 'remember those in bonds as bound with them, and those that suffer adversity, as being herself also in the body;'(Heb. XIII. 3) should she desire that her own sex may no longer be treated as brutes, no longer be bought and sold, and marked like cattle, which the

> Planters' own Gazettes incontrovertibly prove that they are, let her look around the circle of her own relatives and acquaintance, to discover if there be not at least one person who may be awakened to compassionate, and assist, and plead for, our unhappy Slaves, who, living under our dominion, are not protected by our laws, but receive from civilised, enlightened, Christian, Britain, whatever is most painful, humiliating, and dishonouring, in the bitter cup of slavery.[25]

The first theme expressed in this fragment concerns audience. Women's abolitionist writings were almost always aimed exclusively at other women, and through reading them it is possible to see how they understood their place in the social structure of the time, and to prise apart the various meanings of womanhood. Ten years later, a pamphlet addressed to the 'Christian Women of Sheffield' exemplified the way that women's subordinate role in society appeared to be confirmed in this type of propaganda:

> But here we are met by the question, 'What can *Women* do in this cause? We will attempt to answer the inquiry under a deep sense of our limited ability to accomplish what we desire, but with the prayer that we may each receive the gracious commendation of our Lord, '*She hath done what she could.*'
>
> We are happily excluded from the great theatre of public business, from the strife of debate, and the cares of legislation; but this privilege does not exempt us from the duty of exerting our influence, in our own appropriate and retired sphere, over that public opinion, without which no important moral reformation can be accomplished. We desire not to take part in the final adjustment of these affairs, but we may help on towards a decision.[26]

A second theme in women's anti-slavery pamphlets was the emphasis on women's moral responsibility to emancipate the slaves. In the eyes of most abolitionists, slavery was regarded as a sin, and one of their greatest achievements was to make it impossible for any respectable person to defend slavery publicly. Theirs was a moral crusade which claimed Christianity as the true religion of emancipation, which, as the above extract shows, gave women a particular relationship to the movement. As in all philanthropic movements, the language of abolition was infused with biblical metaphors and references. The quote from the Book of Hebrews – 'Remember those in bonds as bound with them' – was one of the most regularly invoked; it was particularly appropriate for a female audience, as women were generally thought to 'feel' and 'suffer' more than men, and would therefore be more able to imagine themselves 'also in the body' of the oppressed slaves, and thereby identify with their powerlessness.

Elizabeth Pease, one of the most radical of all British abolitionists, acknowledged the limits of women's political activity while stressing the power of their moral influence. In a draft of an address from the women of Darlington to the women of Great Britain she wrote:

> Be not afraid; we ask you not to do anything, to incite in anything, unbecoming to your sex:
>
> 'Ours is not the tented field,
> We no earthly weapons yield,
> Light and Love our sword and shield,
> Truth our panoply'[27]

The Sheffield pamphlet also raised the problem that anti-slavery work might tempt women into the political sphere, which was not thought appropriate for them. Again, the authors posed it as a question which could be answered with righteous indignation, and in their reply they extended their sense of their own womanhood to the slaves they were seeking to help:

> Be not turned aside by the oft-repeated objection, that this is a *political* question, with which we, as *women*, have nothing to do. *Nothing to do with Slavery!* Nothing to do in behalf of women, publicly exposed for sale under circumstances the most revolting to human nature – of woman, writhing under the bloody lash – scorned, polluted, ruined, both for time and eternity![28]

The appeal to white women to comprehend the brutality of slavery through empathizing with black women as women is another vital theme running through women's abolitionist propaganda. While women's anti-slavery appeals were often made on behalf of both men and women, it was the fate of female slaves that seemed to provoke the greatest outrage. The literature was often quite explicit about the 'indecencies' that women slaves endured as they were stripped and beaten by male overseers. The destruction of family life and the anguish of wives, mothers and daughters were also recurrent images used by women to aim their propaganda at others of their sex. In doing so they identified the specific oppression of women slaves: either as objects of lust and brutality at the hands of white male overseers, or as victims of a system that denied them any kind of 'natural' domestic existence. The same Birmingham women's *Album* from which the first extract was taken contains three engravings that illustrate these points. One shows an anguished black woman as a mother of a young baby; another, a wife being forcibly separated from her husband who is being sold off to pay his owner's debts; and the third depicts a group of near-naked black women, clearly distressed and ashamed at being paraded before a number of fully clothed white men. There are minimal captions to these particular pictures as the message was expected to be clear to any woman who studied them. Images such as these played a vital role in anti-slavery propaganda and deserve careful study for what they reveal about gender and race relations throughout the struggle of both slaves and abolitionists for emancipation.[29]

The Sheffield pamphlet relied not on actual pictures but on direct appeals to women in their different familial roles as daughters, sisters, wives and mothers. Through identifying with the female slave they could illustrate that she was being denied all the most important components of a woman's existence in a supposedly free society: she was not able to receive the love and care of a mother while growing up, her husband was likely to be sent away from her at any time, and as a mother she had to suffer the pain of seeing her children sold as merchandise. In this way the abolitionist women both reaffirmed their responsibility for the moral and spiritual well-being of the family in their own communities, which helped to sanction their active involvement in a very public and un-feminine activity, and they also confirmed their sense that both black and white were part of the same human family. Reading the pamphlet, it is hard to imagine that women were not moved by the power of this type of propaganda, made even more dramatic by frequent recourse to poetry:

> Women! the fair, the firm, the free,
> Of England's vaunted isle!
> Tell us, if griefs like these shall be,
> And you be still the while?
> No! strong in Christian virtue rise!
> And heed the negro mother's cries!

With plighted hands, a living chain,
Unsevered but to die,–
Crusaders, sally forth again,
To heed that thrilling cry.
A broken heart your ensign be,
Your watchword, *Love and Liberty*![30]

The last line of this poem suggests another theme echoed in the reference to 'civilised, enlightened, Christian' Britain in the Birmingham women's *Album*. The emphasis on the supposedly advanced state of civilization within Britain was often used in abolitionist propaganda to highlight the hypocrisy involved in justifying or condoning the slave system. It also meant that the destruction of slavery could be presented as an inevitable act that would demonstrate the triumph of British, Christian, civilized values. The word 'civilized' had several nuances of meaning – as it still does – which relate to different theories of race, class and gender prevalent at the time of the anti-slavery movement. In his history of Victorian racial attitudes, Douglas Lorimer argues that in the early part of the century there were those who believed that civilization was obtained through education and religion, and that most black people remained in a more 'uncivilized' state merely through lack of opportunity and, more importantly, because of their class position which they shared with sections of white society.[31] One example of this attitude is provided by the philanthropist Hannah Kilham, whose work took her from Ireland to Africa to the slums of London. In 1823 she wrote that the African children who played on the streets of London were disadvantaged by poverty, and were not representative of African children in their own environment:

> In England, people see only a few of those who have been slaves, or mostly beggars, and too often judge from such specimens of Africans in general. . . . But what judgement would even be formed of the English nation were only the most unfavourable specimens presented to view?

Hannah Kilham's experience of missionary work in Africa had taught her that civilizing and educating the poorest whites in London presented in many ways a more difficult prospect than bringing Christianity to 'heathen' lands. It was a similar process, she argued, and 'they would want the same care even from the beginning in the attempt to civilise and Christianise them'.[32] Douglas Lorimer points out that such theories would probably have had the effect of bolstering middle- and upper-class notions of superiority over both Africans and their own less well-off countrymen, and that during this period it is in fact very hard to distinguish between racism and class antipathy.[33] Other writers have laid more emphasis on the long history of racist ideas about black people which predated slavery, and which formed the basis of the more systematic theories of the nineteenth century. Peter Fryer, for example, cites the influence of eighteenth-century writers like Edward Long, who not only identified blacks as a different species from whites but described at length what he saw as the similarities between blacks and apes.[34]

The Sheffield pamphlet is again useful for the way it illustrates a particular moral and religious anti-slavery position, which refers to this kind of racial prejudice as 'unholy'. In the following extract their goal appears more visionary than practical, and possibly calculated to induce satisfaction among the do-gooders rather than their objects of pity:

> We seek to raise the Negro from the depth of misery and degradation into which Slavery and unholy prejudice have thrown him, and bring him out into heaven's sunshine, in the full enjoyment of his birthright privileges. And we seek the attainment of these objects by Christian means and upon Christian principles alone. By the concentrated radiance of *light* and *love*, we would melt the fetters of the slave and let the oppressed go free.[35]

The development of racist ideologies in Britain has been discussed at length, particularly in the context of black history.[36] As we shall see below, black abolitionists who visited Britain during the first half of the nineteenth century gave favourable reports of their treatment there by whites, which is hardly surprising since many of them had experienced slavery at home or at least severe discrimination if they were from the Northern states. However, the same period saw the emergence of the bio-social sciences of racial difference which appeared to establish a rational explanation for human variation. For example, it was during the 1820s that phrenology, or the study of skull shape, first gained credibility as an accepted discipline after the well-known surgeon Sir William Lawrence, published his findings as evidence that culture was biologically determined. In 1819, he wrote: 'The inferiority of the dark to the white races is much more general and strongly marked in the powers of knowledge and reflection, the intellectual facilities . . . than in moral feelings and dispositions. . . . I deem the moral and intellectual character of the Negro inferior, and decidedly so, to that of the European.'[37] His book was at first condemned for its heretical stance on creation (which predated Darwin), but its conclusions were entirely compatible with other supposedly scientific findings.

As science itself became established as a unique form of knowledge it became increasingly hard to contest this type of bio-social theory. Of course, race was not the only object of scientific inquiry: social divisions based on class and gender also required explanation and justification which bio-social theories were able to supply, building on existing ideologies of difference.[38] Yet biology was not always invoked to confirm social and cultural inequality; there were instances of women using a form of phrenology to assert the similarity of the sexes. Barbara Taylor describes how many Owenites turned to physical evidence to reinforce their arguments for 'human perfectability'.

> A lecture delivered by Anna Wheeler in 1829 was typical. Having demonstrated women's moral capacity with historical and literary examples, and their muscular potential with evidence from non-European societies, she went on to cite phrenological studies which had shown that 'all existing differences' in male and female skull topology were a result of education and the 'very different circumstances' of the sexes.[39]

In order to defend themselves against charges that they were innately different from men, and that their supposedly natural talents were confined to the domestic sphere, advocates of women's equality sometimes turned to simplistic forms of ethnography and even zoology to demonstrate the possible range of relationships between males and females. Harriet Taylor, who married the philosopher John Stuart Mill, came near to this approach when she wrote in 1851 in her *Enfranchisement of Women* that the domination of women altered as a society progressed from a 'primitive' state to so-called civilization:

> In the beginning, and among tribes which are still in a primitive condition, women were and are the slaves of men for the purposes of toil. All the hard bodily labour devolves on them. The Australian savage is idle, while women painfully dig up the roots on which he lives. An American Indian, when he has killed a deer, leaves it, and sends a woman to carry it home. In a state

> somewhat more advanced, as in Asia, women were and are the slaves of men for purposes of sensuality.[40]

The use of this kind of ethnographical language was not in itself so remarkable, but it illustrates the way that, by the middle of the century, the sciences of ethnography and, later, anthropology were being freely used to validate theories of racial and cultural difference, and to define the path to true civilization. However, Harriet Taylor was not arguing that women's situation in Europe was necessarily better than what she had described. The domination was here achieved by 'sedulous inculcation on the mind': that is, through a more refined psychological form of bondage which undermined the 'civilized' status of the Western world just as much as racial slavery. In her famous essay she went on to describe the effects of this 'modern' relationship between the sexes in which women had become part of the furniture of the home. It is time to look now at the constraints imposed on abolitionist women by ideologies of gender and class.

## Women's Mission to the Slave

One of the most important themes of early nineteenth-century women's history is the philanthropic role assigned to the women of the emerging middle class. This is sometimes referred to as 'women's mission', a concept which has been usefully summarized by Alex Tyrrell in an essay on women's role in early Victorian pressure-group politics.[41] The first precept was thc hcavy emphasis on the distinctive characteristics and roles of the sexes. Men and women were suited to different tasks in life, both mentally and physically. Second, women were ascribed special qualities of a moral and domestic nature – home was their principle sphere of operation. Third, women's refined sensibility was seen as out of place in the 'real world'. Instead they were expected to use their particular qualities as a reforming influence on their families and friends. The logic of this – which was not quite so widely accepted – was that they had a useful part to play in public societies working for social and moral reform.

Useful as it is, this summary must not be allowed to over-simplify or obscure the ways in which the meanings attributed to womanhood were being contested in nineteenth-century Britain. As many historians have described, there was a certain amount of confusion over definitions of woman's position in society at this time: 'Revivalist doctrines regarding women's role were, in fact, riddled with contradictions which provided a continuous undercurrent of tension and conflict.'[42] Some, for instance, argued that there was spiritual equality between men and women, while others insisted that women were in the moral vanguard of society, and therefore responsible for its moral well-being. Philanthropy became a legitimate form of activity for women since it allowed them to use their moral and spiritual influence for the benefit of their community. Thus it offered a chance to move beyond the private sphere of family into a more public world.

The concept of 'women's mission' has also been discussed at length for its effect on the relationship between women of different classes. Lynda Nead, for example, has written about the way the phrase was used to describe the role of the respectable woman in the reclamation of the fallen, and the way that it differentiated between the deserving and the undeserving poor.[43] One of the contradictions of 'women's mission' was that it undoubtedly helped to regulate the distance between women of different classes. In this context it is also important to consider how it worked to construct relationships between women across race as well. It was a short step for women to channel their supposedly superior moral energies bestowing charity and advice to poor women and their families, to applying themselves to 'compassionate, and assist, and plead for' a more abstract group of poor with whom they had next to no physical contact at all. There was at least one fundamental ideological difference between performing charity work at home and campaigning for the abolition of slavery. For most women in the anti-slavery movement, the increasing numbers of urban poor whom they felt it was their duty to help were perceived to belong to a social hierarchy with which they were more familiar. Their condition might be addressed by readings from the Bible or education in home economics, but hardly by campaigning for their emancipation, let alone their equality. Abolitionism was a political struggle to change hearts, minds and laws; the appeal to British women to recognize sisterhood across race and class could be read as sentimental philanthropy, but it could also signify an assault on racism itself.

Much has been written, particularly in recent years, about the class composition of the anti-slavery movement. One characterization of its leaders maintains that they were not only largely ignorant of the conditions of the urban poor within Britain, but actively colluding, either as factory owners or as politicians. It was not uncommon for meetings to be disrupted by radicals in an attempt to focus on forms of wage slavery nearer home and to expose the sanctimonious ramblings of the abolitionists. It was also the case that the movement addressed and involved people from all classes to a varying degree. Without wanting to comment on this debate at this point it is interesting to note that some women abolitionists both acknowledged these criticisms and took them personally enough to respond. In their second annual report, the Birmingham group quoted at length from a speech about the brutalities of the slave trade given by Thomas Buxton in the House of Commons. They then said:

> Those by whom all this is forgotten, look only on the distress of our own poor at home, and are persuaded that all our sympathy should be expended on the nearest objects of misery; that our charity should not only 'begin at home,' but end there. They are ignorant, or unmindful, of the claims, the much-wronged, helpless slave has on our Justice as well as Mercy; and they forget that if two beggars presented themselves in distress at their door to ask for alms, they would first help the one to whose misery they had contributed, whose sufferings were chargeable to their oppression, their inhumanity, or thoughtlessness.[44]

The comparison of the two beggars who are poor for different reasons, and who therefore need a different order of treatment, is another sign of the complex relation between race and class, articulated through an image of the female philanthropist bestowing charity. The preference for Justice over simple Mercy indicates a moralistic view of why the poor at home were poor in the first place, implying that, unlike the slaves, they were not the innocent victims of a vicious economic and ideological system of domination.

The tone of women's anti-slavery tracts may appear today to be excessively patronizing towards the slaves themselves, but the emphasis on the 'much-wronged, helpless slave' was often matched by an insistence on women's own weakness and frailty. The authors of this extract from the Birmingham *Album* pleaded that through their own shortcomings they were better placed to redeem the slave:

> Why is not this work of mercy more universally and heartily engaged in! The answer which, in Christian charity we may return to such an enquiry, is

> this, the women of England do not know the use they might be of, in a cause in which there is nothing to dishearten them; for, our very weakness and feebleness, furnish additional reasons 'to hope for the pitying aid of God our Saviour,' who has declared – perhaps for the encouragement of the most lightly esteemed of his followers – that he has chosen the 'weak things of the world, and the things that are despised, and the things that are not, to bring to nought the things that are' – 'The race is not always to the swift, nor the battle to the strong.'[45]

This throws more light on to the discourse of affinity between women and other groups marginalized by masculinist and racist hierarchies. Without necessarily appearing to be radical, women were ready to link their own subordination with that of black people by referring to the Christian ideal of inner strength that might be possessed by the physically and mentally weak, which was certainly one way of connecting the hierarchies of gender and race. The similarities between black people and women were suggested more forcefully by the American abolitionist Lydia Maria Child in an argument which is part of this same discourse. In 1843 she wrote:

> In comparison with the Caucasian race, I have often said that they are what woman is in comparison with man. The comparison between women and the colored race as *classes* is striking. Both are exceedingly adhesive in their attachments; both, comparatively speaking, have a tendency to submission, and hence, have been kept in subjection by physical force, and considered rather in the light of property, than as individuals. As the *intellectual* age passes towards the *moral* age, women and the colored race are both rising out of their long degradation.[46]

## 'What have I done for much injur'd Africa?'

It was in this context of performing moral and religious duties that women became legitimately involved in abolitionism, which, as the first great campaign of the early Victorian era, provided women with a means to use their influence in the public sphere. However, as it was one of several areas of philanthropy that they turned to, it has until recently been glossed over by historians as just another example of the compulsory charity work of the middle classes. Women's contribution to abolitionism has even been dismissed as 'sentimental humanitarianism', in a middle-class society where the drawing-room had become 'an abolitionist hotbed'.[47] One historian goes so far as to say:

> To some extent the philanthropic possibilities of the movement attracted the charitable and spare-time activities of idle ladies, and to patronise societies for the emancipation of Negroes became as fashionable as it had been one hundred and fifty years earlier to own one.[48]

One writer who does draw attention to the large numbers of women working in anti-slavery societies describes how they were encouraged to do so within the limits of what was expected of them.[49] By the mid 1820s women were being attracted to meetings in such large numbers that separate committees and auxiliary groups were set up so that they could work more effectively among their own sex. Within a few years the activities of the newly founded women's groups had succeeded in swelling the ranks of the anti-slavery movement beyond its founders' dreams. 'It is a singular fact that none of our Antislavery meetings were well-attended till after it was agreed to admit ladies to be present . . .' wrote Sir George Stephen graciously as he composed his memoirs.[50] However, not all male abolitionists were able to accept even token involvement. William Wilberforce, whom generations of British schoolchildren have been taught was responsible for ending slavery, made his own objections clear.[51] The majority of male abolitionists welcomed women's participation, often producing explicit propaganda exhorting women to take an active part in influencing those in their immediate acquaintance:

> We would remind every lady in the United Kingdom that she has her own sphere of influence, in which she may usefully exert herself in this sacred cause; and the effect of that influence, (even if it were quietly and unobtrusively confined to the family circle, or to the immediate neighbourhood), an awakening sympathy, in diffusing information, in imbuing the rising race with an abhorrence of slavery, and in giving a right direction to the voices of those on whom, under Providence, hang the destinies of the wretched slaves. . .[52]

There were many ways that women could identify themselves with the wider movement, both at a private and at a public level. Wearing or decorating the home with images and emblems was one popular gesture:

pictures of slave ships and other reminders of the horrors of slavery were common in households all over the country. The most famous pendant bore the image of the kneeling slave with the words, 'Am I Not a Man and a Brother?', which was first produced commercially by the Committee to Abolish the Slave Trade in 1787. In 1826, a female version of this emblem was used by the Birmingham Ladies Negroes' Friend Society to decorate the cover of their first report, and it quickly became an effective piece of propaganda in its own right.[53] Outside the home, attendance of public meetings was central to maintaining the momentum of the movement. The network of associations was divided into regions, and lecturers were appointed to cover as many towns and villages as possible. Meetings were often several hours long and it was quite common for halls to be overcrowded with people of both sexes. Reading accounts of these lectures in anti-slavery papers of the time it is possible to get a glimpse of the incredible popularity of the subject by the late 1820s. Hundreds would attend meetings in churches and town halls, queuing up for hours beforehand to be sure of getting a place, particularly if there was to be a visiting speaker from London. Women as well as men attended in large numbers; in Bedford a meeting was arranged for a Friday as Saturday was 'an inconvenient day for families to attend public proceedings'.[54] Women were not expected to speak at these meetings and there is no evidence that any tried to do so, though presumably they made up for it at their own gatherings.

As we have already seen, a significant number of women's protests against slavery had already been registered through their writing. In the early part of the century, three other literary women made particular contributions to the movement, each making an impact far beyond her immediate acquaintance. Hannah More, poet and friend of William Wilberforce, wrote several poems on the theme of slavery which were widely circulated. Although a strict conservative when it came to the issue of women's rights – she was a vocal critic of Mary Wollstonecraft, whose book she claimed she had never actually read[55] – More made her views on the British slavery system well known throughout London's social circle. In 1824, Amelia Opie, poet and writer of romantic novels, wrote a poem entitled: 'The Negro Boy's Tale, a Poem Addressed to Children' which was similarly taken up by abolitionists as ammunition for the cause. But it was Elizabeth Heyrick, a member of the Birmingham Female Society, whose work was 'hurled like a bomb in the midst of battle'.[56] Her pamphlet, *On the Reasons for Immediate Not Gradual Emancipation; Or, an Inquiry into the Shortest, Safest, and Most Effectual Means of Getting Rid of West Indian Slavery* also published in 1824, was to have a decisive effect on the direction and tactics of the movement. It appeared at a time when the London Anti-Slavery Committee, led by such famous names as Wilberforce, Thomas Clarkson, James Stephen and Macaulay, had initiated a campaign for the gradual abolition of slavery. This was largely a means of distancing themselves from radicals who appeared to promote insurrection in the colonies as a quick way of ending slavery, as well as an attempt to adopt what they considered to be realistic tactics. Elizabeth Heyrick's pamphlet provided a coherent and compelling challenge to this reformist position, and was widely circulated among abolitionists in Britain and among the nascent movement in America. She denounced the whole principle of gradualism, condemning the government for negotiating with slave-holders and, most importantly, calling for a boycott of all slave-grown produce in order to achieve immediate and complete emancipation.

Coming from the pen of a woman, this message had very powerful implications for the movement, whose leaders had been careful to avoid any identification of anti-slavery politics with radicalism in any form. Elizabeth Heyrick followed up her argument by personally carrying out a door-to-door survey of households in her home town of Leicester, finding support for the idea of a consumers' boycott. It was around this time that women's auxiliary groups began forming in the Midlands. Heyrick herself was an early member of the Birmingham Female Society for the Relief of British Negro Slaves, founded in 1825. This group made its annual grant to the London society conditional on its declaration in favour of immediatism.[57] Also in 1825, the Sheffield Ladies Anti-Slavery Association deleted the word 'amelioration' from its constitution and pledged itself to immediatism.

By supporting the boycott of slave-grown commodities, women aligned themselves with the progressive wing of the movement, which eventually split off from the more conservative London committee in the years leading up to abolition. Their power as consumers and housekeepers gave them a vital role in implementing tactics, however symbolic, which helped to arouse public feeling all over the country.[58] Women fully recognized their power within the domestic economy, as this extract from a Birmingham report shows:

> The influence of females in the minor departments (as they are usually deemed,) of household affairs is generally such, that it rests with them to determine whether the luxuries indulged in, and the conveniences enjoyed, shall come to them from the employers of free men, or from the oppressors of British slaves.[59]

The women in Birmingham were typical of many of their sisters throughout England, Wales, Scotland and Ireland who called for boycotts of slave-produced sugar. They embroidered work-bags which they filled with pamphlets explaining the iniquities of slavery and the reasons why the price of West Indian sugar was kept at an artificially low level.

In order to argue for the abolition of the slave system, the female activist obviously had to understand the principles of free trade and protectionism. This obliged her to study worldly matters which took her far beyond the area where her conventional domestic expertise was assumed to lie. Economic arguments were used sparingly by the anti-slavery movement as a whole, compared to considerations of religion and human rights; but by the 1820s the changing economic climate throughout Europe led to a general belief that the older system of mercantilist protectionism was out of date in early nineteenth-century Britain, and that free trade was in the nation's self-interest. The copious annual reports of ladies' groups demonstrate that women were convinced that the rejection of all slave-grown produce was an issue of morality first: 'Is it for Christian females', asked the Birmingham women, 'to be bribed by the greater cheapness of this, or the other article of daily consumption, to lend themselves to the support of a flagrant system of blood-guiltiness and oppression, which cries to heaven for vengeance? – and can we think the cry will not be heard?' However, their crusading work also involved persuading other women face to face that they should reject all slave-grown produce. Where moral arguments failed, they were not ashamed to give them economic reasons for being more selective in their housekeeping:

> Only about one sixth of the town of Birmingham yet remains to be visited house by house, to promote this benevolent design. It has been calculated, that, if the 830,000 slaves of Great Britain were divided amongst the whole population of the United Kingdom, it would be found that there was one slave for every twenty five persons; and that, if the towns and neighbourhood, embraced by this Association, contain 300,000 inhabitants, then the

> number of slaves held in bondage by them, would be 12,000. And thus, but for the conscientious rejection of slave produce by many in this populous district, we shall have to record that 'we are paying Thousands of pounds a year, for the perpetuation of this misery and oppression, while we are subscribing less than Three Hundred a year for its extinction.'[60]

This line of reasoning was credited to their sister group in Liverpool. Correspondence between the proliferating women's associations was clearly an important part of their work: the early reports of the Birmingham society list with an anxious and almost proprietory tone the formation and work of new groups. In 1826 the list included Sheffield, Norwich, Manchester, Bristol, Liverpool and Huddersfield, as well as more provincial towns such as Calne, Devizes and Colchester. Over the next twenty-five years women's auxiliary groups were formed all over England, Scotland, Ireland and Wales. This network was crucial in exchanging ideas and tactics as well as testifying to the fact that hundreds of women were being drawn into the public sphere and acquiring, first-hand, experience of basic political organization.

The practical skills that women developed during this time were those essential to any campaign: writing, printing and distributing propaganda, fund-raising, organizing meetings and collecting signatures for petitions. Pamphlets, reprints of speeches or newspaper articles, poetry and prose were produced in phenomenal quantities as the abolitionists attempted to argue their case. This was not just the result of their desire to educate and persuade, but arose out of earlier struggles by working-class activists to gain access to the printed word.[61] The flourishing corresponding societies which had sprung up since the late eighteenth century had led to an increase in literacy among working men and women and this was reflected in the tactics of the anti-slavery movement. The mainly middle-class female organizers expected a high standard of literacy, judging from the contents of the work-bags, portfolios and albums which they sold. Apart from pamphlets explaining the necessity of boycotting slave-grown produce, there were many other documents ranging from extracts from notable anti-slavery speeches to copies of Jamaican papers proving the horrors of the system 'in their own authentic records'. These collections also contained children's books, which were intended to help 'the rising generation to grow up devoted, as one man, to the entirely effacing of this foul stain from the national character'.[62]

Women played a crucial role in sustaining the movement through fund-raising. Money raised from the sale of work-bags was augmented by annual subscriptions, and donated to the central organizing committee. This aspect of their work was particularly significant during the 1830s and 1840s when the movement turned its attention to the colonial system of enforced apprenticeship that replaced slavery after abolition. Some groups were also able to pay the expenses of visiting American abolitionists. In 1840 the African-American lecturer Charles Lennox Remond was sponsored on an eighteen-month visit by the Bangor Female Anti-Slavery Society, the Portland Sewing Circle and the Newport Young Ladies Juvenile Anti-Slavery Society. In turn he represented them at the first international anti-slavery convention which was held in London, and to which women were barred as delegates.

Women were also active in raising money to fund black projects in America as a result of solicitation from visiting African-American abolitionists. Men such as William Douglass, J. W. C. Pennington, William Wells Brown and many others received money to help found black schools or churches. Black newspapers were supported by funds raised in Britain while money was also used to help buy relatives out of slavery.[63] Frederick Douglass achieved his legal freedom as a result of the direct intervention of a woman in Newcastle, without any suggestion or encouragement from himself. A Quaker abolitionist called Ellen Richardson who was working as a headmistress of a girls' school spent a day with Douglass and her brother at the seaside when he visited Britain as a fugitive in the 1840s. She later described the idea of purchasing his freedom coming to her like a flash of inspiration, though she did not discuss it with him for fear he disapproved. Douglass at that time belonged to an organization of American abolitionists who refused to recognize the trade in human flesh. Ellen Richardson first consulted a lawyer friend who reassured her that it was morally right to raise money for the sale and, without telling her own family, she wrote to various influential people asking for their financial support. Money was quickly raised and she managed to negotiate with Douglass's former owner through relatives and a helpful lawyer in America. Douglass had no idea who had arranged his freedom until he revisited Britain several years later, and he remained in close and affectionate contact with Ellen Richardson until the end of their lives.[64] Ellen was also responsible for arranging the freedom of the novelist William Wells Brown, again on her own initiative. Fund-raising for large public organizations obviously entailed keeping detailed accounts, a skill at which many women were adept if they managed domestic budgets. As women developed arguments for boycotting slave-grown produce in their role as housekeepers, many also took the initiative in promoting the sale of alternatives, particularly cotton. Anna Richardson, another Quaker activist in Newcastle, edited the *Slave*, the organ of the Free Labour Association, at various stages throughout the 1840s and 1850s; another woman managed the London Free Labour Depot, and women's committees provided a national network of customers and helpers.[65]

Collecting signatures for petitions was a significant development in both reformist and radical politics during the first half of the nineteenth century. At its peak in the 1830s the anti-slavery movement submitted the highest number of signatures to Parliament in a record four thousand petitions. As Seymour Drescher points out, the significance of this form of political activity goes far beyond the sheer number of names collected together: 'It required the existence of a complex political and social network which could foster the easy circulation of political literature and agitators throughout society, and of associations capable of well-timed agitation on a broad scale'.[66] Women abolitionists were obviously part of this complex network and worked in conjunction with men, but they also reached large numbers of women who would not otherwise have been approached for their opinions. The staggering size of the petitions are an indication of the organization needed to collect them together. In 1833, at the climax of the campaign, four men were needed to carry a single petition of 187,000 signatures of 'ladies of England' into Parliament. The accession of Queen Victoria in 1837 provided a great incentive for women to demonstrate the strength of their feelings. Groups in Scotland and England combined together to produce an address signed by 588,083 women on rolls stretching 11,453 feet.[67]

Over five thousand of these signatures were collected from the Darlington Women's Abolition Society, which the young Elizabeth Pease had helped to found the previous year. It was mainly due to her interest in the international movement, that the Darlington group was the first to respond to the address to the women of England from the ladies' anti-slavery societies in the New England states of America. Their reply, published in the *Durham Chronicle* (16 December 1836), led to the formation of many other women's societies around the country. The tactic of composing formal addresses which were issued from one group of women to another was significant in the development of women's politics. Like most female anti-slavery propaganda, these missives acknowledged the importance of gender both in determining black and white women's experiences and in suggesting a remedy. But they also helped to extend a more symbolic network of women, united by their gender across class and race, from one side of the slave-owning world to the other.

This international solidarity between women was expressed in other ways. In 1837, Elizabeth Pease suggested the publication of the American abolitionist Angelina Grimke's powerful 'Appeal to the Christian Women of the Slave States of America' and wrote to her assuring her that the pamphlet would be circulated 'amongst all grades of society from the nobleman to the humble cottager'. Elizabeth was also responsible for its distribution, along with other members of Scottish and northern anti-slavery societies.[68] The dialogue between British and American women was backed up by gifts and donations which became important symbols of mutual support. The women in the Boston group held an annual anti-slavery bazaar for which they solicited articles made by women in England. Boxes of gifts and handiworks were shipped over and apparently eagerly bought by visitors to the fair. Maria Weston Chapman, one of the organizers, wrote to Elizabeth Pease in 1837:

> Though in greatest haste I cannot let this opportunity pass without thanking you for the beautiful articles for our fair which we receive through Angelina E. Grimke. They were the means of bringing throngs to purchase, who would otherwise [have] passed by on the other side; nothing could have been more opportune than their arrival. Please to express to those to whom, with yourself we are so deeply indebted, our warmest thanks on behalf of the slave. The Address from the Ladies of Darlington, signed by yourself and Miss Wemyss, has been published in all the Anti-Slavery periodicals, & has been the means of encouraging the hearts of thousands.[69]

The warm and heartfelt correspondences that developed across hundreds of miles through letters were sometimes translated into real friendships as both black and white Americans made the trip over the Atlantic to argue for the abolition of slavery in their country.

British audiences welcomed hearing first-hand accounts of the brutalities of slavery and, by the 1850s, anti-slavery meetings were incomplete without a black witness, usually from America.[70] Women were particularly receptive to the fate of slaves, and it appears that many African-American men frequently made pointed references to the sexual abuse of black women, though they were often reluctant to discuss the details openly. William Craft, whose escape from slavery with his wife, Ellen, had become almost a legend, told his packed audiences that 'the wrongs heaped upon women could not be told'.[71] Sarah Parker Remond, who came from a northern family with a long anti-slavery tradition, was more explicit in her description. In her first public speech in Britain in 1859 she told the story of Margaret Garner, who was abused so badly she decided to free herself and her children or die in the attempt.[72] According to the newspaper report of the meeting, held in Warrington, Sarah Remond explained how common this experience was for women:

> Above all sufferers in America, American women who were slaves lived in the most pitiable condition. They could not protect themselves from the licentiousness which met them on every hand – they could not protect their honour from the tyrant. . . . 'Ah!' continued Miss Remond, in deep and thrilling tones, 'what is slavery? who can tell? In the open market place women are exposed for sale – their persons are not always covered. Yes I can tell you English men and women, that women are sold into slavery with cheeks like the lily and the rose, as well as those that might compare to the wing of the raven. They are exposed for sale, and subjected to the most shameful indignities. The more Anglo-Saxon blood that mingles with the blood of the slave, the more gold is poured out when the auctioneer has a woman for sale, because they are sold to be concubines for white Americans. They are not sold for plantation slaves.'[73]

Shortly after her arrival in Warrington, Sarah Remond gave a talk to a group of women. Although she was extremely tired and not feeling well, she spoke to them for a few minutes concentrating entirely on the experience of female slaves. When she finished she was approached by one of the women who said she felt proud to acknowledge her as a sister. She gave her a watch which bore the words: 'Presented to S. P. Remond by Englishwomen, her sisters . . .' The *Warrington Times* reported that Sarah Remond could scarcely speak she was so surprised. At length she said, 'I do not need this testimonial. I have been received here as a sister by white women for the first time in my life. I have been removed from the degradation which overhangs all persons of my complexion . . .'[74] Several months later, when Sarah had travelled all over England, she spoke directly to women in her audience. In a large meeting in Manchester she appealed for 'especial help from the women of England'.[75]

British women's appetite for anti-slavery work was in the early days greatly admired by American women abolitionists and served as an inspiration for them. Between 1830 and 1860 women on both sides of the Atlantic were conscious of each others' efforts as interest and enthusiasm inevitably flagged and needed reviving. After a tour of the northern states in 1836, the controversial British abolitionist George Thompson returned from America with a special appeal to women to become more active. During a visit to the Pease family in Darlington, Thompson charged Elizabeth with the task of organizing local women into an anti-slavery association. 'GT's farewell words to me', she later wrote, 'made a deep impression, and laid a responsibility on me which I know not how to discharge. "Remember," said he, "it rests with you whether anything is done here by women or not." '[76]

International links between women flowed mostly across the Atlantic, but there were also successful attempts to make contacts in Europe. Anne Knight, a Quaker active in her local anti-slavery association in her home town of Chelmsford from 1830 onwards, visited France several times to promote the cause and in 1834 tried to persuade the eminent abolitionist George Thompson to carry out a speaking tour there. When he declined, she decided to do it herself and addressed several large congresses and many other informal meetings.

It is no coincidence that most of the women mentioned so far – Elizabeth Heyrick, Elizabeth Pease, Anne Knight, Ellen and Anna Richardson, for example – were Quakers, as were many other active members of the movement. Their religious Nonconformism often meant that they had long absorbed notions of the equality of man and the iniquities of slavery, and had received, in principle, a reasonably good education. While the skills and experience acquired by anti-slavery women in their campaign work provided a first-hand political training, many would have been familiar with radical ideas through their unorthodox upbringing. In order to trace the ways in which some of these women both experienced and conceptualized the social and political relations of race, class and gender in their own lives, I shall now explore the social networks in which they lived and worked, and particularly the friendships that developed across the Atlantic.

## Connections and Correspondence

It is important to bear in mind that the anti-slavery movement was active during a period of great social and political change. Throughout Europe the first half of the nineteenth century saw working-class and nationalist movements erupt and threaten the stability of their respective governments, and political philosophies moved across the English Channel in both directions. In Britain the key issues were suffrage and representation, Ireland and the price of food, and abolitionists were often key figures exerting an influence on these questions as well as focusing on slavery. The crusade against slavery had helped to make respectable the formerly radical claim that all men were equal, and from this stemmed the demand that women should be equal as well. In the first half of the nineteenth century, Owenite, Chartist and Saint Simonian groups and individuals discussed and called attention to women's rights, demanding the vote, education and greater recognition of women's lower status. In 1847, Anne Knight, who, as we have just seen, was also heavily involved in the anti-slavery movement, published what is thought to be the first leaflet on women's suffrage and this led eventually to a petition in the House of Lords in 1851. However, it was not until 1854 that women actually came together to make specific demands on laws and institutions, and began to create channels of communication to discuss women's issues. It was during this year that Barbara Leigh Smith Bodichon published *A Brief Summary in Plain Language of the Most Important Laws Concerning Women*, and the first group of self-consciously feminist women came together to discuss political strategy.[77] The following year she instigated a petition to reform the legal position of married women. Addressed to all women this petition had collected sixty thousand signatures from around the country by 1857, by which time a growing number of feminists had begun meeting together. The *English Woman's Journal* – the first regular journal to be entirely written and published by women – was founded and several important institutions for female reform were set up.

Both Barbara Bodichon and Anne Knight came from family backgrounds that encouraged daughters to appreciate the value of education and take an interest in politics. As we shall see below, both were active within a network of radical men and women who were in regular contact with their counterparts in Europe and America. Although there was an age difference of forty years between them, both their attitudes to women's rights were profoundly affected by their involvement in anti-slavery politics. Both were deeply affected by an event that took place in London in 1840 which precipitated a surge of interest in the question of women's rights and became a landmark in the development of feminism.

In June of that year the first international anti-slavery convention was held in London. The male delegates made their way to the Freemason's Hall, quite unprepared for the political debates that they were about to witness. When they arrived, others were standing around talking earnestly and there were unexpected groups of American women who appeared to be about to take their seats among the men in the huge hall. Immediately after the chairman had introduced the convention, the young American abolitionist Wendell Phillips rose to propose a motion:

> That a Committee of five be appointed to prepare a correct list of the members of this Convention, with instructions to include in such a list, all persons bearing credentials from any Anti-Slavery body.[78]

The entire first day of the conference was spent discussing whether or not women delegates should be allowed to participate in the proceedings. With few exceptions the British delegates refused even to contemplate that they should do so. One of the committee pointed out that, as soon as they had heard rumours that some of the Americans intended a 'liberal' interpretation of the invitation, the organizers had sent them word that convention delegates were to be 'gentlemen'. Another Englishman, the Reverend J. Burnet, appealed to the women to recognize English custom and conform to English prejudices. His arguments were sarcastically reduced to the following list by George Thompson:

> 1st That English phraseology should be construed according to the English usage.
> 2d That it was never contemplated by the anti-slavery committee that ladies should occupy a seat in this Convention.
> 3d That the ladies of England are not here as delegates.
> 4th That he has no desire to offer an affront to the ladies now present.

After dismissing these 'arguments' as frivolous and groundless, Thompson gave his reasons for supporting the motion:

> The simple question before us is, whether these ladies, taking into account their credentials, the talent they have displayed, the sufferings they have endured, the journey they have undertaken, should be acknowledged by us in virtue of these high titles, or should be shut out for the reasons stated.[79]

The failure of the majority to respect these credentials reflected the dominant view of women's work in the British anti-slavery movement. As Thompson himself pointed out, 'It appears we are prepared to sanction ladies in the employment of all means, so long as they are confessedly unequal with ourselves'. Inevitably the charge was raised that delegates were wasting time on such a 'paltry' question. Opponents of the motion warned that the proposal was in danger of splitting the whole conference, of doing untold damage to the cause for which they had originally assembled. This extract from Phillips's speech illustrates the passions that were aroused by the debate:

> When we have submitted to brick-bats, and the tar tub and feathers in America, rather than yield to the custom prevalent there of not admitting colored brethren into our friendship, shall we yield to parallel custom or prejudice against women in Old England? We can not yield this question if we would; for it is a matter of conscience. But we would not yield it on the ground of expediency. In doing so we should feel that we were striking off the right arm of our enterprise.[80]

At the end of the day a vote was taken and the women were excluded as delegates by an overwhelming majority. For the remainder of the sessions they were obliged to sit behind a curtain – 'similar to those used to screen the choir from the public gaze'.[81]

The exclusion of the American women delegates from the business of the conference and their banishment behind the gauze curtain at the back of the hall would have come as no surprise as they had been warned that this was likely to happen. Their first few days in London were not just spent recovering from the terrible seasickness which seemed to afflict all transatlantic visitors. According to Lucretia Mott, much of the time was spent discussing their right to take part in the convention.[82] They breakfasted with Joseph Sturge, one of the founders of the newly formed British & Foreign Anti-Slavery Society and organizer of the conference, who tried to persuade them not to claim their seats alongside male delegates. A 'pleasurable evening' was spent at the anti-slavery headquarters in conversation with British abolitionists, not all of whom were unsympathetic. Here the women argued for the historical importance of British women in the cause, not just those like Elizabeth Heyrick whose pamphlet was well known in America, but also the thousands of anonymous women whose example had inspired many of their American sisters.

Lucretia Mott, whose diary reflects her renowned energy and enthusiasm for political life, records that there was only one other woman present at this gathering, besides those in the American party: Elizabeth Pease had already called on them in their lodgings – 'a fine, noble-looking girl' – and was to entertain them with her father, Joseph Pease, for breakfast a few days later. Throughout their stay Lucretia and Elizabeth developed a close and supportive friendship which was to become one of many important transatlantic alliances against opposing conservative forces. From 1840 onwards a serious split emerged in the abolitionists' ranks in America, which was replicated in England as organizations and individuals took sides. Although it may be characterized briefly as a rift between the radical and the conservative factions, there were also great differences of religion, politics, morality and, inevitably, personality. At the centre of the radical faction, called the 'Old Organisation' (as opposed to the 'New Organisation', which broke away), was a man called William Lloyd Garrison, who is now remembered as one of the most influential white abolitionists in nineteenth-century America.

Garrison began his political career as a journalist committed to social reform. In 1829 he became associate editor of a paper called *The Genius of Universal Emancipation*, edited by Benjamin Lundy, a Quaker opponent of slavery who had consistently reported on British women's campaigns. For the next three years, Garrison, influenced by the demand for immediatism inspired from England by Elizabeth Heyrick[83] and impressed by the contribution made to the British movement by women generally developed his particular strategy for abolition. During this period Elizabeth Margaret Chandler, a young Philadelphia poet, was appointed to edit 'The Ladies Repository', a section of *The Genius* reserved for 'philanthropy and literature'. Jean Fagan Yellin has described how she used these columns to publish a wide variety of materials on women and slavery, including reports of female anti-slavery societies in England and America, writings by black and white American women, and her own abolitionist essays and poetry.[84]

Whatever the precise reasons for Garrison's interest in women's rights, he was quick to support American female abolitionists when they began their public work in the 1830s. The 'Woman Question', as it was known, became a source of disagreement among American abolitionists as soon as it arose, precipitated by the attempts of the Grimke sisters and others to address public meetings attended by men and women.[85] However, there were other factors which alienated potential supporters: Garrison's unorthodox religious views, in particular his attack on the sanctity of the Sabbath – he insisted on the right to hold his anti-slavery meetings on Sundays – and his alleged fanaticism and unwillingness to compromise. His reputation has survived attempts to demote and blame him for fracturing the forces of anti-slavery in America, and he has likewise enjoyed periods of recognition as a great journalist and influential spokesperson for human rights. One of the distinctive tactics of Garrison's American Anti-Slavery Society (AASS) with which many others took issue was a complete withdrawal from active political life, based on a belief that all human instititutions were corrupt. Slavery was a sin, and any dealings with slaveholders were unacceptable. Frederick Douglass, whose career as a public speaker was first facilitated by the AASS, fell out with many Garrisonians because he allowed friends to negotiate a price for his freedom. He later expressed his irritation at fellow-abolitionists who criticized this transaction for giving credibility to the institution of slavery: 'Viewing it simply in the light of a ransom, or as money extorted by a robber, and my liberty of more value than one hundred and fifty pounds sterling, I could not see either a violation of the laws of morality or of economy.'[86]

Garrison had considerable charisma which particularly affected some of the women who encountered him. Elizabeth Cady Stanton, one of the party of American women who attended the 1840 London convention – not as a delegate herself, but on honeymoon with her abolitionist husband – said twenty years after meeting Garrison:

> In the darkness and gloom of a false theology, I was slowly sawing off the chains of my spiritual bondage, when, for the first time, I met Garrison in London. A few bold strokes from the hammer of his truth, I was free! Only those who have lived all their lives under the dark clouds of vague, undefined fears can appreciate the joy of a doubting soul suddenly born into the kingdom of reason and free thought.[87]

Elizabeth Pease first met Garrison and heard him talk when he paid a visit to London in 1833. Coming from a radical family, she was immediately attracted to his philosophy and interested in his organization. When he arrived at the convention a few days late and took his seat with the women in protest at the way they had been treated, he was inevitably ostracized by the majority of British abolitionists who had at least expected him to participate. Several weeks later the thirty-three-year-old Elizabeth Pease wrote to an anonymous friend in America:

> He [Garrison] knows my mind and heart, we have canvassed everything together, and inexpressible has been the treat and privilege of doing so with me. . . . Thanks to some who have hardly taken him by the hand, abstaining from all intercourse with him, who have sat in judgement, censured and condemned alike both him and many of his opinions. Thanks to such as these I have been privileged with a much larger share of his company than I ever dared to anticipate would fall to my lot – & I feel that the fault is my own if I have not been benefitted and instructed by it.[88]

According to George Thompson, with whom she worked, she appeared 'quite in love with W.L.G. & to find in his name and virtues an exhaustless theme for her prolific pen. She seems to mourn his departure with a deep and unaffected sorrow.'[89]

Despite their relatively small numbers, Garrison's supporters in Britain formed an important part of the British anti-slavery movement. They were based mainly in the provinces with strong groups in Ireland, Bristol and the West Country, Scotland and the north of England. As in America, they tended to come from Unitarian or Quaker backgrounds, but were freer of religious dogma than the older generation of Quakers who gave financial and moral support to the rival British and Foreign Anti-Slavery Society. Like the Garrisonians in Boston and Philadelphia, they also connected and supported a wide range of humanitarian and sometimes revolutionary causes – from Irish nationalism, Chartism and the Anti-Corn Law League to women's rights. However, judging from the correspondence that survives, this last question was given less prominence in Britain than in America, whereas the letters from Britain to America are full of news and discussion about Chartism, poverty and the Irish question.

It was during the aftermath of the 1840 convention that we can see the clearest picture of women's rights emerging as a political issue among the

British abolitionists. A month after the convention, Lucretia Mott wrote from Dublin to her friend in Boston, Maria Weston Chapman, giving her all the details about what had happened. It is worth quoting from her letter at length for the differences it reveals between the positions of American and British women:

> Of course we would not 'thrust ourselves forward' into such a meeting, but having come so far to see what could be done for the slave, & being thus prevented doing anything ourselves, we were willing to be mere lookers on & listeners from without, as by doing so we should be the means of many more women having an invitation to sit as spectators – which we found was accounted a very high privilege in this land – by their women who had hitherto most submissively gone forth into all the streets, lanes, highways and byepaths to get signers to petitions, & had been lauded – long and loud for this drudgery, but who had not been permitted even to sit with their brethren, nor indeed much by themselves in public meetings – having transacted their business, as we were informed, by committees.[90]

Lucretia Mott had earlier made a rather disparaging note in her diary after meeting some unnamed women anti-slavery activists in London: ' A stiff company of Anti-Slavery ladies at our lodgings, a poor affair. We find little confidence in women's action either separately or conjointly with men, except as drudges . . .'[91] However, in her letter to Boston she described their attempts to rouse women on the question of their own rights:

> In vain we endeavoured to have a public meeting called for women – although a few Anne Knight, Elizh Pease &c – did all they could to promote it. At length we gave up in despair & left London satisfied – that 'when for the time they ought to be teachers, they have need that one teach them which be the first principles' of Human Freedom.[92]

She went on to speculate that the British public, for whose sakes the women were banned from the convention, would not have been as outraged as they were given to understand, judging from the reaction that she and her colleagues had met in public meetings.

Elizabeth Pease gave her own version of their attempts to organize a women's meeting in London:

> Every obstacle was thrown in the way & no public opportunity was afforded them for a free interchange of sentiment with their English sisters. I

> regretted it deeply & several of us mourned over our utter inability to help it – had we been at our homes, we might have exerted an influence, but here we felt ourselves to be powerless . . . [93]

As we have seen, Elizabeth already had positive experience of setting up a women's group in her home town, and corresponding with other such associations both nationally and in America. It is significant that this was not enough to overcome the barriers set up to prevent women organizing away from 'home', especially around issues that did not comply with the legitimate female task of philanthropy. A letter from the veteran American abolitionist Sarah Grimke, written two years after the convention, indicates that Elizabeth Pease turned to her for support in raising the question of women's rights within the British abolitionist movement. After reassuring her that the behaviour of the British men had been 'an unwarrantable assumption of power', the older American woman told her: 'I cannot see my dear friend that the public expression of my opinion on the subject of the rights of women, would at all tend to set at rest the strife and animosity of the parties of the anti-slavery cause.' It is interesting to note that, in her view, the dispute over the woman question was a pretext for sectarian fighting, and not the real cause of dissension. Even if it had been, she claimed that the sectarian behaviour of the women's supporters since then had shown them to have identified 'self with the principles they were defending'. Meanwhile she believed that 'God calls now to other duties, to the living out of our anti slavery principles in every day life, to assert our unchanged opinions as to the equality of the sexes at the family altar, around the social board and on all the occasions which may and do arise in domestic life.'[94]

The fiasco of the 1840 convention also prompted Anne Knight to write to the Grimke sisters: 'Yes dear Angelina dear Sarah your noble spirits lighted a flame which has warmed, enlightened, we thought not of *our* bondage . . .'[95] She also wrote to Maria Weston Chapman in Boston: 'How much have we felt thy absence during our convention! A new and grand principle launched in our little island and shipwrecked as it were in its birth . . .'[96] The principle to which she referred was, of course, women's rights. The British women were aware that Lucretia Mott and Elizabeth Cady Stanton had decided to organize a women's rights convention when they returned home.[97] It seems that the endless discussions they must have all had on the subject affected Anne in a particular way. From then on all her writings show a new political philosophy in which she attributed all social ills to the suppression of women's 'diviner instinct'.[98] She appeared to believe that it was a religious issue, that women had been created by God to prevent any mischief caused by man. Ten years later in a correspondence to the *Brighton Herald* concerning women's suffrage she wrote:

> It is not fighting powers we want in that House (of Commons); we already have a horrible majority of slaughter-men there. Women could not suffer war; she would soon change the sword for the ploughshare, the spear for the pruning hook; although for power of fighting, her deeds in battle have shewn what she can do, from Boadicea downwards; but the day of battle and war with her is gone. She would soon take the tools of murder from the hands of her brute force brother and he would learn war no more.[99]

The previous year she had written to Lord Brougham about the manner in which women had learned of their own oppression: 'Ah! We have been taught another lesson, by our idle brothers driving us out into the battle-field to combat slavery and war, and every monster that is grasping the throat of our trampled and peeled country, taught of another slavery than black! Compelled to fight with hands tyed these foes to our welfar; and now we see and know the evil, some of us; we are demanding the remedy.'[100]

The stubborn refusal of the convention's organizers to admit women delegates was fiercely contested by some of the male members of the American delegation who joined the banished women behind their curtain in silent protest. But they also took satisfaction in the way that the issue of women's rights had been forced on to the agenda. Garrison wrote to his wife shortly after the conference: ' . . . We have not visited this country in vain. The "woman question" has been fairly started, and will be canvassed from the Lands End to John O'Groats' house.'[101] Two months later he reported to a friend and colleague that 'the rejection of the American female delegation by the London Convention, and the refusal of Rogers, Remond, Adams and myself, to become members of the same, have done more to bring up for consideration of Europe the rights of women, than could have been accomplished in any other manner'.[102]

Charles Lennox Remond, the African-American delegate who was attending the convention as a representative of three women's groups in north-west Wales, wrote a report of the incident to the only American reform paper directed at a black audience, the *Colored American* – unlike his fellow-countrymen who only informed white anti-slavery papers. In a letter to the editor Remond wrote:

> Thanks be to Providence, I have yet to learn, that the emancipation of the American slave, from the sepulchre of American slavery, is not of more importance than the rejection of females from the platform of any Anti-Slavery Society, Convention, or Conference. In the name of heaven, and in the name of the bleeding, dying slave, I ask if I shall scruple the propriety of female action, of whatever kind or description. I trust not – I hope not – I pray not, until the bastard system is annihilated, and not a vestige remains to remind the future traveller, that such a system ever cursed our country . . .[103]

Remond was consistently interested in the work of women's groups and was the first black abolitionist to collect items for the Boston Anti-Slavery Bazaar. On a highly successful tour of Ireland in 1841, he helped found the Cork Ladies Anti-Slavery Society, which became the most active women's abolitionist group in the country.

The correspondence generated by the 1840 convention is fascinating for its comment on a number of social and political issues. The Garrisonians were shocked by the appalling poverty they witnessed on their visit, and the callous treatment of the working class by an aristocratic and landed government. Garrison himself wrote to a friend as soon as he arrived back in Boston:

> Oppression, degradation, vice, starvation are there, side by side with monarchy, royalty, aristocracy, monopoly. . . . I could not enjoy the beautiful landscape of England, because of the suffering and want staring me in the face, on the one hand, and the opulence and splendour dazzling my vision, on the other.[104]

He predicted that England was sitting on a volcano which was about to erupt, and that should Queen Victoria suddenly die, a republican revolution would bring down the monarchy and the present system of government. (Like many other radicals, Garrison found Scotland much more to his liking.) Just over two years later Garrison wrote to his friend Elizabeth Pease in a much more militant tone:

> The present condition of England strikes me not only as extremely melancholy, but as absolutely frightful. What a spectacle, in a country famous for its industry and its fertility, to see vast multitudes of the people famishing for bread! What is to be the end of all this? Of all your reform parties, not one goes far enough, not one is based on the broad immovable foundation of human rights – not one raises the standard of Christian revolt against the power of darkness. . . . The watchword should be, – at the risk of martyrdom, or execution for high treason, – Down with the throne! Down with the aristocracy! Down with the accursed union between Church and State![105]

The political climate in Britain was so volatile that radical women found their energies dispersed into a number of urgent causes, of which women's rights was just one. However, through involving themselves in a wide range of political issues they were able to see connections between different groups of oppressed people. This experience, combined with the active support of those they worked with, radically influenced their perceptions of their own oppression as women. Some, like Elizabeth Pease, Harriet Martineau, Eliza Wigham and Mary Estlin, juggled their feminism within a broad concern for human equality.[106] Others, like Anne Knight and Barbara Bodichon, increasingly concentrated on women's issues while retaining their commitment to other social causes. For all these women, regular contact with radicals in Britain, America and Europe was crucial in sustaining their energy and confidence, and it was this that helped to provide the grounding under the feet of the incipient women's movement.

## Elizabeth Pease

Elizabeth Pease, being a Quaker, was a pacifist, but it is clear that her own views were not so far from those of the outspoken American whom she admired so much. A biography, written shortly after her death in 1896, describes a significant moment in her political development. Travelling to Birmingham with her father, Joseph Pease, to celebrate the anti-slavery jubilee in 1836, they were joined by the Irish nationalist Daniel O'Connell. She listened while the two men talked: 'I felt myself in a sort of elysium while listening to the conversation of two men, who, to so large an extent, practically carried our principle "that all men are created free and equal, and have an equal right to life, liberty, and the pursuit of happiness".'[107] During that same year, Joseph Pease began organizing in earnest around the subject of slavery in India. The jubilee in Birmingham had been called to celebrate the passing of the act that dismantled enforced apprenticeship in the Caribbean, but former slave owners had already turned to India for cheap labour, importing what were known as 'hill coolies' to Mauritius and Guyana. Besides this virtual slave trade, plantations in India relied on vast pools of native labour whose plight was gradually becoming known to English abolitionists through increased traffic between the two countries. Both O'Connell and George Thompson became involved in Joseph Pease's campaign, and a network of local groups, formed 'for the protection of the natives of British India', quickly spread in conjunction with existing anti-slavery groups. By 1839, the British India Society had been founded with Elizabeth Pease as the unofficial secretary. For several months she had worked closely with both Thompson and her father, writing their letters, discussing strategies and deciding policies. She continued to do so for as long as her health permitted, and her biography describes the dependence with which the two men relied on her.

> It was a rare position, in those days of prejudice and misconception, to stand at the side of the men who were proclaiming a great crusade, to be consulted on every step taken, supported in every suggestion, to have her prompt business-like arrangements carried out in every detail; to be in a sense the source of their resources, and the executive of the measures which she inspired.[108]

The relationship between Elizabeth and her father was not particularly unusual in anti-slavery circles; in fact, the role of the daughter-confidante would make a very rewarding study. For instance, both Eliza Cropper and Priscilla Buxton, daughters of leading abolitionists in the early days of the movement, played an important part behind the scenes. In her role as secretary, Elizabeth consistently asked her American friends for support for the British India Society and found them to be extremely willing to help. Articles were exchanged, often written by Elizabeth herself, on many different aspects of the Indian situation, including the opium question and the great famines exacerbated by the system of British rule. She also found time to write a pamphlet criticizing American Quakers for their exclusion of black Friends from New England meeting houses. This was widely circulated in both England and America and helped to earn Elizabeth a reputation as a radical well before the 1840 convention.

Many of Elizabeth's surviving letters illustrate how she incorporated the struggles of blacks, women and the working class into her politics. In one to a Boston friend, Anne Warren Weston, she wrote directly and honestly about her feelings:

> With regard to my political tendencies, about which thou enquires – I return an answer which my friends here wd. term very ungenteel – for they are ultra radical; to sympathise with the poor oppressed Chartists is considered vulgar – but I do most sincerely – condemning of course in them as I wd. in any, an appeal to physical force – but their transgressions in this way have been wonderfully few – considering the oppression they are enduring, & their deprivation of rights as human beings, I am often filled with astonishment at their patience and forbearance. I know I am not capable of taking a comprehensive view of what wd. be the effect of their principles, were they carried out in action – but it appears to me that they ask nothing more than what accords with the grand principle of the natural equality of man – a principal alas! almost buried, in this land, beneath the rubbish of an hereditary aristocracy & the farce of a state religion – the natural consequences of which are the love of patronage & power in the great – the domination of the few over the many, & the destruction of the rights of the great mass of the people. The five points of the Charter, are these, Universal Suffrage, vote by ballot, annual parliaments, no money qualifications for members, & a salary for members of parliament. It is thought most unaccountable for a gentleman to say he sees nothing wrong in these – but for a lady to do so is almost outrageous – I have nevertheless frequently done so, & am generally answered – that the people are not ready for all this – now this appears to me, nothing but a slaveholder's argument – the slave was not prepared for liberty – & the people are not prepared for their rights. How, I shd. like to know, are they to become prepared for them if they continue to be withheld?[109]

Later that year she wrote to the same friend again, describing the progress of the anti-bread tax agitation. In this letter she welcomed the education this campaign provided for the middle classes:

> It is teaching the middle classes their powerlessness to resist the Aristocracy & Landocracy & shewing them that the political liberty & equality of the people, whose rights they have too long treated with neglect or disdain, is necessary to their own independence.[110]

She continued to expand on the realities of the class system in England. For many middle-class radicals, it was impossible not to be deeply affected by the conditions of the men, women and children who had been drawn to the manufacturing centres in search of work. Like Garrison, Elizabeth Pease was particularly sickened by the contrast between the idle, landowning rich and the starving, homeless masses in the towns:

> We treat the working classes as aliens, as foreigners, as interests, except when we want to carry some measure of self-interest – then we appeal to them as rational & intelligent beings, capable of reasoning & deciding of questions of Justice & Injustice – so long as they are called on to judge on the extension of some privilege to ourselves – but, if they dare to exercise this judgement in favour of their own privileges, or rights even, then, forsooth they are ignorant, misled by passion & incapable of coming to a just conclusion. Ah, my dear Friend, the slaveocrat spirit is not confined to the Southern States of America . . .[111]

In this same letter she marvelled at the forbearance of the labouring classes in not rising up to 'steep the nation in bloodshed and rebellion'. She ended quite abruptly, as she ran out of space, reflecting on the miseries of her countrymen 'my brethren, my equals', and on the wickedness of those who perpetrate such cruelty, not just towards those in England but throughout the Empire. She added:

> Think too of our atrocities in heathen Lands, wherever the English have colonised – & now behold them carrying devastation & war into China, because, they have the morality to refuse our poison. Was such iniquity ever heard of before, yet we call ourselves a Xtian nation![112]

In another letter to close friends in Boston, this time to Wendell and Ann Phillips, she wrote about the Chartists in more detail. First, however, she thanked them for their questions on the subject which 'taught me how little I really knew on the subject notwithstanding that I reckon myself one of their body.' Although she had to write to a mutual friend for clarification on some of their questions, she talked at length about her own experience and opinions:

> Surely it is to class Legislation that nearly all the evils which affect Gt. Britain & render her a curse, instead of a blessing, to other nations – is to be

> attributed and so long as this hydra-headed monster is suffered to remain, it is vain to strike off one of its heads – in the shape of the Corn Laws, Monopoly, union of church & state or aught else; – till it is destroyed utterly – blood, bones & sinews – like the fabled monster of old, two heads will spring up to fill the place of one.[113]

After this she seemed vague about the Chartist position on women's rights – 'I believe, the Chartists generally hold the doctrine of the equality of women's rights' – and she admitted to being unsure of the status of married women, and whether or not they were expected to merge their political rights with their husbands'. In this letter she did not give any opinion on this question.

Reading these extracts written by and about Elizabeth Pease I am struck by how reticent she was on the subject of gender, as opposed to race and class. This may have been related to the independence of her own life-style which made her less concerned about her subordination as a woman, or it may have just been that she felt a great deal more angry about the hierarchies of class and race. In any event, it would seem that she was not ready to connect the way that women were systematically excluded from political and economic life with the oppression of the 'starving homeless masses' in Britain and slaves in America, India or the Caribbean. The confusion she expresses in her letters is a useful reminder that political consciousness is bound to be uneven and contradictory, even in the most committed and militant activists.

Elizabeth's politics were inextricably connected to her religious beliefs as a member of the Society of Friends. In both America and Britain Quakers played a significant role in the abolitionist movement, and although they were feminists neither in principle nor practice, their commitment to humanitarian principles gave many women a grounding in early feminism. However, as Olive Banks points out, it is clear that even a deep involvement in such issues did not necessarily lead women to question their traditional role.[114] Elizabeth Fry, famous for her work on prison reform in the early nineteenth century, justified her role in social welfare through entirely conventional means. Her life provided a clear example of the contradictory nature of women's philanthropic work. Her 'mission' as a woman was to apply her moral and spiritual strength to helping the poor and needy. By applying herself to the appalling conditions of prisoners she inevitably involved herself in the public domain and from there in social reform.

Elizabeth Pease belonged to that strand of Quakers that refused any kind of sectarianism or religious dogma. Her belief in the fundamental equality of mankind was derived as much from the Gospels as from the iniquities she saw around her. For her, Christianity was a 'religion of love, which teaches the universal brotherhood of Man'. Her dislike of sectarianism was reflected in her readiness to befriend Lucretia Mott, who belonged to a branch of the Quakers that was considered heretical by the orthodox. Later in her own life she came up against sectarianism among her own community: when Elizabeth married in 1852 she was disowned by her local branch of Friends as her husband was not a Quaker. It appears, though, that they were more reluctant to expel her than she was to leave, and it was probably the case that her expulsion hastened the end of the rule that Friends could not marry outside.

During the 1850s Elizabeth was occupied by ill-health and her happy but all too brief marriage. Her husband, Professor John Nichol, who was a widower, was an ardent supporter of national liberation movements in Europe, and personally acquainted with the Italian and Hungarian leaders, Mazzini and Kossuth. In the few years they enjoyed together the couple formed an important part of the radical network in Glasgow, where Elizabeth was closer to long-time friends and allies Jane Smeal and Eliza Wigham. However, she kept up her correspondences with American friends and was visited by Garrison before his death in 1879.

Elizabeth Pease was by all accounts a very remarkable woman. She was a port of call for many important American abolitionists who visited Britain. In 1849 the novelist William Wells Brown wrote to her shortly before he arrived in Liverpool, introducing himself and passing on letters from Garrison and other mutual friends. He asked for her help in arranging a lecture tour: 'As I am a stranger, and wish to consult the friends of the slave, upon my future course, any suggestions from you, will be gratefully received and highly appreciated. . . . Respectfully yours for the slave.'[115] J. A. Collins, who toured the country during the winter of 1840–41 trying to raise support for the American Anti-Slavery Society, wrote home to Garrison about his experiences: 'But the most noble of all the English spirits I have met with is Elizabeth Pease. What an enlarged and free mind! How faithful and uncompromising! How liberal and self-denying! How sociable and amiable. She possesses qualifications sufficient to constitute her emphatically, a noble woman.'[116]

## Anne Knight

Where Elizabeth Pease has provided this legacy of written material, Anne Knight remains more of a mystery. I was able to find only a few scattered (and almost unintelligible – she used no punctuation whatsoever) writings and a number of references to her being the first author of a women's suffrage pamphlet.[117] It is frustrating not to know more about the friendship that developed between Anne and Elizabeth as a result of their anti-slavery work in the 1830s. They would have had much in common: both women came from or were related to leading Quaker families and had been allowed to develop an interest in both intellectual and artistic subjects. Anne, being older, became involved in her local anti-slavery association in Chelmsford as early as 1830 and throughout the decade met many of the abolitionist leaders and activists, including Elizabeth. By 1838 she was already in affectionate correspondence with William Lloyd Garrison and other Boston abolitionists in the radical camp. In July 1838, she wrote to Garrison from Paris bemoaning the fact that the abolition of slavery had not managed to improve the lives of the former slaves:

> My dear friend & brother
>
> I hope the hideous enthralment is coming to an end for every vessel brings to our ports tidings of other planters coming to emancipation from motives of self interest! They only wanted to see if & how much more they could plunder from an outraged people in the form of compensation we have all reasons to hope that for the Africans liberty may be obtained – and then – then – the Hill Coolies![118]

Although Anne may have felt more strongly on the 'woman question' than Elizabeth Pease – or at least felt more compelled to express her beliefs on the matter – she was similarly connected to other radical movements of the period. She also counted herself a Chartist sympathizer and had many friends in the Owenite movement. After she had published her leaflet on women's suffrage in 1847, she was approached by a leading socialist in Sheffield, Isaac Ironside, who passed on to her the names of seven Chartist women who were interested in organizing together on this issue. She immediately wrote to them and a month later the Sheffield Association for Female Franchise was founded – the first recorded women's suffrage organization. It was as a result of this that the first petition demanding the vote for women was delivered to the House of Lords in 1851. Shortly after this Anne left England to live in Europe, returning periodically for visits.

## C. S. Toll

However tantalizing it is to have only fragments of correspondence between Anne Knight, Elizabeth Pease and their friends, these sources do at least make it possible to claim some knowledge of their family backgrounds and political contacts. There is no suggestion that they were unique, either in their intellectual or political lives, however difficult it is to find written evidence of other women who shared their political passions. The following extracts from letters from and about C. S. Toll, who is far less well known, suggest that a significant number of women involved in anti-slavery campaigns were more ready to make connections with their own oppression than has so far been thought.

Clare Taylor's collection of abolitionist correspondence between America and Britain includes an extraordinary letter from a woman called Margaret New in London to Maria Weston Chapman in Boston, written in September 1841. She began by explaining that she was writing out of support for the work being done to end slavery by the women in America, describing how ashamed she felt when reading of their treatment at the hands of those calling themselves 'Gentlemen'. She then begged for more information about their activities, before launching into a revealing plea for women's emancipation:

> If you can now and then spare a few minutes of your valuable time, and will write to me, how proud and happy I shall be. . . . It is a selfish wish, but it is mine, that you would use all your energies towards bettering the condition both political and social of women of this country, we are in such a fearful state of bondage tis dreadful to contemplate, and we have so few women of moral courage sufficient to attempt a change. My friend Mrs. Toll is one of the few she is a woman following in your own footsteps. Thrice blessed are the women who do advance some steps from the old beaten path

> and do not heed the sneers of the world, but go right onward in their right doing . . .[119]

We hear no more of Margaret New in this collection, but are fortunate enough to have a letter from Mrs Toll herself, also addressed to Maria Weston Chapman. It appears that C. S. Toll lived in Birmingham where she was involved in a campaign to pass a law against the employment of women in coal mines. In this letter, written in 1844, she explained to the American woman that with the help of 'many good and noble hearts' and the signatures of many local women they were successful in getting a law passed, although it was being evaded by mine owners. Her letter is a mixture of anger and despair at social conditions she saw and heard around her: the use of the military against the Irish, the strikes in the cities and the poverty of the working people in the towns and villages throughout Britain. She was particularly concerned about the fate of women:

> On the right of suffrage – on the cruelties and horrors of our Poor Law, and on the abject and suffering condition of our labourers, particularly females, there is an enormous deal to be done . . .[120]

But C. S. Toll had written to the Boston Anti-Slavery Society principally because she wanted to express her solidarity with their work. 'If I were in your land,' she began in the same letter, 'I must join your ranks, I could not possibly be apathetic, neither can I conceive how any woman calling herself a Christian and a woman, can stand by contented with professing herself opposed to slavery.' She ended with a warm message of support from herself and her young daughter for 'those good and right-thinking women who act with you in trying to rescue their fellow creatures from the curse of slavery'.

## Barbara Bodichon

Barbara Bodichon (or Barbara Leigh Smith as she was known before her marriage,) was only thirteen years old in 1840, but a childhood spent in radical anti-slavery circles would have made her well aware of the excitement generated by the London convention. Both Lucretia Mott and Elizabeth Cady Stanton visited her house as guests of her father, Benjamin, who was a radical MP like his father before him. As Unitarians, members of the family were also in touch with political refugees from Europe and other visiting abolitionists, as well as radicals and socialists in Britain. Barbara's education was unconventional but equal to that of her brothers: they attended a school run along Owenite lines, founded and paid for by their father, and her independence and freedom to involve herself in politics was greatly helped when she was given an independent income by her father at the age of twenty-one.

Barbara Bodichon's contribution to the Victorian women's movement has been documented elsewhere.[121] Her attachment to other reformist and radical causes was important to her and expressed in a variety of different ways including important alliances with other writers, artists and activists. The importance of anti-slavery politics in Barbara's life revealed itself early on in her political career. A trip to America in 1857–58 with her husband, Eugene Bodichon, brought her into contact with defenders of slavery as well as slaves themselves.[122] During the seven-month visit she spent six weeks in New Orleans before travelling up the east coast to Canada. She also followed up her contacts with women such as Lucy Stone, an active feminist who had come to women's politics through the abolitionist movement. Barbara wrote in her diary that questions of slavery and women's rights were inescapable:

> It is less perverting to the mind to hold the most monstrously absurd doctrines of religious faith than to believe a man has a right to breed slaves [and] to sell his own children . . . [or] to believe that men have rights over women. . . . Every day men acting on this false belief destroy their perception of justice and blunt their moral nature. . . . Slavery is a greater injustice but it is allied to the injustice to women so closely that I cannot see one without thinking of the other . . .[123]

After she returned home she published unedited extracts from her diaries in the *English Woman's Journal* which she had helped to found just before she left England. One of her aims was to inform British women of the issues involved in the American Civil War. Her views were strongly anti-slavery, and she went out of her way to gather information about life among black people in the Southern cities she visited. She also spent time trying to analyse the effects of slavery on the white population, rapidly coming to the conclusion that it was they who fared worse from the institution:

> It is impossible, almost, for you to conceive the utter depravity in all ideas of

> justice caused by slavery; I still think the whites suffer most, spiritually and physically.[124]

She was particularly critical of the white women she encountered, noting their extreme hypochondria, fear of work and obsession with their appearances, all of which she attributed to slavery rather than the most usual explanation: the unhealthy climate. She also remarked on the cruelty of many slave-owning women she encountered. In one extract Barbara recorded an extraordinary conversation she took part in with a group of strangers on board a boat on the Mississippi. All her companions were united in their disgust that Barbara should have gone to school with a 'mulatto' girl and that there were 'mulattoes' in England 'who were not unlikely to marry with white people'. When Barbara pointed out that 'your little children all find it possible to come in close contact with negro nurses, and seem very fond of them', proving that there was no 'natural antipathy', the Southerners replied that: ' . . . there is an inborn disgust which prevents amalgamation'. Barbara noted at this point that 'only half the negroes in the United States are full-blooded Africans; the rest born of white fathers and black mothers'. The conversation then turned to women's rights, which the strangers inevitably dismissed as rubbish, although Mrs B did confess to having been carried away by Lucy Stone's eloquence when she first heard her speak. Barbara steered the conversation back to slavery as she wanted to push them further on the subject of education, and to argue for the right of black people to learn to read and write. The general argument ran that education made slaves discontented and encouraged them to run away; any form of emancipation was out of the question: 'They were inferior to whites and likely to remain so'. The encounter ran into deeper water when Mrs B asked Barbara if she had read *Uncle Tom's Cabin*. When she said she had, Mrs B replied: 'If there's a creature living I hate, it's that Mrs Beecher'. 'This was said with an expression of bitter feeling which distorted her good face until every vestige of humanity disappeared.' Barbara noted more than once the frequency with which *Uncle Tom's Cabin* was cited by white Southerners, although it was certainly not available in the slave-owning states.

Barbara concluded her report of this conversation with a comment on white racism:

> I do not know how others may feel, but I cannot come amongst these people

> without the perception that every standard of right and wrong is unconsciously lost, and that they are wretched in themselves and degraded by this one falsehood in the midst of which they dwell – to live in the belief of a vital falsehood poisons all the springs of life.[125]

Despite her abhorrence of the system which caused families to be split up and sold off – she once witnessed a slave auction which she described in great detail for her English readers – Barbara's own writing betrays deep-rooted ideas about racial privilege. Many of her character sketches of black people are demeaning in their attempts to portray their humanity, and her observations about the benefits of education to the African race are fairly insulting. In one passage she described herself not as an abolitionist who believed in immediate emancipation, but as a gradualist: 'What I wish for is gradual freedom for the blacks, but freedom in all the states to buy themselves, and freedom to educate themselves.' She was interested in what she saw as the relative capabilities of the races, observing in one extract that 'the race is not so low in the human scale as I had supposed before I came here. Probably the field hands are inferior'.[126] Elsewhere she noted that 'the mulatto and quadroon are equal in mental endowments to many European races'.

For all their mid-Victorian arrogance and sentimentality, the diaries give a valuable impression of life in the American South before the Civil War. They revealed, for example, that black women often expressed an interest in Queen Victoria and her marriage, seeing her as both a symbol of liberation and as an expert in fashion.[127] Barbara's research took her to black churches, where she was welcomed with interest, and where she made many thoughtful, if again patronizing, observations about black life and strategies for survival. She was most affected by the singing and chanting she heard:

> The voices of the negroes are beautiful; some day great singers will come out of that people. . . . Sometimes when I hear them sing, the thought of slavery, and what it really is, makes me utterly miserable: one can do nothing, and I see little hope; it makes me wring my hands with anguish, sometimes, being so helpless to help.[128]

One of the features of the slave system that most appalled Barbara was the way the law either discriminated against black people, free or slave, or was used to oppress them even further. It was forbidden by law to teach blacks to read or write, for example, which forced people to learn and to teach in secret. While in Savannah she wrote: 'The negroes tell me it is hardly worth while to be free, the laws are so hard on them now. If they stay in the State of Alabama . . . they must have a nominal owner, and go up to be registered at certain times, and comply with all sorts of vexatious regulations, some of which are expensive.'[129] The institutional inequality between black and white was shocking enough for a British visitor, especially one who had grown up as a child of the anti-slavery movement. But Barbara had other reasons to identify the legal structure as a source of particular oppression: three years before her visit she had written her famous pamphlet, *A Brief Summary*, which, as I have already noted, coincided with the first feminist gathering in Britain. The first law to be targeted by feminists was the notorious Married Women's Property Act, which deprived women of control of their earnings or property once they were married, and gave husbands legal custody of the children. In 1855, Barbara instigated a petition calling for reform of this law, drawing together a group of women called the 'Langham Place Circle'. In the petition she wrote about the power of the law to retain all women in a state of powerlessness and vulnerability: she ended it with the words:

> . . . it is time that legal protection be thrown over the produce of their labour and that in entering the state of marriage, they no longer pass from freedom into the condition of the slave, all whose earnings belong to his master and not to himself.[130]

Barbara used the metaphor of slavery with peculiar passion, but she knew it was not an original analogy. Her ideas and political development had been shaped by her contact with other radicals, and this included a vocabulary which repeatedly referred to slavery as the ultimate state of legalized – and uncivilized – inequality.

## From Bondage to Liberation

In 1825, just as the first female anti-slavery associations were being formed, an Irish Socialist called William Thompson published a book called *Appeal of one-half the human race, Women, against the pretensions of the other half, Men, to retain them in political, and thence in civil and domestic, Slavery*. Written with Anna Wheeler, a feminist active in the Co-operative and Saint-Simonian movements, the book documented the precise forms of women's domination by men and suggested remedies to overcome this. It became recognized as one of the classic philosophical texts on women's rights, spanning the eighty years between Mary Wollstonecraft's *Vindication* in 1792 and John Stuart Mill's *Subjection of Women*, which was published in 1869.

At the core of Thompson and Wheeler's argument was the idea that women – particularly married women – were systematically deprived of any chance of happiness or fulfilment as human beings. Man's domination was achieved first by rendering women powerless by law, and this was then consolidated by arbitrary moral and physical codes which maintained women in a state of ignorance, idleness and frivolity, much as if they were part of the furniture of the home. A central and recurring theme of the book was that women in Britain had been reduced – literally not metaphorically – to a condition which at least equalled that of slaves in the West Indies:

> A domestic, a civil, a political slave, in the plain unsophisticated sense of the word – in no metaphorical sense – is every married woman.[131]

Thompson and Wheeler relied on public condemnation of West Indian slavery, which was just gathering momentum in another wave of campaigning, to supply graphic illustrations of women's dependence on men.[132] Although slavery was always condemned in all its forms throughout the *Appeal*, the urge to prove that British wives of all classes were suffering under a similar condition sometimes required a simplistic picture of life on the plantations. In one section they tried to prove that British women were actually worse off than female slaves, arguing that for all the evils of slavery, female slaves were not required to submit to 'a second state of individual domestic slavery to the male slaves'.

> No female slave is obliged, for the sake of existence, to vow obedience to all the despotic commands of a male slave, to resign her privileges, such as the task master leaves to all, of going out and coming in, of moving from place to place within the desolate sphere of common bonds, of forming acquain-

> tance, friendship, and attachment, at her pleasure, with any individuals of her fellow-slaves . . .[133]

They argued that British women were totally dependent on their husbands for permission to move outside the home, 'Is there a female slave in the West Indies,' they asked, 'who would submit to such dictation from any male slave, if her companion, her equal, and no more than her equal, in degradation and misery?'[134] Black men and women were united in slavery, since there was no property to make claims to and no rights over the children anyway. While female slaves were 'liable to the *occasional* despotic will, to the lust or caprice of the common tyrant of all', married women in Britain were 'liable to the uncontrolled and eternal caprices of an ever-jealous and ever-present tyrant'.[135]

Other comparisons – the psychological effects of slavery, the brainwashing required to keep people in submission, and the degradation of everyday life – were carefully argued through by Thompson and Wheeler in unrelenting prose. The marriage contract was likened to the contract between master and slave – 'the law of the stronger imposed on the weaker, in contempt of the interests and wishes of the weaker'.[136] They argued that neither women nor slaves had any choice as to whether they entered this contract. Daughters were groomed for marriage as soon as they could speak, although in passing from single to married status they lost all civil rights and returned 'into the state of children or idiots, the passive property of their owners'.[137]

Thirty years earlier, Mary Wollstonecraft had also likened British women to slaves, though she was far more allegorical. In the final paragraph of the *Vindication* Mary appealed to her male readers not to be like Egyptian task-masters, resorting to Old Testament references rather than examples nearer to hand. She used the vocabulary of slavery freely, only rarely qualifying her choice of words. When she did so she was quite precise:

> When therefore I call women slaves, I mean in a political and civil sense; for indirectly they obtain too much power, and they are debased by their exertions to obtain illicit sway.[138]

Elsewhere she displayed a somewhat dismissive view of black slaves in a section on the way women are forced to occupy themselves with trivial pastimes and an obsession with their appearances:

> . . . even the hellish yoke of slavery cannot stifle the savage desire of admiration which the black heroes inherit from both their parents, for all the hardly earned savings of a slave are commonly expended in a little tawdry finery. . . . An immoderate fondness for dress, for pleasure, and for sway, are the passions of savages; the passions that occupy those uncivilised beings who have not yet extended the dominion of the mind, or even learned to think with the energy necessary to concatenate that abstract train of thought which produces principles.[139]

This discussion is not intended to diminish Mary Wollstonecraft's status as a political writer, but instead to invite a reading of her work that is sensitive to her perception of racial subordination and its possible connections with the oppression of women. In fact it is precisely because of her status that this kind of interrogation is needed, since the *Vindication* has so often been celebrated for its unequivocal demands for social, political and legal equality between men and women. Discussing Mary Wollstonecraft's role in the formation of feminist sexual politics, Cora Kaplan writes that the reputation of the *Vindication* as the founding text of Anglo-American feminism 'generally precedes and in part constructs our reading of it'.[140] This has often meant that 'its troubling historical meanings and contradictions drop away, so that we may take away from it an unproblematic feminist inheritance'. I would also argue that this same warning should be applied to other influential writing on women's equality.

John Stuart Mill's famous tract *The Subjection of Women* echoed many of the themes found in the *Appeal* when it was published over forty years later, but the political climate that received it had altered considerably. Slavery in the Caribbean and in America had been abolished by then, but the memory of the abolitionist cause was kept alive by those who had lived through its most active days, some of whom had endeavoured to co-ordinate new campaigns in support of blacks living under British domination. Mill had a particular relationship to the expanding British Empire: at the instigation of his father he worked for the East India Company from 1822 until its demise in 1858, the year after the Indian uprising.[141] As a Liberal MP in 1865 he acted as one of the leaders of the Jamaica Committee in Parliament, arguing with great eloquence against the excesses of the

British army in the Morant Bay uprising and for the removal of Governor Eyre.[142] On the subject of women he wrote that 'the law of servitude in marriage is a monstrous contradiction to all the principles of the modern world, and to all the experience through which those principles have been slowly and painfully worked out.'[143] The only slaves that remained were the ones married to men under British law. Slavery was viewed from a historical point of view as a state of legal dispossession in which individuals were forbidden from owning property and were treated as property by their masters.

Mill wrote at length about the evolutionary nature of women's oppression, concurring with the *Appeal*'s position that women in modern Europe were experiencing a milder form of dependence which had its 'brutal' origins in primitive slavery. Where the *Appeal* had argued that the 'brand of inferiority' was impressed on women at birth, 'indelible like the skin of the Black', Mill discussed at great length the ways in which men justified their domination of others by claiming it to be natural. He cited the slave owners in the Southern states of America:

> Did they not call heaven and earth to witness that the domination of the white man over the black is natural, that the black race is by nature incapable of freedom, and marked out for slavery?[144]

The historical context of each of these texts determined the weight each gave to slavery. The *Vindication* appeared at the outset of the earliest popular wave of agitation against the slave trade; the *Appeal* just as the campaign for abolition caught the philanthropic imagination; the *Subjection* after slavery in America and the Caribbean had been officially abolished, but during a period of imperial expansion justified by economic and ideological arguments. Both the *Appeal* and the *Subjection* relied on popular sentiment against the institution of slavery, arguing meticulously that the oppression of women was identical in many respects, and therefore worthy of the same, if not a greater, degree of condemnation. To quote John Stuart Mill once again:

> I am far from pretending that wives are in general no better treated than slaves; but no slave is a slave to the same lengths, and in so full a sense of the word, as a wife is.[145]

All three texts argued for changes in laws relating to property, as well as drawing out the psychological effects of bondage – which included the extinction of any will to resist as well as the moral corruption of the slave-owning class. Lack of education or opportunity for intellectual development, and absence of any political or civil rights were also frequently discussed as means by which British married women were reduced to a state of servitude. Their constant references to slavery – even Mary Wollstonecraft's unqualified use of the adjective 'slavish' – provided a powerful philosophical basis for all three writers wanting to make both rhetorical and literal points about women's subordination.

While the language of slavery was often used in the context of other oppressed groups, its role in the articulation of early feminism, suggested by this superficial reading of some classic texts, provokes important questions about connections between race and gender during the first half of the nineteenth century. For instance, what did the concept of slavery represent in terms of a political understanding of race, either as an analytic category comparable to gender, or as a system of domination of which they were part? How was the power of anti-slavery rhetoric affected by the popularization of science and by the legitimation of scientific racism? To what extent was race seen as a gendered category, and under what circumstances did race, class and gender take precedence over one another? I have suggested that a new synthesis of the disparate strands of history is needed and that I think women's abolitionist work provides untapped opportunities for finding a dynamic between sex, race and gender in the first part of the nineteenth century.

There are several approaches to looking at the connections between race, class and gender during this period. The first is to examine how racial difference was expressed, or obliterated, in relation to gender and class. For instance, the fact that British women claimed an unbroken sisterhood with female slaves must have had implications for the meaning of womanhood which bound them in their own communities. To deny that there was any difference between the basic expectations and experiences of black slaves and free white women and to assert a sort of spiritual sisterhood would have had the effect both of confirming conservative ideas of what constituted a woman and of what imprisoned her at the same time. Since feminism took on the task of constantly redefining the boundaries of womanhood, the significance of race or class difference between women was always present in some form, as it continues to be today.

Second, it is important to examine women's anti-slavery language in the context of changing attitudes to race. The permeation of political discourse with concepts and language drawn from the natural sciences created new and often contradictory ways of constructing the hierarchies of race and gender within both a developing feminist ideology and the wider political culture of which it was a part. The first half of the nineteenth century witnessed the beginnings of scientific culture, which produced a different order of struggle against domination by race, class and gender. In order to contest, or alternatively legitimate, existing social divisions, political philosophy was increasingly drawn into a dialogue with the new sciences of ethnography, anthropology, biology and other branches of study of the human race. In other words, it became more and more difficult to discuss the particularity of women without reference to other apparently natural differences, particularly race, since both white women and black people differed visibly from white men against whom all difference was measured.

Each of these three works on women's rights convey an implicit rejection of 'unholy prejudice' which lies beneath the forceful condemnation of slavery in all its forms. Yet, as in many abolitionist tracts, the discussion of the realities of West Indian slavery or the cultural patterns of non-European societies frequently betrayed assumptions of white superiority. As Nancy Stepan discusses in *The Idea of Race in Science*, there is a complex and contradictory relationship between racism and the various stages of abolitionism:

> A fundamental question about the history of racism in the first half of the nineteenth century is why it was that, just as the battle against slavery was being won by abolitionists, the war against racism was being lost. The Negro was legally freed by the Emancipation Act of 1833, but in the British mind he was still mentally, morally and physically a slave.[146]

A third area of inquiry must be the relationship between the politics of women's rights and black people's struggles for emancipation and equality. I have tried to show how the nineteenth-century movement for women's rights was at first inextricably connected to the rights of black people for equality, humanity and some kind of liberty. Through analogies with slavery, women's rights activists could claim that theirs was a respectable moral cause, not a revolutionary demand that threatened the whole structure of society. The identity of slavery with sin and barbarism, and of abolitionism with true Christian civilization, paved the way for a new reformist movement for the emancipation of women. 'As your bondage has chained down man to the ignorance and vices of despotism,' wrote George Thompson and Anna Wheeler in the final sentence of the *Appeal*, 'so will your liberation reward him with knowledge, with freedom and with happiness.'[147]

These three areas of inquiry all lead to a further question: What happened to those interweaving strands of race and gender when slavery was formally abolished? Although some would continue to argue that the real slaves were the working class, the dismantling of racial slavery in the Caribbean, and later in the United States, marked the end of the most intense form of oppression recognized in Western culture. The existence of a popular movement against the slavery of blacks in the Caribbean and later America provided a cornerstone for the building of a women's rights movement in Britain. Concepts of equality, legal and economic bondage, liberation and all the metaphors of servitude which were freely used by abolitionists were consistently borrowed by pioneers for women's rights to link their struggle to the wider one of human rights. Today this might seem an obvious point as the language of slavery has been endlessly diluted, but for those who were acquainted in any way with the realities of the plantation systems and the trade in human souls, it had a specific and powerful resonance. As the movement for women's rights progressed, women were able to exploit the power of the slavery analogy in interpreting their own servitude but without needing any longer to refer to the slaves whose bondage had once outraged and inspired them. However idealized or unconscious their identification with black slaves had been, it began to ebb away as a fresh sense of the politics of female subordination emerged and became the site of new public struggles. By then, however, the geography of racial conflict had itself altered. The struggles of black people for liberation from British control had ranged further across the world and the Empire had been extended into new territories. Woman's mission to the slaves was accomplished, but her relationship to the 'natives' was still evolving.

## Notes

1 *An Appeal to the Christian Women of Sheffield from the Association for the Universal Abolition of Slavery*, Sheffield 1837. Rhodes House Library, Oxford.

2 Judith Butler, 'Gender Trouble, Feminist Theory, and Psychoanalytic Discourse', in Linda J. Nicholson, ed., *Feminism/Postmodernism*, Routledge, New York/London 1990, pp. 324–5.

3 Louis Billington and Rosamund Billington, ' "A Burning Zeal for Righteousness": Women in the British Anti-Slavery Movement', in Jane Rendall, ed., *Equal But Different: Women's Politics in Britain 1800–1914*, Basil Blackwell, Oxford 1987. This is one of the most detailed accounts published recently.

4 For a fuller discussion of the historical significance of *Oroonoko* see David Brion Davis, *The Problem of Slavery in Western Culture*, Cornell University Press, Ithaca/London 1966, pp. 472–9. See also Ania Loomba, *Gender, Race, Renaissance Drama* (Manchester University Press, New York/Manchester 1989) which presents a much more complex, feminist, view of race and gender in literature before Behn's time.

5 Strangely enough, Maureen Duffy in her introduction to a recent edition of *Oroonoko* (*Aphra Behn: Oroonoko & Other Stories*, Methuen, London 1986) attributes Oroonoko's failure to complete the suicide pact to physical weakness, which is a misleading simplification that denies him the passions that illustrate my argument. In *Oroonoko* (p. 94) Aphra Behn describes how her hero's 'grief swell'd up to rage' as he looked upon his wife's dead face:

> He tore, he raved, he roar'd like some monster of the wood', but as he called out Imoinda's name his rage and desire for revenge turned to grief and he lay weeping by her side, powerless to move. After two days he was indeed too weak to kill himself, but when his English enemies found him he still found enough strength and pride to kill one of them and disembowel himself before they carried him off.

6 David Brion Davis, p. 474.

7 Duffy, p. 33.

8 Angeline Goreau, *Reconstructing Aphra: A Social Biography of Aphra Behn*, Oxford University Press, Oxford, pp. 41–69.

9 Duffy, p. 70.

10 Dancer and choreographer Bill T. Jones based an incredible three-hour epic performance (called 'The Last Supper at Uncle Tom's Cabin/The Promised Land') on the character of Uncle Tom, which he used as a springboard to explore themes of sexuality, race, gender, faith and AIDS. In an interview in *Elle* (November 1990, US edn) he explained:

> I've been called an 'Uncle Tom' before. I wanted to set the record straight. Nobody knows the story now – let's see who Uncle Tom really was. He is such an incredible part of our Western consciousness: the epitome of the American liberal impulse, with all its hypocrisy, inconsistency, and idealism. People think they know the novel but they don't. It deserves to be examined on a much deeper level.

11 Samuel Sillen, 'Mrs Stowe's Best Seller – the Hundredth Anniversary of an American Classic', *Masses & Mainstream*, vol. 5, no. 3, March 1952, p. 23.

12 Some of the Scottish anti-slavery groups took the initiative in capitalizing on the success of the novel. The Edinburgh group held a large public meeting at which it was agreed that all readers of *Uncle Tom's Cabin* should subscribe a penny (minimum) towards anti-slavery funds. Many other groups followed suit. Glasgow groups wrote to Harriet Beecher Stowe inviting her to visit, and she was offered a free passage by the owner of the steamer, *Glasgow*, which she accepted. However, there was some doubt expressed as to the value of all this excitement: for example, Jane Wigham, a radical abolitionist in Edinburgh, wrote to a friend in Boston that, 'The great excitement caused by "Uncle Tom's Cabin" – is unlikely to do much good, and we were grieved to see H. C. W. trying to undervalue the

book – we should be thankful for every auxiliary – even though it be not entirely according to our standard.' See Clare Taylor, *British and American Abolitionism: An Episode in Transatlantic Understanding*, Edinburgh University Press, Edinburgh 1974, pp. 390–1.

13 'The Key To "Uncle Tom's Cabin" ', *Frederick Douglass's Paper*, 29 April 1853. Frederick Douglass was one of the most famous black figures in nineteenth-century America. Born into slavery, he escaped and was propelled into the abolitionist limelight by the Garrisonians in Boston. He was a brilliant orator and later edited his own newspaper. He travelled to England several times and was an important figure in the transatlantic anti-slavery movement. He was also the first man in America to call publicly for women's suffrage and, despite fundamental differences, he remained a close friend of many leading feminists throughout his life.

14 C. Peter Ripley, ed., *The Black Abolitionist Papers'* vol. 1: *The British Isles, 1830–1865*, University of North Carolina Press, Chapel Hill/London 1985, p. 344.

15 Cited in Ellen Moers, *Literary Women*, The Women's Press, London 1980 p. 4.

16 Langston Hughes in an introduction to *Uncle Tom's Cabin*, Great Illustrated Classics, Dodd, Mead & Co., New York 1952.

17 Harriet Beecher Stowe, *The Key to Uncle Tom's Cabin*, Clark Beeton & Co., London 1853.

18 Harriet Beecher Stowe, *Uncle Tom's Cabin*, Penguin, Harmondsworth 1986, p. 84.

19 Ibid., pp. 153–4.

20 For a list of earlier critical books, see Margaret Holbrook Hildreth, *Harriet Beecher Stowe: A Bibliography*, Archon Books, Hamden, CT 1976. For more recent feminist criticism see Gillian Brown, *Domestic Individualism: Imagining Self in Nineteenth-Century America*, University of California Press, Berkeley and Oxford 1990, Part 1.

21 Harriet Beecher Stowe received many approaches from black people to tell their stories of escape from slavery. Harriet Brent Jacobs, a former slave, suggested through an intermediary that Stowe should take her daughter Louisa, who had received a good education, on her proposed visit to Britain as a 'representative of a Southern slave'. Stowe's reply was a bitter disappointment: 'She was afraid that if her situation as a slave should be known it would subject her to much petting and patronizing which would be more pleasing to a young Girl than useful and the English were very apt to do it and she was very much opposed to it with this class of people.' This last remark made Harriet Jacobs extremely angry and she later wrote: 'What a pity we poor blacks can't have the firmness and stability of character that you white people have'. Dorothy Sterling, ed., *We Are Your Sisters: Black Women in the 19th century*, W. W. Norton, New York/London 1984, pp. 76–7. Following this she travelled to England herself and began to write her own life story – *Incidents in the Life of a Slave Girl* – which was later published in Boston with the help of Lydia Maria Child, becoming the only autobiography of a woman fugitive to be published before the Civil War. See Harriet A. Jacobs, Lydia Mary Child and Jean Fagan Yellin, ed., *Incidents in the Life of a Slave Girl, Written by Herself*, Harvard University Press, Cambridge, MA 1987.

22 Elaine Campbell, 'Oroonoko's Heir: The West Indies in Late Eighteenth Century Novels', *Caribbean Quarterly*, vol. 25, nos 1 and 2, March–June 1979.

23 See Moira Fergusson, *Subject to Others: British Women Writers and Colonial Slavery, 1678–1834*, Routledge, London 1991.

24 Herbert Aptheker, for instance, argues that abolitionism was more of a successful revolutionary movement than a simple reform movement. See *Abolitionism: A Revolutionary Movement*, Twayne, Boston 1989. For a good account of these debates, and of the dynamics

of anti-slavery generally, see Robin Blackburn, *The Overthrow of Colonial Slavery 1776–1848*, Verso, London/New York 1988.

25 *Album* of the Female Society for Birmingham for the Relief of British Negro Slaves, R. Peart, Birmingham *c.* 1828, p. 1.

26 'An Appeal to the Christian Women of Sheffield', from the Association for the Universal Abolition of Slavery.

27 Anna M. Stoddart, *Saintly Lives: E. Pease Nichol*, J. M. Dent, London 1899, p. 64.

28 'An Appeal', p. 13.

29 See Jean Fagan Yellin, *Women and Sisters: The Anti-Slavery Feminists in American Culture*, Yale University Press, New Haven/London 1989. This book takes the classic abolitionist emblem of the kneeling slave asking, 'Am I Not a Woman and a Sister?' and uses it to examine the discourse of the anti-slavery feminists. Thanks, Isaac.

30 'An Appeal', p. 12.

31 Douglas Lorimer, *Colour, Class and the Victorians – English Attitudes to the Negro in the Mid-Nineteenth Century*, Leicester University Press, Leicester 1978, ch. 1.

32 Hannah Kilham wrote her memoirs (*The memoirs of Hannah Kilham*, ed., S. Biller, 1837) which reveal many interesting insights into the nature of charity, Christian missionary work and the contradictory position of middle-class women in the early nineteenth century. Quotes cited in Lorimer, pp. 34–5, 294–5.

33 Lorimer, p. 35.

34 Peter Fryer, *Staying Power: The History of Black People in Britain*, Pluto, London 1984, pp. 157–61.

35 'An Appeal', p. 14.

36 See Lorimer for a discussion of Victorian racism. Also Fryer, ch. 7; Ripley, pp. 33–5; Nancy Stepan *The Idea of Race in Science – Great Britain 1800–1960*, Macmillan, London 1982.

37 Fryer, pp. 171–2.

38 Despite a huge literature on the development of biosocial science, as far as I am aware there has been little published on the intersection between theories of race, class and gender difference. See Stephen Jay Gould, *The Mismeasure of Man*, W. W. Norton, New York 1981; Nancy Leys Stepan, 'Race and Gender: The Role of Analogy in Science', in David Theo Goldberg, ed., *Anatomy of Racism*, University of Minnesota press, Minneapolis 1990. This essay also cites John S. Haller and Robin S. Haller, *The Physician and Sexuality in Victorian America*, University of Illinois Press, Urbana, 1974.

39 Barbara Taylor, *Eve and the New Jerusalem: Socialism and Feminism in the Nineteenth Century*, Virago, London, 1983, p. 27.

40 Harriet Taylor Mill, *Enfranchisement of Women*, Virago, London 1983, p. 25.

41 Alex Tyrrell, 'Women's Mission and Pressure Group Politics in Britain (1825–1860)', *Bulletin of the John Rylands University Library*, vol. 63, no. 1, 1980, pp. 194–230. I am indebted to Barbara Taylor for sending me a copy of this article in 1981.

42 Barbara Taylor, p. 124.

43 Lynda Nead, *Myths of Sexuality: Representations of Women in Victorian Britain*, Blackwell, Oxford/New York 1988, pp. 196–7.

44 'Second Report of the Female Society of Birmingham', contained in Birmingham *Album*, pp. 13–14.

45 Ibid., p. 26.

46 Yellin, p. 58.

47 Gordon K. Lewis, *Slavery, Imperialism and Freedom: Studies in English Radical Thought*, Monthly Review Press, New York 1978, p. 40.

48 Kenneth Little, *Negroes in Britain: A Study of Racial Relations in English Society*, Routledge & Kegan Paul, London/Boston, revised edn 1972, pp. 228–9.

49 James Walvin, 'The Propaganda of Slavery', in Walvin, ed., *Slavery & British Society 1776–1846*, Macmillan, London 1982, pp. 61–63.

50 Sir George Stephen, *Anti-Slavery Recollections*, London 1854, pp. 196–8, cited in Tyrrell, p. 207.

51 Barbara Taylor, p. 127.

52 Ladies Anti-Slavery Associations, 5 (n.d.). Goldsmith's Library, Senate House, University of London (quoted in Walvin, p. 62).

53 See Yellin, pp. 3–26 for a discussion of the various readings of this image and its history.

54 Walvin, p. 56.

55 Barbara Taylor, p. 14.

56 Betty Fladeland, *Men & Brothers: Anglo-American Antislavery Co-operation*, University of Illinois Press, Urbana/London 1972, p. 181 This metaphor would not have pleased Elizabeth Heyrick as she was a Quaker and therefore a pacifist.

57 Tyrrell, pp. 224–5.

58 David Brion Davis, *Slavery and Human Progress*, Oxford University Press, Oxford/New York 1984.

59 'Second Report', p. 16.

60 Ibid., pp. 15–16.

61 See Olivia Smith, *The Politics of Language 1791– 1819*, Oxford University Press, New York/Oxford 1984.

62 'Second Report'.

63 Ripley, pp. 29–3.

64 Alfreda B. Duster, ed., *Crusade for Justice: The Autobiography of Ida B. Wells*, University of Chicago Press, Chicago/London 1970.

65 Tyrrell, p. 212.

66 Seymore Drescher, 'Public Opinion and the Destruction of Slavery', in Walvin, ed., *Slavery & British Society*, p. 25.

67 Tyrrell, p. 213.

68 Stoddart, p. 53.

69 Clare Taylor, *British and American Abolitionists*, p. 63. Finding a copy of this book made an enormous difference to this essay as it provided many of the key pieces for the jigsaw.

70 Between 1830 and 1865 African-American women were very much in the minority as visitors to Britain. Only eight out of the eighty whose presence is recorded in this book were women. However, many black lecturers frequently made reference to the work of women's groups, and called for boycotts of slave-grown produce, using similar arguments to those made by British women since the 1820s. See Ripley, and R. J. M. Blackett, *Building an Antislavery Wall: Black Americans in the Atlantic Abolitionist Movement, 1830–1860*, Louisiana State University Press, Baton Rouge/London 1983.

71 Ripley, p. 23.

72 Margaret Garner was recaptured, but when she realized she was cornered she killed one of her children with her own hands rather than submit her to slavery. She was brought

to trial and charged with murder. Julius Yanuck, 'The Garner Fugitive Slave Case', *Mississippi Valley Historical Review*, 40, June 1953, pp. 47–66.

73 Ripley, p. 438. As a young woman, Sarah Parker Remond campaigned actively against slavery and Northern racial prejudice throughout New England, becoming one of the first black women to lecture regularly before anti-slavery audiences. While she was in England on a speaking tour she continued her formal education, enrolling in women's courses at Bedford College in London. She remained in England during the Civil War, working for the London Emancipation Society and the Freedmen's Aid Society. She attracted the admiration of early feminist reformers through her anti-slavery work and part of her autobiography was reproduced in the *Englishwoman's Review* (vol. 7, June 1861). In 1866 she went to Florence, Italy, where she trained as a doctor. She subsequently married, and died in 1894. See B. J. Loewenberg and R. Bogin, eds, *Black Women in Nineteenth-Century American Life: Their Words, Their Thoughts, Their Feelings*, Pennsylvania State University Press, University Park/London 1976, pp. 222–33.

74 Ripley, pp. 445–6.

75 Ibid., p. 459.

76 Stoddart, p. 51.

77 Jane Rendall, *The Origins of Modern Feminism: Women in Britain, France and the United States 1780–1860*, Macmillan, London 1985, p. 228.

78 Mari Jo and Paul Buhle, *The Concise History of Women's Suffrage: Selections from the Classic Work of Stanton, Anthony, Gage, and Harper*, University of Illinois Press, Urbana/London 1978, p. 79.

79 Buhle, p. 82.

80 Buhle, p. 83.

81 Buhle, p. 85.

82 Frederick B. Tolles, ed., *Slavery and the Women's Question: Lucretia Mott's Diary 1840* Friends' House Historical Society, Haverford Penn and Friends' House, London 1952, pp. 22–5.

83 George M. Fredrickson, *The Arrogance of Race: Historical Perspective on Slavery, Racism and Social Inequality*, Wesleyan University Press, Middletown, CT 1988, p. 74.

84 Yellin, p. 12.

85 There is a substantial literature on abolitionism and the early women's movement in America: see, for example, Buhle; Angela Y. Davis, *Women, Race & Class*, Random House, New York 1981; L. Perryl and M. Fellman, eds, *Anti-Slavery Reconsidered*, Louisiana State University Press, Baton Rouge 1979.

86 Frederick Douglass, *Life and Times of Frederick Douglass* (1892), Collier Macmillan, New York/London 1962, p. 255.

87 Ellen Carol Dubois, ed., *Elizabeth Cady Stanton, Susan B. Anthony: Correspondence, Writings, Speeches*, Schocken Books, New York 1981, p. 80.

88 Clare Taylor, *British and American Abolitionists*, p. 101.

89 Clare Taylor, p. 109.

90 Clare Taylor, p. 104.

91 Tolles, p. 49.

92 Clare Taylor, p. 104.

93 Clare Taylor, p. 102.

94 Clare Taylor, pp. 163–4.

95 Gail Malmgreen, 'Anne Knight, 1786–1862' (unpublished paper, 1978) p. 4. I am grateful to Barbara Taylor for drawing my attention to this quote and telling me about this

essay, later published in J. O. Baylen, ed., *Biographical Dictionary of Modern British Radicals*, Harvester Press, Brighton 1986.

96 Ibid.

97 Lucretia Mott and Elizabeth Cady Stanton were partly responsible for organizing the Seneca Falls convention in 1848, the first national gathering of American women and the beginnings of the movement for women's rights.

98 Gail Malmgreen, 'Anne Knight and the Radical Subculture' *Quaker History*, 71 (Fall 1982), pp. 100–13.

99 Letter to the *Brighton Herald* about the situation of women in the French Republic, February 1850. Friends' Houses Archives, London, Ref 0.230.

100 Ibid.

101 Clare Taylor, p. 92.

102 Clare Taylor, p. 110.

103 Ripley, p. 73.

104 Clare Taylor, p. 114.

105 Clare Taylor, p. 188.

106 Harriet Martineau is one of the better-known female anti-slavery activists of the early to mid nineteenth century. I have chosen not to write about her at length because she was in many ways exceptional. Eliza Wigham came from a Quaker family with strong anti-slavery connections in Edinburgh. Another Quaker, Mary Estlin (1820–1902), was the daughter of John Estlin, an oculist who founded the Bristol Eye Dispensary in 1812. She was his close companion and worked with him in abolitionist circles. The Bristol Anti-Slavery Society was pro-Garrisonian, and further correspondence in Clare Taylor's book shows that both father and daughter were committed liberals with strong links to other radicals in England and America. In an obituary in the *Englishwoman's Review* Mary was described as 'strongly advocating the rights of her own sex'. She was one of the original members of the Bristol Women's Suffrage Society and continued her father's work by supervising the eye dispensary and establishing the 'Hospital for Women' in Berkeley Square.

107 Stoddart, p. 70.

108 Stoddart, pp. 80–1.

109 Clare Taylor, pp. 154–5.

110 Clare Taylor, p. 159.

111 Ibid.

112 Ibid.

113 Clare Taylor, p. 183.

114 Olive Banks, *Faces of Feminism: A Study of Feminism as a Social Movement*, Macmillan, London 1981, pp. 24–6.

115 Ripley, p. 152.

116 Clare Taylor, p. 134.

117 Malmgreen; Banks, p. 25.

118 Clare Taylor, p. 65.

119 Clare Taylor, p. 178.

120 Clare Taylor, p. 210.

121 See, for example, Jacquie Matthews, 'Barbara Bodichon: Integrity in Diversity', in Dale Spender, ed., *Feminist Theorists*, The Women's Press, London 1983; Sheila R. Herstein, *A Mid-Victorian Feminist: Barbara Leigh Smith Bodichon*, Yale University Press, New Haven/London 1985.

122 Matthews (p. 104) mentions that Eugene Bodichon was often mistaken for a 'coloured' man while travelling in the South, which must have provided Barbara with further insights into the slave-owning mentality.

123 Joseph W. Reed Jr, ed., *An American Diary 1857–8*, Routledge & Kegan Paul, London 1972, p. 63, quoted in Matthews, pp. 105–6.

124 *English Woman's Journal*, vol. 8, October 1861, p. 117.

125 *English Woman's Journal*, vol. 8, December 1861, pp. 264–5.

126 Ibid., p. 263.

127 Ibid., p. 262.

128 *English Woman's Journal*, vol. 8, November 1861, p. 186.

129 Ibid., p. 184.

130 Matthews, p. 97.

131 William Thompson, *An Appeal of One-Half the Human Race, Women, Against the Pretensions of the Other Half, Men*, Virago, London 1983, p. 67.

132 The Anti-Slavery Society was formed in 1823 at the start of a new drive towards emancipation. Elizabeth Heyrick's pamphlet calling for immediatism appeared in 1824.

133 Thompson, p. 83.

134 Ibid., p. 84.

135 Ibid., p. 88.

136 Ibid., p. 56.

137 Ibid., p. 59.

138 Mary Wollstonecraft, *Vindication of the Rights of Woman*, Penguin, Harmondsworth 1985, p. 286.

139 Ibid., pp. 310–11.

140 Cora Kaplan, *Sea Changes: Essays on Culture and Feminism*, Verso, London 1986, p. 34.

141 Patrick Brantlinger, *Rule of Darkness: British Literature and Imperialism 1830–1914*, Cornell University Press, Ithaca/London 1988, p. 82.

142 See Catherine Hall, 'The Economy of Intellectual Prestige: Thomas Carlyle, John Stuart Mill, and the Case of Governor Eyre', in *Cultural Critique*, no. 12, Spring 1989. This fascinating essay explores the response of particular intellectuals to the Governor Eyre controversy. Among other things, Hall discusses the way in which questions of race and gender were in the process of being transformed by a new articulation of racism that became popularized by the supporters of Governor Eyre. Mill played a central role in opposing the concept of 'natural' difference between male and female, black and white.

143 John Stuart Mill, *The Subjection of Women* (1869), Virago, London 1983, p. 147.

144 Mill, pp. 20–1.

145 Mill, pp. 56–7.

146 Nancy Stepan, *The Idea of Race in Science: Great Britain 1800–1960*, Macmillan, London, 1982, p. 1.

147 Thompson, p. 213.

Part Three

# Britannia's Other Daughters

Feminism
in the Age of Imperialism

Daisy Bates with Aboriginal skull, Pyap 1938

The birth of organized feminism in Britain took place against a background of anti-slavery enthusiasm, but its development was consolidated during a period of popular imperialism. The 1870s marked the beginning of a new style of expansionist foreign policy involving military and geographical conquests that caused great popular excitement and agitation at home. This decade saw the disappearance and death of David Livingstone, the Ashanti campaign, the purchase of the Suez Canal shares, the Russo-Turkish War of 1878 and the Afghanistan and Zulu disasters of 1879. The invasion of Egypt in 1882 and the death of Gordon at Khartoum in 1885 'raised imperialist sentiment to a fever pitch that hardly abated even after the "revenge" for Gordon at Omdurman in 1898'.[1] However, according to John Mackenzie, it would be a mistake to concentrate too much on these 'imperial characteristics, popular reactions to specific events, dramatic displays of chauvinistic emotions. These were merely the surface ripples, occasionally whipped up into storms, of a much deeper intellectual and social current which had been set up by the second half of the nineteenth century'.[2]

There has been great speculation and debate on the development and the nature of Victorian imperialism and all its manifestations. Mackenzie, who has made innovative studies of imperialism and popular culture, has described it as an 'ideological cluster' that was made up of 'a renewed militarism, a devotion to royalty, an identification and worship of national heroes, together with a contemporary cult of personality, and racial ideas associated with Social Darwinism'.[3] Patrick Brantlinger discusses the idea that imperialism had the effect of being an 'ideological safety valve' in response to domestic crises: declining industrial growth, the great depression between 1873 and the 1890s, and the question of Irish Home Rule were among the main issues facing politicians in Britain.[4]

Mackenzie, Brantlinger and others have dealt very interestingly with the subject, studying many of the components of the 'ideological cluster' that made up Victorian imperialism. While class and race have figured heavily in these discussions, the configurations of class, race and gender are still a relatively uncharted territory for social historians. This essay is concerned with the ways in which late nineteenth-century imperialism articulated with feminism, and it starts from the premiss that feminist ideology and practice were shaped by the social, economic and political forces of imperialism to a far greater extent than has been acknowledged.

At a time when evolutionary theories defining women's physical and mental capabilities were beginning to pass into the realms of 'common sense,'[5] the Empire provided both a physical and an ideological space in which the different meanings of femininity could be explored or contested. Corresponding ideas about racial or cultural difference provided a context for these conflicts to be played out in their full complexity, so that, for example, the Englishwoman abroad could be at once a many-faceted figure: from an intrepid adventuress defying racial and sexual boundaries to heroic mother responsible for the preservation of the white 'race'; from the devoted missionary overseeing black souls to the guardian of white morals; from determined pioneer and companion to the white man to a vulnerable, defenceless piece of his property – 'the greatest gift God gave to man'. These various images of white women's femininity obviously had implications for relationships between men and women, but they also worked as part of the dynamic between black and white, both in the colonies and at home.

We can safely assume that the dominant view of British women's relationship to Empire was a conservative one, since it was women who were expected to provide domestic continuity as well as to breed new citizens. One question that arises from this is how feminists, who contested many of the traditional restrictions on women, conceived of their role within or outside the imperialist framework of society, both at home and in the colonies. According to one feminist historian, one of the achievements of the Victorian women's movement was 'the adoption of an alternative set of values',[6] but there seems to have been little research into whether their politics offered, consciously or unconsciously, an alternative view of popular imperialism. Recognizing that Victorian feminists were in no way a homogeneous group, this essay excavates the racial dimension of their struggles to improve conditions for themselves and for other women. Taking the examples of two British women whose lives and work were bound up with Indian women, I examine the ways in which they saw their influence, as politically active women, in the wider world of colonialism. Their stories are told in order to find out how they connected their own idea of womanhood to those whom they perceived to be of different cultures and races, as well as how they dealt with difference itself.

### The Indian Social Reform Movement in Britain

> At the present moment a thousand Hindu houses are open to receive and welcome English governesses – well-trained, acccomplished English ladies, capable of doing good to their Indian sisters, both by instruction and personal example. . . . I speak to you not for one, not for fifty, but for millions of Indian sisters, whose lamentations and wails penetrate the skies and seem to come over to England to stir up the hearts of their English sisters.
>
> Keshub Chunder Sen[7]

In the autumn of 1870, Annette Ackroyd attended a lecture by Keshub Chunder Sen, a Bengali who was visiting England as leader of the Brahmo Somaj, an association for Indian social and political reform. Sen outlined the need for basic education for Indian people, especially what he perceived to be the neglected area of women's education, and he appealed directly to English women to go out to teach their 'Indian sisters'. Annette Ackroyd, who came from a Nonconformist, liberal background, was one of many

Annette Ackroyd (1842–1929) with her pupils in March 1875

women who responded enthusiastically to his message. Two years after hearing Sen speak, at the age of twenty-nine, she travelled to Calcutta to start a school for Hindu girls. Her mission was to prove a failure, although she worked at it dutifully for two years on her own, but after marrying a progressive British administrator she made her home in India and stayed there for most of her adult life.

Her personal story is useful because it reveals some of the complexities of a Victorian feminist's response to questions of race, class and gender. When she first arrived in Delhi, Annette Ackroyd was shocked by the attitudes of the other British people – known then as Anglo-Indians – towards Indian people and culture; ten years later, however, she was active in the debate surrounding the Ilbert Bill, a relatively progressive piece of legislation introduced by the viceroy, Lord Ripon, which aimed to expand the territories in which Indian judges could try subjects on criminal charges. Annette Ackroyd was in the forefront of opposition to it since it meant that European women would have to stand before Indian judges. In a letter to *The Englishman* she argued her case:

> I am not afraid to assert that I speak the feeling of all Englishwomen in India when I say that we regard the proposal to subject us to the jurisdiction of native judges as an insult.
>
> It is not pride of race which dictates this feeling – it is the pride of womanhood. This is a form of respect which we are not prepared to abrogate in order to give such advantages to others as are offered by Mr Ilbert's Bill to its beneficiaries.[8]

In the same letter she claimed that all Indian women would agree that the Bill was an outrage. Her concept of womanhood allowed her to speak on behalf of all women against a measure of social reform in the colony; she clearly felt that the bond between women across racial lines was stronger than any desire for political independence felt by the Indian nation as a whole. By tracing the circumstances of her decision to go to India and her experiences once she got there, I hope to illustrate how she came to hold these views, and what significance they hold for us today.

Annette Ackroyd's Indian venture is evidence that there was a lively connection between progressives in the heart of the Empire and those at its margins, and that women were active in maintaining these links. From the first days of the Brahmo Somaj in England, a significant number of women had attended their meetings. An indication of the degree of their support is suggested by the fact that the primary source of information about the activities of the association in Britain can be found in the writings of two women. One of them, Sophie Dobson Collett, was only ten or eleven years old when she first heard the founder of the Brahmo Somaj, Rammohun Roy, speak at South Place Chapel in London. Born in 1822 into a family which had connections with India going back to 1719, she retained a lifelong commitment to the movement. She learned Bengali in order to study Brahmo texts, and despite the fact that she was bedridden for much of the time, was active in propagating the history and ideas of the association in England: she produced three books on the subject, including a substantial and scholarly biography of Roy.[9] The other contemporary English study of Roy was Mary Carpenter's *Last Days in England of the Rajah Rammohun Roy*, written in 1866.[10] Like Sophia Dobson Collett, Mary Carpenter had encountered Roy as a child, when he had been a guest at her father's house in Bristol.

Before addressing the question of why the message of these Indian social reformers appealed to so many British women, it is necessary to look briefly at the background to their movement. The association, which sought to reform Indian society through eradicating idolatry, polytheism and caste had been founded in 1830 by Rammohun Roy, a Bengali, who himself had spent two years in England, where he died in October 1832. He was a complex figure: a brahmin by birth, he had converted to Christianity, yet he maintained caste rules while in England,

> . . . not [from] any lingering attachment to the superstitions of his country, or to early associations, but [from] a desire to avoid everything which might impair his usefulness among his countrymen, or diminish the influence of his teachings.[11]

Despite his conversion and his belief in the conservative nature of the Hinduism of his day, Roy was no Anglophile. He saw the need for change in India, but he challenged the British view of India as backward and was deeply critical of British political and religious institutions. In July 1832, he wrote to a correspondent in Liverpool:

> I am now happy to find myself fully justified in congratulating you . . . on the complete success of the Reform Bills, notwithstanding the violent opposition and want of political principle on the part of the aristocrats.

> As I publicly avowed that in the event of the Reform Bill being defeated I would renounce my connection with this country [he had talked of going to America], I refrained from writing to you or any other friend in Liverpool until I knew the result. Thank heaven I can now feel proud of being one of your fellow subjects.[12]

Roy was an aristocrat who advocated democracy and allied himself to the cause of the working people of India and throughout the world. In Britain he won friends among liberals and Nonconformists of all classes. But it was his support for women's rights above all which must account for the admiration which he received from British women.

Among the questions which were of deep concern to Roy, *sati*, the practice of widow-burning, was perhaps his major preoccupation.[13] Roy took up this issue, inspired 'by the personal shock he experienced when his sister-in-law became sati'. His work in this area typified his overall approach: to reform Hinduism through a rereading of primary texts. In a series of papers published between 1818 and 1830, each of which he translated into English, he opposed the understanding of *sati* as a religious rite.

> It is not from religious prejudices and early impressions only that Hindoo widows burn themselves on the piles of their deceased husbands, but also from their witnessing the distress in which widows of the same rank in life are involved, and the insults and slights to which they are daily subjected, that they become in a great measure regardless of existence after the death of their husbands; and this indifference, accompanied with the hope of future reward held out to them, leads them to the horrible act of suicide.[14]

Seeing *sati* as intimately bound up with women's economic dependence he argued for the rights of women to hold property. Like John Stuart Mill, forty years later, Roy realized that what was widely regarded as essential feminine character was in fact the outcome of a very particular process of socialization. He saw that social, religious and economic factors were crucial in shaping the female individual's sense of self and often mocked the evolutionist argument that men were by nature superior:

> The faults which you have imputed to women are not planted in their constitution by nature; it would be, therefore, grossly criminal to condemn

> them to death merely from precaution . . .
>
> As to their inferiority in point of understanding, when did you ever afford them a fair opportunity of exhibiting their natural capacity? How then can you accuse them of want of understanding? . . .
>
> As you keep women generally void of education and arguments, you cannot, therefore, in justice, pronounce on their inferiority . . .
>
> You charge them with want of resolution, at which I feel exceedingly surprised; for we constantly perceive, in a country where the name of death makes the male shudder, that the female, from her firmness of mind, offers to burn with the corpse of her deceased husband.[15]

While Roy wrote about Hindu women his articulation of the injustice of their situation clearly struck a chord for the British women who encountered the man and his work. His commitment to Indian women's rights, 'his feeling for women in general' according to another admirer, Lucy Aikins, and evident pleasure in the 'mental accomplishments of English ladies' he met with, won him a wide reputation. After reading one of his papers, Lucy Aikins, who met Roy a number of times, wrote in 1832:

> Afterwards, he details the many cruelties and oppressions to which females in his country are subjected by the injustice and barbarity of the stronger sex, and pleads for pity towards them with such powerful, heartfelt eloquence as no woman, I think, can peruse without tears and fervent invocations of blessings on his head.[16]

Keshub Chunder Sen, who became leader of the Brahmo Somaj in the late 1850s, shared Roy's belief that there were radicals in Britain who might be enlisted to help their cause, and he inherited some of the same contacts. In May 1870, he delivered a lecture on 'England's Duties to India' in which he argued that 'the first great duty which the British nation owes to India is to promote education far and wide'.[17]

In Sen's view, mass education was central to progressive change in India; it was through education that people would come to question idolatry, polytheism and the immutability of caste. In particular he was concerned about the lack of educational opportunities for Indian women and girls, which prevented the spread of literacy throughout the population. What India lacked, he argued, were women qualified to teach. For though increasing numbers of girls were receiving some sort of elementary schooling, early marriage prevented them from reaching a level of education which would fit them for teaching the next generation. Sen suggested that among widows in particular, there was a rich resource of women who would benefit from teaching as an occupation, but at that time there were no women equipped to train them as teachers. He believed that English women had a unique role to play in this interim work, which was why he appealed to the educated women who were among his supporters to travel to India as teachers.

## The Civilizing Mission

It is relatively easy to understand the positive way that many women responded to this call, particularly when Sen claimed to speak on behalf of 'millions of Indian sisters'. First, it was unusual for women's intellectual skills to be sought after; Sen's appeal was direct to 'well-trained, accomplished English ladies, capable of doing good to their Indian sisters, both by instruction and by personal example'. During the second half of the nineteenth century, many educated women were faced with stultifying boredom as there were so few opportunities for satisfying employment. Being a governess in Britain was an obvious choice for many young women as it was considered a 'genteel' and respectable way of earning a living. However, according to Barbara Bodichon, writing in 1860, it was in reality a gruesome fate. In the rigid class structure of the Victorian family the governess was not considered as a social equal either by her employers or the other servants: 'The governess, however well conducted, remains a governess; may starve *genteely*[sic], and sink into her grave friendless and alone.'[18]

One solution was for women to consider looking further afield for more satisfying work. One of the most immediate ways in which women – including feminists – in Britain were connected to the expansion of the Empire was through emigration and the opportunities it provided for female independence and employment. According to A. J. Hammerton, between 1862 and 1914 voluntary societies helped more than twenty thousand women of various classes to emigrate to British colonies. The first of these, and probably the most controversial, was the Female Middle Class Emigration Society, which was set up in 1862 as a feminist response to the increasing demand from middle-class women for new forms of employment. The serious disproportion of men and women in Britain, caused partly by the emigration of men to work in the Empire, meant that many women could not rely on marriage as a guaranteed means of support. Feminists were often attracted to the idea of working overseas as governesses and teachers to the children of white settlers. However, the short history of the FMCES demonstrates that in general the question of organized emigration remained a problematic one for feminists during this period. By 1886 the FMCES had become absorbed into the recently formed Colonial Emigration Society, and emigration propaganda had acquired strong anti-feminist connotations.

One reason why feminists did not unequivocally support the emigration movement was that the motives of the new society were readily misinterpreted by the right-wing press as being little more than those of a marriage agency; although some professed to be shocked at this, for many others it seemed a perfectly logical way of reducing the number of 'distressed gentlewomen' in Britain and increasing the stock of white women in the colonies. The challenges of the feminist movement and the demands of the 'new woman' for social and political reform might simply be dispersed by sending feminists into the far corners of the world where they would be occupied in setting up homes and raising families. A second, and perhaps more conclusive factor that discouraged many feminists from emigration was the reports that began to flow back from women whose jobs as governesses had amounted to little more than domestic service of a kind which would not be contemplated by women of the same class in Britain. As Hammerton points out, 'Colonial social conditions required a reordering of traditional British categories of class, status and female employment, a difficult task for women whose class-consciousness overshadowed their feminism.'[19] Although successive leaders of the society attempted to steer a course between acceptable feminist principles and the genuine need for employment, the contradictions made many women wary of the whole idea. There were thousands of others, however, who left Britain to work in the colonies in whatever capacity was available. Working-class women were needed as domestic servants, nurses and home-makers, and while there was always the prospect of danger and risks in travelling round the world to countries like Australia and New Zealand, it was invariably measured against the likelihood of poverty and unemployment at home.

Nevertheless, Sen's plea was well received, for it accorded with the idea that British women had a unique duty to bring civilization to the uncivilized. This was invoked in relation to the poor in the cities at home, the new English settlements abroad or the colonized people living in heathen lands. As I discussed in Part 2, one of the channels for women's energies from the early 1800s had been philanthropic activities. By the 1870s the charitable work of the Evangelical middle-class woman was still aimed at educating her working-class counterpart in religion, morality and sanitation but, as the ideology of Empire developed, her sphere of influence was expanding to wherever the British flag was flying. As one writer puts it: 'Notions of imperial destiny and class and racial superiority were grafted onto the traditional views of refined English motherhood to produce a concept of the Englishwoman as an invincible global civilising agent.'[20]

Although women from more radical backgrounds would not necessarily have seen themselves in this light, and would have had a variety of different responses to ideas of duty and patriotism, they undoubtedly would have felt that they were better educated than women elsewhere. Many of those who heard Keshub Chunder Sen's appeal must have been distressed at his description of the plight of Indian women, though not especially surprised. Ever since the British had first begun to settle in India, the practice of *sati*, commonly represented as a product of a pagan religious system which had produced all manner of strange and backward social practices, not least the caste system, had aroused curiosity about the way Hindu women were treated by men. It seems that, before the movement for women's rights intervened in public debate, there was a variety of ways of characterizing gender relations in India, mostly, though not always, from the point of view of white supremacy. For example, the matrilineal system of the Nairs of Western India had been held up as a utopian example of freedom between the sexes.[21] Eliza Fay, writing home from Calcutta at the turn of the eighteenth century, began a description of East Indian customs and ceremonies with a discussion of widow-burning in which she acknowledged that men in most countries had not failed to 'invent a sufficient number of rules to render the weaker sex totally subservient to their authority'. The same letter was probably a good indication of British attitudes towards Indian women themselves; it was not so much their status that intrigued, but rather their different approach to femininity:

> The Hindoo ladies are never seen abroad; when they go out their carriages are closely covered with curtains, so that one has little chance of satisfying curiosity. I once saw two apparently very beautiful women; they use so much art however, as renders it very difficult to judge what claim they *really* have

> to that appellation – their whole time is taken up in decorating their person: the hair – eye-lids – eye-brows – teeth – hands and nails, all undergo certain processes to render them more completely fascinating; nor can one seriously blame their having recourse to these, or the like artifices – the motive being to secure the affections of a husband, or to counteract the plans of a rival.[22]

By the 1870s when Annette Ackroyd went to Calcutta, the dominant image of Indian women in the minds of the British public can be characterized as one of intense suffering behind closed doors. This was partly because of the spread of missionary work throughout the subcontinent which influenced the way that Indian culture was represented in Britain. Descriptions of purdah and zenana life, the provision of education for high-caste Hindu women within the women's quarters, where they lived without contact with men outside the family, abounded with metaphors of darkness and imprisonment which had become synonymous in the British mind with Indian women's whole existence. Mission writings created an imperative for women's mission work by denouncing purdah as inherently evil. In the minds of many Europeans, the world of Hindu and Muslim women, largely hidden from their view, provoked suspicions too awful to name,

> In all the homes, the purdah is strictly kept, and alas! who can tell what dark deeds are *occasionally* done in these secluded homes.[23]

An increased awareness of feminism and the different forms of women's subordination at home meant that gender relations in other countries were viewed more critically by many observers. Hindu women were increasingly portrayed by feminists as victims of barbaric cultural customs from which they needed help to escape. In the British feminist journal *Englishwoman's Review* in 1868, Mrs Bayle Bernard contrasted two books written about life in India. She scorned the first in a few paragraphs because of its attention to 'frivolous details' and its 'slipshod slangy style', but devoted several pages to Mary Carpenter's *Six Months in India*. Mary Carpenter had a lifelong interest in India – her father was responsible for inviting Rammohun Roy to Britain in 1830 – but she only travelled there in her fifties when she became involved in the Indian educational reform movement. Her published diaries, which were the subject of this review, provide a revealing glimpse of Indian life seen through the eyes of a British liberal feminist.

Mrs Bernard quoted her as saying, 'From the first to the last day of a residence in India, the point which most painfully strikes the mind is the position of Hindoo women', and then proceeded to paraphrase parts of the book which addressed this question. However, the review also drew attention to Mary Carpenter's description of educational projects set up in different parts of India by Indians themselves, including the Brahmo Somaj, and it emphasized 'how earnest the women of India themselves are in desiring their own improvement', a point demonstrated by the enthusiasm with which women greeted Mary Carpenter when they heard about her mission. Mrs Bayle Bernard ended her review with a plea for British women to get involved, her last sentence providing an interesting example of an explicitly feminist attitude to Empire and the sense of duty which it demanded:

> Let them throw their hearts and souls into the work, and determine never to rest until they have raised their Eastern sisters to their own level; and then may the women of India at last attain a position honourable to themselves and to England, instead of, as is now so generally the case, filling one which can only be contemplated with feelings of shame and sorrow.[24]

Interestingly, although there was often a blanket condemnation of both Hinduism and Islam by the British within and outside India, these religions were not always understood as being equally oppressive to women. Five years later, another review article focused on the 'condition of women in mahometan countries', the first sentence setting the tone for what was to follow:

> At a time when we are congratulating ourselves that a better day for women has dawned in Christian Europe and America, and that the harsh laws, engendered by ages of ignorance and barbarism, are being one by one repealed, it is satisfactory to be told that in countries under Mohammedan rule, a similar advance is taking place, and that the women of the far off East are not the hopeless helpless victims we have long thought them.[25]

During this same period the *Englishwoman's Review* carried an announcement of the founding of the Indian Association, which was set up to promote understanding between the two countries and to support 'enlightened natives of India in their efforts for the improvement of their countrymen'. The fact that Mary Carpenter was one of the society's founders and editor of its journal was given as proof that it was a worthy cause, and the article took a critical view of British administration in India, mainly because it seemed to have carried out so little reform. It quoted with approval the basis of the new association, supported by Indian reformers such as Keshub Chunder Sen and Dadabhai Naoroji (who was later to become a member of the British Parliament), that 'the Government principle of non-interference in religious and social customs is to be strictly maintained'; one of its aims was 'to promote by *voluntary effort* the enlightenment and improvement of our Hindu fellow subjects'.[26] The education of women was inevitably high on the agenda, along with sanitary improvements which were seen to be essential to the moral and physical health of the nation.

The 'Government principle' referred to was a recurrent question in the colonial administration of the subcontinent. The 1857 national uprising, known to the British as 'The Mutiny', had been sparked off by a cynical disregard of Indian religious practices. This much was agreed upon by all observers and interested parties, but there were disagreements as to what should be done to secure Indian rule once the rebellion had been suppressed. At one extreme, there was a body of opinion in mission circles that the uprising would have been averted by more 'interference' in Indian culture rather than less. It was understood by missionaries in both India and Great Britain as a sign of divine displeasure that the British authorities had been tolerating false religions and neglecting Christianity. There was a belief that if missionaries had been allowed access to the Indian soldiers, the uprising would never have happened. Extracts from church magazines of the period give the impression of an attitude of supreme confidence that mission work was in the best interests not only of the church but also of the state. In the same year as the rebellion, one article in the *Church Missionary Intelligencer* claimed that: Christianity strengthens lawful authority, concurs with it in action, makes the man more loyal, more submissive to his superiors, more attentive to their commands.'[27]

The church view did not necessarily represent the official position. Queen Victoria's response was that Crown rule must respect the autonomy of Indian people's religions. She took this stance in opposition to the particular events which had led to the uprising, but made it clear that she had disapproved of the increasingly aggressive government of the country by the East India Company, which had evolved from a once peaceful mercantile trading company through military aggrandisment into a sort of benevolent despot. By the 1830s, developing ideologies of racial and cultural supremacy in England had led to a belief that those beyond the reach of Western civilization needed rescuing from their own primitive customs and religions.[28] The fifty years prior to 1857 had reflected this change, as the Company's policy had shifted steadily from a readiness to coexist with Indian culture to a practice of active intervention into the private lives of Indian people. First, the Company's prohibition on missionary work had been dropped in 1813, heralding an influx of churchmen and women into the country; equally damaging was the Education Minute of 1835 which decreed that English education became official Company policy. Political theorists with progressive views on other subjects were ready to support the imperial project in India, in the name of disrupting the 'despotism of custom'. Patrick Brantlinger points out that John Stuart Mill, for example, who worked for the Company under his father, argued that Indians needed protection from both European aggression and from their own despotism of custom; before 1857 he believed that the East India Company was the best agent for supervising this civilizing mission.[29] Queen Victoria was thus addressing those who would rule India under her as much as the Indian people when she insisted that the following passage, which she reputedly wrote herself, be included in the proclamation which explained the passing of India's rule from the East India Company to the Crown in 1858:

> Firmly relying ourselves on the truth of Christianity and acknowledging with gratitude the solace of religion, we disclaim alike the right and the desire to impose our convictions on any of our subjects. . . . We do strictly charge and enjoin all those who may be in authority under us that they abstain from all interference with the religious belief or worship of any of our subjects on pain of our highest displeasure.[30]

There is no mistaking that this was a pragmatic benevolence. She had seen that the uprising of 1857 had been caused by such 'interference' and sought to ensure the continuation of her rule. Hence the proclamation went on: 'In their prosperity will be our strength; in their contentment our security'.[31]

Closer study of Victoria's life reveals, however, that she often displayed both sympathy and warmth towards Indian people that went beyond mere pragmatism.[32] Aside from her official role as Empress of India, she took a particularly active interest in Indian affairs and in the situation of Indian women. When Keshub Chunder Sen visited England in 1870, he was invited to the palace where a vegetarian lunch was provided for him. He later reported that 'both the Queen and the Princess were glad to hear that India is a great field of philanthropic labour and that Mr Sen had requested many of his lady friends in England to go thither to undertake the work of female education'. She was also said to have

> . . . expressed much satisfaction at the progress of female education in India, and the improvements made in several respects by her Indian subjects in consequence of the spread of English education. She was glad that the suttee had been abolished and showed great concern for the miserable condition of Hindu women.[33]

Victoria herself saw no contradiction in applauding 'the spread of English education' while promoting the official principle of cultural autonomy. So though the uprising caused the British ruling elite to question the wisdom of outright reform of Indian society along Western lines, the promotion of both Western education and religion continued steadily. However, the concept of education without interference in religious or social customs was an ideal shared by the more enlightened policy makers and many Indian reformers alike. In Keshub Chunder Sen's lecture on 'Female Education' he spoke forcefully against the imposition of European cultural norms, and clearly found enthusiastic support in his audience:

> With all my respect and admiration for civilization as it prevails in England, I have always been foremost in protesting against the demoralisation of India by importing English customs into it.(Cheers) Though I can respect learned, intelligent, philanthropic and generous-hearted ladies in England, I could not for one moment persuade myself to believe that for the interest of India I ought to introduce their customs and institutions. The growth of society must be indigenous, native and natural. (hear, hear)[34]

After the national uprising in 1857, many more people in England, whether Tory, radical or Evangelical, took an interest in the question of how a colony like India should be governed, and in particular to what extent the 'native' culture should be allowed to coexist with the dominant cultural ways of the British Raj, as it came to be known. The perceived relation between class and gender in Indian beliefs and cultural practices was central to these debates, and it is highly likely that a woman like Annette Ackroyd, who came from a radical Unitarian background, would have been familiar with the subject even before she became involved with the Brahmo Somaj.

## Annette Ackroyd in India

Annette Ackroyd owed her belief in education to her Unitarian father, William, who saw it as a vital social issue. He had begun his working life as an artisan but worked his way up to become a successful businessman with wide-ranging involvements – a gas company, engineering, banking. He was a prominent local figure who, according to his biographer, Annette's son William Beveridge, maintained a strong sense of identification with his working-class background and devoted more time to unpaid work as a poor law guardian, against the Corn Laws, and as a Liberal candidate, than to his business. He had been involved in setting up the first public library in Stourbridge and in private he encouraged his daughters to take their education to the limits available at the time.

After leaving school, Annette studied for three years in London at Bedford College, a nondenominational college for women, the nearest thing to a university available. Having excelled in her courses there, she returned to her father's house in Stourbridge in 1863, where she remained for the next five years. Her diaries show that she was active in several different aspects of education available in the town – she taught at Sunday School and at a local Ragged School, regularly distributed tracts, took classes in sketching, geology, singing and metaphysics, and attended all sorts of performances such as the opera, choral events and penny entertainment. During this time she was also involved in founding a Working Women's College in London where she taught intermittently after it opened in 1866. She appears to have led a busy life, yet occasional remarks in her diary suggest a level of intellectual frustration and dissatisfaction:

FEBRUARY 22ND 1865:

> Bachelor's Ball. Very Great Fun in some things. Not very lively (mentally). Good Dancing.

SUNDAY 9TH JULY 1865:

To Church to hear a mission sermon, more brains in the parson than usual but very slow still.

SUNDAY 16TH JULY 1865:

To Church, very slow indeed. Won't waste my time again.

2ND MAY 1866:

To Town doing frittering business.[35]

Twice she approached her father about the possibility of his employing her in his firm, but it seems that such a suggestion was beyond the scope of William Ackroyd's imagination, and he refused. Yet Annette's attachment to her father and home were such that seeking a more fulfilling life away from Stourbridge does not seem to have suggested itself to her until her father's unexpected death, after a brief illness in early 1869.

That year, the remaining family moved to London, and at her stepmother's wish, Annette and her sister Fanny rented a furnished house of their own. Annette then spent almost a year with her sister and another friend on a European tour during which time Keshub Chunder Sen arrived in England. The Unitarians, who were committed to progressive reform in India and had supported the organization for over thirty years, were prominent among Sen's supporters, so Annette Ackroyd became aware of his lectures while she was still travelling on the Continent, attending one shortly after her return. By that time she was twenty-nine years old, unmarried and frustrated by the lack of intellectual stimulus in her life. Since her father's death she had felt particularly rootless. Writing to her sister Fanny some years later, she confided, 'I know you have felt as I have, that home was gone'.

The situation described by Sen must have appeared straightforward to her. Indian women were 'crying out' for her help; her skills, which seemed so underused in England, were apparently needed to free them from a burden of suffering. Educated, progressive Indians she met in England encouraged her to go to Calcutta. Though immediately attracted by the idea, it was some time before Annette actually made the decision to go. Meanwhile she taught English at the Working Women's College and her diary shows that she pursued her interest in Indian affairs as she met a number of other Indian visitors – Sisipada Banerjee who was on a lecture tour in 1871, Krishna Govinda Gupta and Mr Manmohan Ghose. In July

1871 she noted in her diary that she had told Fanny of her decision to go to India.

During 1872, she began to prepare herself by taking Bengali lessons and a governess course at the Home and Colonial College, and she finally left for India later that year. She spent her first months living at the house of Mr and Mrs Manmohan Ghose in Calcutta, from where she started her work of establishing a school. Her copious notebooks and diaries provide a unique picture of her responses to her new environment and the nature of the problems which she experienced. Her initial reaction was one of detached disapproval towards the British establishment. It is worth quoting at length from an entry in her notebook five months after arriving in India.

> To Government House a large party – very nice music – but! This is a country where there is always a but! and this but! is of painful dimensions. Day after day as I go into Anglo-Indian society, I am convinced of the falseness of our position here. All allowances made for some little insular prejudice, for we cannot at once get over this narrowness – there is a cruel amount of difficulty between the races. What wonder! I sit among a group of ladies and hear one lisping to a gentleman that the 'natives' come so early, sit downstairs in the anteroom, with their feet on the sofa, ie. oriental fashion, as if they were at home – (query? who has most right to feel that, the people who pay for the house, or those who make them pay?) I hear at Belvedere of ladies who say 'Ah! No! I never spoke to a native', when asked to help to entertain and talk to some of the numerous Indians present and of another who said, 'Let us sit on the verandah to get out of the natives.' If this were said of men who have no refined ideas, . . . I should not wonder, but when all are classed together – men of learning from whom these empty-hearted women might learn much, and men of proud feelings – I get a sickening heartache and terror of life here. How these sweet and feminine souls, whose sympathy is so tender and sensibilities so acute can be so destitute not only of humanity but of simple courtesy and consideration for the feelings of others, is a problem I cannot pretend to solve.[36]

Annette Ackroyd not only disagreed with, but was surprised to encounter, the attitudes of the white people in Calcutta, suggesting that she had not encountered such 'colour prejudice' against Indian visitors in England.

The differences in attitudes to race in Great Britain itself and in the colonial territories is repeatedly noted by the black and white travellers who moved in both directions between India and Britain in the nineteenth century. Rozina Visram makes this point in her discussion of the visit of Rammohun Roy to England in 1831. She shows that he was enthusiastically received by a cross-section of English society – he was 'mobbed' by the workers in a Manchester factory which he visited, and then presented to William IV as a distinguished visitor. Among the English he met, it was Anglo-Indians who expressed racial prejudice towards Roy. A contemporary commentator, Mrs Le Breton, wrote of one such incident:

> At a party a friend of ours – Captain Mauleverer, who had known the Rajah in India and was very much attached to him – we . . . overheard one of the guests, an Indian officer of rank, say angrily 'What is that *black fellow* doing here?' A shocking speech to those who loved and honoured him so much.[37]

In the eyes of many people in Britain, the life of their fellow-countrymen in India was characterized by idleness, frivolity and decadence. Mrs Bayle Bernard, in the review discussed earlier, endorsed Mary Carpenter's crusade for educating Indian women, and appealed to all Englishwomen in India to use their influence to better the lives of 'native females', as much to benefit themselves as their charges. 'Have they no other alternative than to indulge in sinful excitements, or to pass day after day and year after year in a monotonous fulfilment of mere animal functions?' she asked. The founding of the Indian Association in Britain was prompted by the impossibility of any respectful dialogue between black and white in India itself. 'We have been assured more than once by a distinguished native, that the English in England are like a different race to the English in India', wrote the *Englishwoman's Review* in 1871, and this seems to have been a common view:

> We may regret the fact (but can hardly deny), that our young English gentlemen, when placed in positions of responsibility and trust over life, limb, and property, for which at home, if ever obtained, they would wait till they were grey-haired men, have not the good name of England more at heart, than to let it be the synonym for contempt of and overbearing discourtesy towards 'niggers'.[38]

During the same decade, the anti-imperialist journal, *Anti-Caste*, carried another revealing report of prevailing British attitudes towards Indians:

> A correspondent of *The Inquirer* who has been travelling for eight weeks in India sends home a saddening picture of the tone of Anglo-Indian society with regard to the native races. At one hotel he heard a resident of many years inveighing roundly against the natives, asserting that thrashing them was the only mode of treatment. 'Thrash them! Thrash them!' he said – 'Every blow that misses is a blow wasted!' He spoke feelingly of the 'good old times' when, if your servant vexed you, you sent him with a note to the nearest police station – 'please give bearer twenty-five (or fifty) lashes' and it was done. This is described as an 'extreme case', though some young English officers chimed in with it heartily, and the writer met with many who apparently were in accord with this view; and whose panacea was to swear at and kick the 'niggers' as they call them. Others, less rabid, assured him that it was impossible to like the natives, and that the longer you live amongst them the more you hate them. Others, again, were very indignant at the educational policy of late years, whereby natives were qualified to fill posts which used to be perquisites of youths from the old country. The contempt with which well-educated natives are treated in India by Europeans is described as a real grievance. . .[39]

The racism described by Annette Ackroyd distressed her for two reasons: on the one hand, it showed a dismissal of the worth of Indians regardless of their class or personal characteristics and, on the other, it completely denied them any cultural autonomy. In the first instance what bothered her was the way that all Indians were 'classed together' and she was particularly mortified that the English women should be so insensitive. But the main point of this notebook entry was to take issue with the predominant attitude to Indian culture. In her 'query' she questioned the logic whereby the English could assert their cultural norms over those of the indigenous people of India – that the English should be the racial group allowed to feel 'at home'. However, although Annette Ackroyd is likely to have gone out to India with a firm belief in the importance of respecting local autonomy, it is important to see the unevenness in her own attitude, for her notebook reveals very contradictory responses to cultural difference. The first notebook entry, made on 15 December 1872, reads:

> The features of Calcutta life which have struck me as most curious are the crows, the jackals and the difficulty of taking exercise! This is because I have never realised all these things before, while the servants, the semi- and demi- semi- clothed people are quite familiar to my imagination.

Though she claimed that she was prepared for the 'culture shock' of Indian costume, continuous comments in the first month's notebook entries show that she was actually very preoccupied with the way that Indian people dressed. Her remarks about clothes are particularly interesting for they contrast starkly with her professed stance of non-intervention into Indian culture. On 26 December she noted,

> As regards the question of the dress of Bengalee women there seems to me to be the greatest need to teach them harmony of colour. . . . . There must be a decided change too in the lower garments. They cannot go into public places in such costumes. They may cover themselves up, but the very huddling of themselves up in swathes of muslin suggests immodesty.

On 27 December she visited a school which Keshub Chunder Sen was involved in running and which his wife attended. They were received by a Mr Bose, who, she wrote, 'really looked so uncivilised that I could hardly shake hands with him. He was clothed in a huge shawl which swung round him in folds, had socks in wrinkles and shoes, but showed a quantity of brown leg, most distasteful to the eye and to the sense of decency.'

Once in the classroom, she commented on the 'immodesty' of the girls' dress, dwelling particularly on their jewellery. But,

> the thing which shocked me most was to see Mrs. Sen, ignorant of English, while her husband speaks so fluently – dressed like a poor wife of some uncultivated Hindoo – in red silk, no shoes or stockings, . . . She sat like a savage who had never heard of dignity or modesty – her back to her husband, veil pulled over her face – altogether a painful exhibition – the conduct of a petted foolish child it seemed to me, as I watched her playing with her rings and jewels.

Whereas Eliza Fay, almost one hundred years earlier, had shown intense curiosity about the different manifestations of Indian women's femininity, to the Victorian mind of Annette Ackroyd, their jewellery, the red silk, the bare feet, the ways they exposed or concealed parts of their bodies, were all clearly and uncomfortably suggestive both of sexuality and of sexual subordination. Mrs Sen's appearance only seemed to make the English woman aware of how little she had in common with her, and encouraged her to apply harsh moral judgements to the Indian people she met: the 'uncivilised' Mr Bose, whom she can 'hardly shake hands with', Mrs Sen, who 'sat like a savage', or the 'immodest' schoolgirls. Thus Annette Ackroyd had already become typical of the British in India where the sense of moral superiority triggered by such issues as dress was a crucial element in reinforcing in Europeans in India a certainty of their rightful position as the ruling race. This is clear in the language of her notebook: having critically quoted other Europeans' use of the word 'native', she used markedly more derogatory terms herself – 'uncivilised' and 'savage' – in describing Mr Bose and Mrs Sen.

If Annette Ackroyd had expected to find instant solidarity with Indian women, this encounter certainly disappointed her. In addition she objected to what she perceived as an untenable inequality between Mr and Mrs Sen. In her eyes, Mrs Sen was not a suitable wife for the leader of the Brahmo Somaj or for a man who had advocated the rights of Indian women, not merely because of her appearance but because she was unable to speak English. For this, she blamed Sen and perceived him as a hypocrite, although there was no evidence for this. Sen advocated education for women and his wife was indeed attending school. There was nothing here which could not have been predicted from Sen's English lectures on the position of Indian women and the need for their education.

Aside from encountering attitudes which shocked her, Annette Ackroyd also found the practical tasks of renting a school building and finding staff extremely difficult. Many of her diary entries are brusque, irritated reports of abortive meetings with prospective landlords and of seeing premises which, because of their state of repair seemed entirely unsuitable to her. Her diaries suggest a frustration brought about by an expectation that things should be just as they would be in London. Despite a busy social life, she felt isolated. In January 1873, she wrote: 'I do not know where to begin! or how to begin, and long for several impossibilities in the shape of help and womanly help.'

She failed to develop any close relationships with Indian women, though she stayed for nearly a year with Mrs Ghose, and mentioned a number of other middle-class Indian women whom she visited. As far as other white women were concerned, she felt alienated from the Government House crowd – the wives and daughters of Civil Servants and army officers – finding them conservative and unsympathetic.

There was certainly no possibility of friendship with any of the mission women in Calcutta. They disapproved of her project and made sure that she knew. On 3 April 1873, she noted that she had been called on by an American, Miss Seeley, who told her plainly that, 'education is not our mission but to save souls'. On another occasion she wrote, 'I learn from Babu Sisapada Banerjee that a missionary had been telling his cousin that our school was going to make all the girls infidels.'

While the missionaries thought her school would provide too little spiritual teaching, there was criticism on the other hand from Indian men, who questioned the wisdom of any intervention by European women into the lives of Indian women. In her notebook of March 1873 Annette Ackroyd transcribed two letters which had recently been printed in *The Indian Daily News*, an Indian-language paper, which announced their opposition to her school. One of them read:

> It is a grievous mistake that our people have fallen into, when they think that our social condition will be improved by our women pursuing instruction according to the customs of European society. We have seen that the wives of all the Europeans that live here are utterly shameless. Where women cast off their modesty and associate with men, that which principally constitutes female virtue is destroyed.

Though many of the British administrators may have seen no contradiction between a policy of cultural non-intervention and the propagation of European-style education, these letters expressed the views of those who did. They also posed a challenge to the arguably naive view of those like Sen who hoped that English women could teach without 'importing English customs'. To these writers, in terms of their very life-style, European women were clearly unsuitable as sources of guidance or authority. The author of this letter had begun by saying that though he believed her to be a 'holy woman', Annette Ackroyd's unmarried state was contrary to religious law. The second correspondent also made a pointed mention of Mary Carpenter's marital status:

> At the present time, many are earnestly making efforts to improve the condition of Hindoo females. Are our women really so degraded that there is no other object to which compassion may be extended?
>
> A short time ago, Miss Carpenter, an English unmarried lady, came to Calcutta for this purpose, and the present lady has come to promote their improvement as the former did . . .

> What improvement of Hindoo females can be effected by an English woman? What does she know of our social customs, that our women should be really elevated by her instructions? Such errors pave the way for the destruction of our society.

It is possible that these letters were intended as much as an attack on Sen as on Annette Ackroyd's school. Her first six months in Calcutta coincided with a period of crisis in the Brahmo Somaj, in which Annette Ackroyd, having come to Calcutta at Sen's invitation, was inevitably entangled. It is hard to tell from her papers what was the exact nature of the crisis within the Brahmo Somaj but it led to the breakdown of relations between Annette Ackroyd and Sen. She had begun to express criticism of Sen soon after her arrival, partly, as we have seen, because of her experience of meeting his wife whom she considered to be shockingly repressed. From then on, she had little positive to say about him. She was antagonistic to his politics, his religious views and what she perceived to be his morality.

When she first arrived, she had considered going into partnership with Sen, forming a new school which would amalgamate with the school which Sen already ran. But she soon dismissed the idea. After sitting in on a class taught by Sen she was also critical of his teaching method, as she wrote early in 1873:

> The girls were mostly listless and inattentive. Mr Sen went on talking for a long time, but I must confess I was sadly disappointed. He never looked to see if the class attended, and the whole affair was pointless and diffuse.

As for his religious views, she was outraged by his evangelical style of delivering sermons and by his belief in the Fall, which was anathema to her. Before long she could only view his actions and involvements with a critical and suspicious eye. She decided that he was corrupt – citing his part-ownership of a newspaper which supported him. She even suspected that he had made dishonest claims for expenses on his trip to England.

The antipathy was clearly mutual. In June 1873, after only three months, Sen resigned from the management committee of her school. Nevertheless, she retained significant support among Indians in Calcutta. In reply to the critical letters in *The Indian Daily News* a letter of support appeared with twenty-three signatures.

Almost a year of difficulties and delays passed between Ackroyd's arrival in Calcutta and taking up residence at 22 Baniapookur Lane with her first five pupils in November 1873. During this time she had investigated existing educational provision and built up support for her school. A list of financial contributors shows that around thirty men and women, most of them Indians, made donations amounting to over £3,000. A number of these were personal friends of Annette – professional people whom she mentioned in her diaries. Another twenty or so made monthly subscriptions – the Bristol-based National Indian Association provided a scholarship for one girl in the sum of £20 a month, and Mary Carpenter personally provided two 'widows' scholarships' at £40 a month.

Among those whose names appeared in both the monthly and the one-off subscriptions to the school was Henry Beveridge. Annette had become acquainted with him through a relative, whom she had got to know during the voyage out. He started to write to her after their first meeting in Calcutta and his many letters fill out the partial picture of events which can be gleaned from Annette Ackroyd's diary and notebook. His attitudes also provide a revealing counterpoint to hers.

Henry Beveridge had been serving in the Indian Civil Service in Bengal since 1857. Like Annette, he was a liberal, though of a less orthodox character as he was also an agnostic. His son and biographer suggests that his political attitudes made him unpopular with his superiors and hindered his advancement. His letters to Annette certainly reveal a critical attitude to British rule. In an early letter written in the midst of her conflicts with Sen in March 1873, he adopted a position sympathetic to those who were criticizing her:

> Every European in India is more or less in a false position. The longer you stay in this country the more you will feel that at heart the natives fear and dislike us and that they look with suspicion on all our schemes even when they really are for their benefit. You will feel too that their dislike and distrust of us are reasonable and that it will be long before they are removed or even mitigated. . . . I am not writing to discourage you and I hope that you will not think I am taking a despondent view of your enterprise. I believe that you will do good and are undoubtedly on the right track.

Beveridge offered her advice and support. He made inquiries among his acquaintances on the merits of a boarding or day school and, coming out in favour of the former, he told her that he believed the prospects of boarders were good. In general he suggested that she proceed slowly and encouraged her to try to understand and respect Bengali people and their culture.

Later in 1873 he suggested a reconciliation with Sen. 'I fancy Keshub is a good man,' he wrote, 'but the leader of a party is always to some extent its slave.' Further than that, he questioned the political implications of the alliances she was making in Calcutta:

> May I venture to say that there is a danger in your being too much identified with the anglicised Bengalees. . . . I have nothing to say against Mr and Mrs Ghose, who were kind to me, but I do not believe that they represent the best section of young Bengal or that Bengal will eventually follow in the track that they are going.

But Annette seemed to have been unresponsive to his advice. In her frequent letters home to her sister, dominated at this point by her enthusiasm about Fanny's engagement, she made no reference to Beveridge's substantial correspondence. When she eventually mentioned him in early 1874, after a year in which he had been writing regularly to her, it was, though complimentary, in quite impersonal terms: 'He seems to have an unusually earnest good character . . .'

They met rarely as he was stationed six days' journey away from Calcutta. But he came to stay in the city the following February and after meeting on a number of occasions he proposed to her. His letters showed that he was aware that this may have seemed hasty but that he was so sure of his feelings for her that it was foolish to delay. Civil Service life in India was inflexible; he was now on furlough and would be visiting England later in the year and did not want to miss this rare opportunity for her to accompany him if she accepted his offer of marriage.

At first she turned him down, but in the face of a barrage of love letters, which included a lengthy discussion of John Stuart Mill's views on marriage, she conceded. After she had agreed to marry him, he sent her a number of letters daily, setting out in disarming detail his feelings for her and his high hopes for the marriage. Henry's courtship of Annette showed him to have progressive views on sexual politics. In one letter he wrote about his fear that he 'never could aspire to be the husband of a young lady who wrote that she was going to read Mill's *Autobiography* as a holiday treat.'[40]

By the time of the engagement Annette's school had been open for nearly eighteen months. Her letters to Fanny gave the impression that things were going satisfactorily – by the end of 1874 she had fourteen pupils. But her diary entries revealed the stresses. In January 1875, she wrote across five days: 'Not able to get out as there was no-one to leave in charge.' After a three day break later in the month her entry read: 'School, most of the girls not returning.' Despite writing at length to her sister of her fondness for a particular pupil, she found the girls in general difficult to understand:

> I am often puzzled as to whether they do like me or not. . . . There are not the same lights and shades in brown as in white faces and they are not so easily understood by strangers.[41]

After two and a half years in India she still experienced a profound sense of difference between black and white people and felt alienated from her Indian surroundings – an approach which contrasted with Henry Beveridge's. In her notebook she made frequent reference to what she perceived as the squalor around her – the 'dirty courts, offensive smells', untidy children – which, had one been observing in Victorian England, she would have read as products of ignorance and ill-breeding. She continued to react unsympathetically to evidence of cultural difference – for example, regarding one pupil's vegetarianism as a whim. On one occasion she wrote to Fanny that a number of girls had refused to eat their lunch because a sweeper had been in the kitchen – a breach of caste rules. Her attitude was disdainful, treating their behaviour as attention-seeking, though she made sure that a breach of this sort did not happen again. However, there were problems with both staff and pupils, which suggest that there was dissatisfaction on both sides:

> FEB 27TH/28TH:
> A good deal of worry in school through the rudeness and disobedience of one or two girls.
>
> APRIL 13TH:
> All the servants absented themselves in the evening.

Her disillusion is plain from her diary. She wrote: 'As for the widespread desire for the education of women – it does not exist.'[42] It appears that by March 1875 when Henry Beveridge proposed to her, Annette Ackroyd had already made up her mind to give up the school. In a letter to her on 5

April, the day before their wedding, Henry noted that in leaving Baniapookur Lane today 'you have only anticipated your intended departure by a month or two.'

Annette Ackroyd attributed the failure of her school less to the behaviour of the girls than to the attitudes of Indian men. As her son wrote years later:

> [This] early experience of where women stood in Indian society had a profound effect on Annette's mind. She did not as a result sympathise any more with what she had described as the Anglo-Indian attitude of most of her English sisters. But she began to feel less in sympathy with the generality of Indian men.[43]

Ever since she had first arrived in Calcutta, her difficult relationship with Sen had been the focus for this antagonism, which soon became a distaste for Indian men in general. Her account of an open-air political meeting 'of quite the lowest classes in the Bengalee quarter', which was addressed by Sen, led her to make the following observations:

> I do not think there were three women amongst the crowd, and certainly I was the only lady. In consequence of the infrequent appearance of a woman the people looked at me with profound amazement, and for the first time I realised how uncivilised are their notions about women. I read it in their eyes, not so much in the eyes of those who looked impertinently at me, for this is an expression not unknown to civilisation! as in the blank wonder with which most scrutinised me.[44]

The absence of women (or rather of *ladies*) was proof to her, not that Sen and the Brahmo Somaj were right to place such emphasis on educating females, but that Indian culture was hopelessly backward. This was evidently a decisive moment for her as she surveyed the men around her, completely ill at ease in the face of their undisguised curiosity. It is interesting that she was less bothered by the plainly sexual attention than by what she interpreted as a vacant stare. Taking on the role of the ethnographer, she made her own mental notes of the men's physical characteristics:

> Many of the men were fine looking fellows. There were three very distinct types among them – the keen delicate featured . . . the heavy, thick-

> featured Roman face, like the Tiberius type, and the type of the physically degenerate. There were some very abject people, with almost black skin, small-pox marked and most wretched.[45]

Annette Ackroyd was to retain a deep hostility towards Indian men long after she gave up her efforts to work in education. Her sympathy continued to lie with Indian women, but she was convinced that they were victims of a form of enslavement which British rule seemed powerless to disrupt. Reading her public statement against the Ilbert Bill in 1883 it is clear that another decade in India, as the wife of a colonial administrator, had only hardened her views:

> In this discussion as in most 'il y a question de femmes' – and in this discussion the ignorant and neglected women of India rise up against their enslavement in evidence against their masters. They testify to the justice of the resentment which Englishwomen feel at Mr Ilbert's proposal to subject civilised women to the jurisdiction of men who have done little or nothing to redeem the women of their own race, and whose social ideas are still on the outer verges of civilisation.[46]

The rhetoric of slavery and civilization are by now familiar to us. As I pointed out at the beginning of this essay, Annette Ackroyd assumed that the bonds between women ought to be stronger than those of class and race; and thus she brought in Indian women as witnesses to support her objection. She clearly believed that they were more likely to feel oppressed by male dominance in their own culture than by the system of British rule represented by this piece of colonial legislation.[47] In this instance she showed herself to have accepted the dominant ideology of imperialism: that it was only through contact with Western civilization that the 'natives' had any chance of being delivered from their own tyrannical customs.

### Josephine Butler and the Pride of Womanhood

The fact that an articulate and well-placed Englishwoman set herself up as an opponent of reform might be enough for many people to dismiss her as a white supremacist. But to overlook Annette Ackroyd on these grounds would be to lose an opportunity to learn more about the history of feminism as a social and political movement, and its uneven relationship to parallel struggles against domination by class and race. Her story raises uncomfortable questions that are just as relevant to feminism today as they were in Victorian times: for example, what does it mean when a white feminist aligns herself on her own terms with black women against black men? The legacies of the same colonial period continue to haunt the way women might answer this question now, echoing similar patterns of alliance, opposition or conflict in response to certain situations.

Annette Ackroyd's stand on the Ilbert Bill does not necessarily tell us whether she was justified in her claim to speak on behalf all English women, although there were undoubtedly many who were against Indians having any more power on any grounds. While it was generally acknowledged by Anglo-Indian society that Indian women were oppressed by their men, there is not a great deal of evidence to suggest that British women in India were moved to feel any sense of connection to them as women. Annette Ackroyd, in this respect, was different because she identified her own feminism with the attempts of Indian women to reform the institutions that oppressed them – even though it was an identity based on her own terms. Both her claim to speak for Indian women, and her despair at ever seeing any change in Indian society, must be seen as part of a complex process of communication between women in Britain and India.

As a way of starting to explore this historical relationship I want to examine in more detail precisely what British women felt they shared with women in other parts of the world, particularly in India, during the last two decades of the nineteenth century. This period also saw intense struggles over the meaning of the concept 'womanhood' – struggles which need to be examined as part of the 'ideological cluster' of imperialism. As feminists began to make a more concerted challenge to oppressive laws and institutions from the 1850s onwards, the forces of opposition laid even more stress on the virtues of supposedly traditional womanhood. In their essay, 'The Englishwoman', Pat Thane and Jane Mackay describe different nationalist images of women during the period 1880 to 1920, arguing that the image of the ideal Englishwoman – or indeed any woman – was based on essentially domestic and maternal qualities. However, although the category of womanhood was generally thought to transcend race, class or culture, Englishwomen often found that they were being compared with women of other nationalities, not always favourably:

> . . . Englishwomen, it seemed, had difficulty in living up to that ideal. Not

> only were they trained and cajoled from their earliest years to recognise the primacy of domesticity, but throughout life faced criticism for the inadequacy of their performance, even in comparison with women of other countries.[48]

The development of feminism, however, meant that women were quite capable of defining their own qualities. In her study of Victorian feminism, Philippa Levine writes that feminists in this period accepted the significance of sexual difference while at the same time rejecting the categories which male politics reserved for them.[49] Similarly, Olive Banks points out that many feminists shared with their opponents a sense of women's essential qualities, a point which they often used in their own defence, but

> this is not to suggest, of course, that the feminists accepted the traditional view of women as they found it. In the hands of even the most conservative of them the cult of domesticity became transformed into the ideal of female superiority, and the doctrine of separate spheres into the attempted invasion of the masculine world not simply by women but, potentially even more revolutionary in its impact, by womanly values.[50]

While there were many women attempting to win reform through more rational argument, there were others who promoted these 'womanly values' of greater sensitivity, spiritual purity and general goodness as a means of changing society from within. At the turn of the century, the writer and campaigner Ellice Hopkins wrote a book called *The Power of Womanhood; or Mothers and Sons. A book for parents and those in loco parentis* which contained a chapter entitled 'Imperial Aspects'. It illustrates perfectly how British women were able to turn their supposedly innate feminine qualities into a force for power in a world increasingly occupied by their fellow-countrymen:

> The great British Empire, the greatest civilizing, order-spreading, christianizing world power ever known, can only be saved by a solemn league and covenant of her women to bring back simplicity of life, plain living, high thinking, reverence for marriage, chivalrous respect for all womanhood, and a high standard of purity for men and women alike.[51]

The argument put forward by Ellice Hopkins was simple: morality was the basis of all great civilizations, and the way that women were treated was an index of a nation's racial purity and strength:

> All history teaches us that the welfare and very life of a nation is determined by moral causes; and that it is the pure races – the races that respect their women and guard them jealously from defilement – that are the tough, prolific, ascendant races, the noblest in type, the most enduring in progress, and the most fruitful in propagating themselves.

It was now British women's responsibility to lead the crusade for restoring a sense of morality to the world. This extract appeared in 1900 in an edition of *The Storm Bell*, a small journal edited by Josephine Butler, another prominent Victorian woman. In her accompanying review of the book, Josephine Butler extended her thanks to Ellice Hopkins for putting these thoughts so clearly – 'thoughts which have been pressing heavily on the minds of a multitude of true British women, whose jealously [sic] for the honour of their dear mother country has never lessened their sympathy for the womanhood of the whole world, and the ardour of their zeal that justice should be done to them, – to the women of every race and colour.'

These words need to be considered in the context of the moral purity movement inspired by the campaign against the Contagious Diseases Acts, which had brought about new alliances between men and women of all classes, and had given a new edge to notions of women's traditional moral qualities. The Acts also provided an example of policies being enacted simultaneously within Britain and India and highlighted the connections and differences between women in both countries. State regulation of prostitutes was largely the result of imperialist foreign policies which required the maintenance of huge armies both at home and in the occupied countries. It may also have been the case that the experience of state governments in India in controlling the movement of prostitutes at the beginning of the nineteenth century influenced government legislation in Britain later on. The fullest analysis of this movement in Britain appears in Judith Walkowitz's *Prostitution and Victorian Society* in which she argues that an initially radical campaign for the repeal of the Acts was superseded by a reactionary movement for 'social purity', whose aims contradicted those of the original organization.[52] An account of the parallel campaigns in India is found in *Race, Sex and Class under the Raj* by Kenneth Ballhatchet, which provides valuable information about India in this period but makes no links with feminist campaigns in Britain.[53]

In Britain the first Contagious Diseases Act was passed in 1864. It received comparatively little attention among civilians, partly as it was limited to providing for the 'sanitary inspection' of prostitutes in specific military depots in southern England and Ireland. The problem of venereal disease among the troops was not new, but the inadequacy of medical treatment of soldiers in the Crimean War had brought about a report by the Royal Commission on the Health of the Army in 1857, which demanded that some action be taken. The report specifically called for an end to routine inspection of the men as it was bad for morale and self-respect. It also stressed the difficult living conditions of men stationed abroad, particularly the boredom of celibacy and the terrible sanitary conditions. Regulation of prostitutes was therefore proposed as a remedy. This so-called humanitarian approach was backed up by statistics showing the raging epidemics of venereal disease among troops in India where local administrations had been experimenting with different 'solutions' for over fifty years. Two more Acts were passed in 1866 and 1869, both extending the powers of the first.

Public opposition surfaced in the early 1870s when coalitions of middle-class Nonconformists, feminists and radical working men challenged the Acts as immoral and unconstitutional. In 1869 Josephine Butler, already a well-known social campaigner, helped to found the Ladies National Association (LNA) which denounced the Acts as blatant examples of class and sex discrimination, not only depriving poor women of their rights but also sanctioning double standards of morality. During the next few years, feminists were drawn for the first time into campaigns which challenged the police, Parliament, medical and military establishments.

Meanwhile in India the first national Contagious Diseases Act was passed in 1868. Drafted along the same lines as the British legislation, it called for compulsory registration of brothels and prostitutes, periodical medical examinations and compulsory treatment of 'diseased' prostitutes. It differed from the law in Britain in that it made it compulsory for women to register, while in Britain action could only be taken after the police had been passed information about a particular woman.

As in all the British colonies, the administrators were in a position to carry out policies that were not necessarily approved by Parliament, but which it rarely opposed. The system of lock hospitals for VD suspects was widely used in India and it was accepted almost everywhere that it should be the women not the soldiers who were detained for treatment. In the state of Madras, hospitals for 'diseased' women were first established at the end of the seventeenth century, and in 1805 the governor appointed special police to deal with prostitutes and to subject women to compulsory medical examinations. The government in London endorsed this with some hesitation, asking for more detailed statistics and costings. The statistics showed that the number of European soldiers suffering from VD had more than doubled since the lock hospitals had been set up. However, closing the hospitals only aroused protests from the military.

This was to be a pattern in India throughout the nineteenth century: the military was only concerned with maintaining an efficient and 'healthy' army, composed of single, young, working-class men who enjoyed 'natural' appetites for sex. They faced a moral opposition, both in India and in Britain, which either refused to accept the legalization of prostitution at all, or objected to the blatancy with which it was institutionalized. Some suggested that the troops should be allowed to marry, comparing their promiscuous behaviour with the orderly and disciplined lives of the Indian soldiers who lived with their families in the barracks. But the prevailing theory was that unmarried men made better soldiers. Apart from this, opponents of marriage claimed that the cost of maintaining thousands of British women would have been prohibitive, and would have enormous and undesirable consequences on the social lives of both settlers and colonized.

While the arguments over the regulation of prostitution and its alternatives continued, the epidemics of VD in India reached crisis proportions in 1868. The Royal Commission on the Sanitary State of the Army in India was set up to prepare legislation, and the result was the Indian Contagious Diseases Act of 1868. This sparked off a great deal of opposition, both in India and back in Britain. The Nonconformists were the most vocal in their condemnation, arguing that it sanctioned prostitution, but the Act's supporters in India claimed that being a 'courtesan' was a respected profession there. The opposition from Indians was also extremely vocal; many people saw the Act as yet another extension of police powers which affected whole communities.

However, the reform movement in India was still overshadowed by the campaign against the British Contagious Diseases Acts, although the law was suspended in Calcutta and Bombay during the 1870s, mainly for financial reasons. By 1886, when the Act was abolished in Britain, reformers in Britain were free to turn their attention to India. The questions asked in the House of Commons by the opponents of the Act proved highly embarrassing to the government, partly because it became clear that the military authorities in India were carrying out policies that were expedient to them, almost regardless of any opposition. Delegations were sent out to India to report on the condition of the troops and of the women who were encamped nearby. Alfred Dyer, a leading Quaker campaigner, went on one of these missions in 1887, reporting in his journal, *The Sentinel*, that there was clear evidence that prostitutes had been injured by soldiers and that the system of camp followers developed over the years encouraged the British soldiers to despise Indians. Although his first dispatches affected public opinion, this had very little impact on the administration of the Acts in India. A new crisis for the government arose when a document, known as 'The Infamous Memorandum' was published in the English press. According to a biography of Josephine Butler, the document was reported to have been sent by the quarter master general in India to officers commanding troops there, saying that there had been complaints about the quality and quantity of the women supplied for the troops. It ordered an improvement in both, suggesting that if the matron in charge of a brothel could not do better she should be replaced. After much denying and disowning it was finally established that the document was authentic, and the Indian government was immediately ordered to abolish all regulation of prostitution.[54] It was clear, though, that the military authorities in India were intent on making their own arrangements, and the abolitionists were forced to counterattack. The campaign for reform decided that a new delegation should be sent out, this time consisting of women who would be able to visit the prostitutes and hear their side of the story. In 1891, two American women who had heard about the campaign volunteered to travel to India to present a report. Mrs Elizabeth Andrews and Dr Kate Bushnell, both members of the World's Women's Christian Temperance Union – the first international women's organization – had professional qualifications for the job, since one was a doctor and the other the wife of a Methodist minister.

From December 1891 until the warmer weather of the following year, the two women visited first the military encampments, which yielded little new information, and then, after learning enough of the language, the areas nearby where the prostitutes were housed. They found that many of the women were young widows who had been sold off by families who could not afford to keep them. They lived in premises provided by the army and were paid a regular but minute amount of money by the 'town magistrate' for their services. They were forced to submit to regular examination and were given tickets countersigned by the army surgeon to certify their state of health. The two women delegates also discovered that the women were under the authority of an older woman, called a 'Moldaharni', whose duty it was to bring in new girls when the supply was down, for which she received three rupees a head.

The delegates' report was met with the usual denials and attempts to cover up the activities of the military authorities, but enough of the truth was established to embarrass the British government further. Dr Bushnell and her partner returned to England to publicize their findings through endless lectures, articles and, eventually, a book called *The Queen's Daughters in India*. In 1895 the abolitionists claimed victory of a sort when the government of India was forced to order the closing down of all brothels within cantonments and to end all compulsory medical examination. Within a year, however, the army's medical officers were reporting enormous increases in venereal disease, which was hardly surprising since they had also shut down many hospitals and treatment centres on the ground that they were useless without compulsion. Statistics were also used to demonstrate that the troops returning from India were infecting the population in Britain and, encouraged by the return of a Conservative government, the lobby in favour of the domestic CD Acts quickly reasserted itself.

Josephine Butler, who by this time was approaching her seventies, was again at the forefront of the campaign for abolition. Her writing and editing throws much light on the relationship of women across Victorian barriers of both class and race during this period, because of both what she challenged and what she fought for. Although her personal life and her involvement in the campaign for abolition of the CD Acts has been dealt with elsewhere, her international work has attracted less attention.

Josephine Butler's attitude towards Indian women is best explored through her well-documented belief in a universal sisterhood and the primacy of gender over class. An essay by Nancy Boyd, which otherwise makes no reference to India, rather curiously describes her as a British brahmin who chose to associate herself with outcasts who were like the 'garbage sweepers of Hindu society'.[55] In her writing, Josephine Butler frequently challenged the idea that prostitutes had no souls and therefore deserved no rights, and consistently asserted that women who were prostitutes were as good as any other. Nancy Boyd illustrates how Butler's

Josephine Butler (1828–1906), taken in 1903

work with middle-class women consisted largely in showing them the importance of the spiritual bonds that existed between all women:

> Womanhood is *solidaire*. We cannot successfuly elevate the standard of public opinion in the matter of justice to woman, and of equality of all in its truest sense, if we are content that a practical, hideous, calculated, manufactured and legally maintained portion of womanhood is allowed to go on before the eyes of all. 'Remember them that are in bonds, as being bound with them'. Even if we lack the sympathy which makes us feel the chains which bind our enslaved sisters are pressing on us also, we cannot escape the fact that we are one womanhood, who cannot be wholly and truly free.[56]

In a discussion of Josephine Butler's ideas about women's claims to equality with men, Jenny Uglow cites Judith Walkowitz in pointing out that although she approached prostitutes as sisters, she was also capable of presenting her campaign as one in which 'mothers' would save 'daughters':

> Butler's defence of motherhood was a political device, aimed at subverting and superseding patriarchal authority: it gave mothers, not fathers the right to control sexual access to the daughters. In this way Butler sanctioned an authority relationship between the older middle-class women and young working women that, although caring and protective, was also hierarchical and custodial.[57]

I would also argue that Josephine Butler carried these contradictory views of women into her international work, and that she saw Indian women as being potentially equal to all women in their role as the moral guardians of society, while at the same time being victims of laws and practices from which only their spiritual mothers, British women, could free them. Unlike Annette Ackroyd, however, she attributed their oppression to the behaviour of British men as much as to Indian culture. In 1898, several years after Dr Bushnell and Elizabeth Andrews had returned from their visit to India, Josephine Butler expressed this view when she reported a meeting at which they had 'pleaded' for the 'Queen's daughters in India'. The imagery that she employed to endorse the delegates' analysis reads today as an appalling example of Victorian racism, informed by a desperate desire to publicize the oppression of Indian women:

> Mrs Andrews spoke of the Queen's daughters in India, the poor Indian women sacrificed by our rulers to the base theory of the necessity of sinful indulgence for our army in India, as being ground between the 'upper and the nether millstone;' on the one hand the native Indian laws and customs which oppress and degrade their women – the child marriages, child widowhood, the condition of the widow as a despised outcast etc; and on the other hand, the foul and heavy-handed injustice exercised towards them by the English authorities in India (backed by the English Home Government) in entrapping and enslaving them, oppressing and tormenting them, and doing them to death under their unlawful system of officially regulated fornication.
>
> They are indeed between the upper and nether millstone, helpless, voiceless, hopeless. Their helplessness appeals to the heart, somewhat in the same way in which the helplessness and suffering of a dumb animal does, under the knife of the vivisector.
>
> We have heard of the meekness and patience of dogs, (the dearest and noblest of beasts), under the inhuman tortures of the great vivisector; even of their licking the hand which held the scalpel, in a mute appeal for pity. It is

> that dumbness, that impossibility of resistance, that complete helplessness of the subjected animal which appeals to our hearts (some of our hearts at least), with a sense of peculiar pain, and of a resentment against their tormentors, which in its way is unique.
>
> The tortured human being, we hope, we believe, has, in some instances the intelligence, dim as that may be, of a Divine power above all earth's cruelty, which may be exercised on behalf of the tortured.
>
> The Martyr Saints at the stake or on the rack, however terrible their sufferings, were enabled to rise above them, and even to rejoice and sing in the midst of their anguish,
>
> Somewhere, half way between the Martyr Saints and the tortured 'friend of man' the noble dog, stand, it seems to me, these pitiful Indian women, girls, children, as many of them are. They have not even the small power of resistance which the western women may have, under the tyranny of the executive of this base system. The western woman may have some clearer knowledge of a just and pitiful God to whom she may make her mute appeal. She has occasionally perhaps the consciousness that among her countrymen and those outside this tyranny there are some who are pleading her cause. This, I believe, has brought to some a faint hope, though it is no more than a faint hope for the future rather than for the present.[58]

It is hard to pass this extract by without discussing the metaphor of the 'dumb animal' but I shall return to it in my conclusion. I should note, however, that it was used at a time when the campaign against vivisection was becoming increasingly vocal in the political circles in which Josephine Butler moved; Alfred Dyer, mentioned earlier, was an ardent opponent, and his journal, *The Sentinel*, often carried information relating to the inhumane treatment of animals. I find it significant that the image of the animal under the vivisector's knife should have replaced the familiar reference to slavery, and wonder how far it represents Josephine Butler's determination to find a new and more powerful politically charged language to express her views on the oppression of women, rather than being a simple ellision of primitive native and docile animal.

The analogy of the millstone used by Bushnell and Andrews was very complex, for on the one hand it conveyed very graphically the sense of complete powerlessness which Josephine Butler attributed to Indian women, while on the other it suggested they they suffered from a 'double oppression' of being women under colonial rule. On both counts the women were victims, unable to help themselves, but she also pointed out that 'western' women were only at a slight advantage in that they could always make a 'mute' appeal to their superior God. It is interesting to compare the language of the above extract with the paragraph quoted earlier in this chapter written by Mrs Bayle Bernard in the *Englishwoman's Review* in 1868. In the earlier piece Indian women were described as 'filling [a position] which can only be contemplated with feelings of shame and sorrow', and British women were charged with the task of raising 'their Eastern sisters to their own level'. In Josephine Butler's account of Bushnell and Andrews's meeting, the shame and sorrow came not from Indian women's position relative to their men so much as from their treatment by British men. Leaving aside the language in which it was expressed, the argument reflected the connections being made in India between the incipient feminist movement and the nationalists, as well as demonstrating the influence of the nationalists upon the campaign in Britain. Indian nationalists such as the MP Dadabhai Naoroji were extremely vocal in the campaign against the state regulation of brothels, since it proved beyond measure that British rule was unjust. In 1893 Josephine Butler reported a meeting addressed by Naoroji at which he prophesied rebellion:

> Mr Naoroji went on to show that, after all, the English Government was a foreign government to the native Indians, and the various rills of injustice and senses of injury were gradually accumulating and nourishing a turbulent spirit in the native breast, which would sooner or later bring it Nemesis upon the responsible British people and British Government. Mr Naoroji's closing words of warning were very solemn, and a tone of profound sorrowfulness in them must have touched many hearts.[59]

Although Josephine Butler was herself highly critical of British rule in India, she continued to hold on to her belief that the Empire represented an opportunity for good in the world. Towards the end of her life she made the following statement in a pamphlet published in 1900 about the Boer War called *Native Races and the War*:

> It is my deep conviction that Great Britain will in future be judged, condemned or justified, according to her treatment of those innumerable coloured races, heathen or partly Christianized, over whom her rule extends, or who, beyond the sphere of her rule, claim her sympathy and help as a Christian and civilising power to whom a great trust has been committed.[60]

Unlike Annette Ackroyd, who 'disdained all connections with Christianizing institutions',[61] Josephine Butler believed that Christianity was the means by which the world would be saved. She was a deeply religious woman whose faith had been strengthened by her own personal suffering as well as through witnessing the misery of the women and children involved in prostitution. Like other prominent Christian women of her day she shared a vision of a society which would be like an extended family under the care of the Father in heaven – a family which respected equality between men and women. However conservative this vision might appear in its attempt to preserve the idea of familial relations under a patriarchal figure, there was little compromise in Josephine Butler's language when she addressed the oppression of women, in Britain or anywhere else. 'We are in times of battle', she wrote. 'We are living amidst the convulsions, a vision of Armageddon that heralds the end of the world.' Through working with God to abolish injustice and oppression,

> The groaning and travailing earth shall be released from her bondage, and the rod of the oppressor shall be broken! Fetters shall no longer be wrought out of the intelligence and civilisation of one zone to entrap the unwary simplicity and enslave the generations of another. The light of day will fall upon all the dark places of the earth, now full of the habitations of cruelty, and there shall come forth, at the call of the Deliverer, the thousands and tens of thousands of the daughters of men now enslaved in all lands to cruelty and lust.[62]

## Loyal to Civilization

The contrast between these two women, Josephine Butler and Annette Ackroyd, provides a useful indication of some of the ways in which Victorian feminists in this period conceived of their relationship to non-white women throughout the Empire. Obviously they worked in completely different fields and had very dissimilar approaches to their work, but the differences serve to highlight a range of possible connections that were made between British and Indian women.

Annette Ackroyd and Josephine Butler shared several basic characteristics. They both expressed their early political beliefs by working with or on behalf of poor women in Britain: Annette was involved in the movement to extend education to working-class women, while Josephine chose to defend the rights of working-class prostitutes. In this they each transformed the ideology of 'women's mission' by addressing the subordination of women by class and gender. Both came from liberal family backgrounds and had grown up with an awareness of the political campaigns of the 1830s and 1840s which had occupied their parents. Unlike Josephine, who was born into a well-off family, Annette's father was from a working-class background. His political activity and belief in universal education was a decisive influence on his daughters, particularly Annette. Josephine was especially proud of her anti-slavery pedigree. Towards the end of her life, in 1900, she wrote: 'My father was one of the energetic promoters of the Abolition of Slavery in the years before 1834, a friend of Clarkson and Wilberforce. The horror of slavery in every form, and under whatever name, which I have probably partly inherited, has been intensified as life went on.'[63] This was true of many other feminists in the nineteenth century. Philippa Levine describes how 'there were women within feminism who had learned their first political lessons at an early age. Many came from politically active families or had married men with political careers'. This is not to say that this was the main route into political activity for women. 'Most came from more ordinary backgrounds, though sometimes from families where religious nonconformity had perhaps promoted an early understanding of injustice and prejudice.'[64]

It is also likely that their family backgrounds contributed to their sense of international solidarity which propelled them to work outside Britain and to apply feminist principles to non-white, non-Christian women. In any event, its own history had demonstrated that from the start nineteenth-century feminism was an international movement in which women throughout Europe and America had received impetus and inspiration from one another. Yet although feminism provided women with a potential understanding both of their common experience and their differences across class and race as well as a new language of sisterhood, this international solidarity did not guarantee that their motives were necessarily progressive or radical, particularly as the Empire expanded and the numbers of British subjects grew. The very idea of a shared sisterhood was dangerously close to the imperialist ideologies of a universal womanhood which in theory also applied equally to women in all countries. However, for imperialists the qualities shared by women could only be skin deep; developing theories of racial difference and eugenics contradicted any notion of equality or even similarity by claiming that the English were a superior race, which gave them the authority to hold their Empire together through force of both character and culture:

> For most Victorians, whether they lived early or late in the queen's reign, the British were inherently, by 'blood', a conquering, governing, and civilizing 'race'; the 'dark races' whom they conquered were inherently incapable of governing and civilizing themselves.[65]

The writings of Annette Ackroyd and Josephine Butler show a critical awareness of racial and cultural supremacy, but this was sometimes overshadowed or contradicted by their views on other subjects. Josephine Butler made it clear that her project had nothing to do with enforcing Christian religion or 'foreign culture' on her Indian pupils, but she seemed to feel very deeply that Christianity would be the force that ultimately saved the world. She did not proselytize among Indian women directly because she was not in a position to do so, but she expressed her own mission and the aims of the campaign in uncompromisingly religious language. That is not to say that she did not support the demands of secular feminists wherever they were, but she was honest about her own motivation.

The difference between the two women's sense of their work in India and their attitudes to racism becomes clearer when we consider how they related to Indian women and the different emphasis they placed on aspects of 'womanhood'. For Annette Ackroyd, the links were made through an awareness of shared oppression, demonstrated by Indian women's lack of social and economic independence. She saw education as a major tool in helping them achieve more power in society, and greatly resented what she saw as the behaviour of Indian men in perpetuating women's low status. Apart from her strong dislike of the British colonial elite in India, her views on colonialism itself are less evident. Josephine Butler believed that women everywhere were united through suffering physical abuse at the hands of men, and that in India it was both British and Indian men who were responsible, although in different ways. However, she continued to maintain a strong sense of Britain's responsibility, as a 'christian and civilizing power', to protect the weaker nations of the world. This weakness might be measured by a country's ability to resist the colonizing impulse of the European nations; but it usually referred to a state of economic and cultural backwardness in relation to the capitalist, Christian powers. In the eyes of those supporting masculinist ideologies or those opposing them, the treatment of women by men could be read as an important index of a society's progress on the evolutionary scale of civilization.

The complexity of these two women's views on race and gender is further underscored by the ways each responded to cultural difference. For Butler, the way that Indian women behaved, dressed, talked and lived their lives was almost irrelevant in the face of their outrageous oppression at the hands of men. Nor did she ever visit India, although she was acquainted with Indians in London. Ackroyd, on the other hand, left behind a detailed record of her reaction to meeting and working with Indian women of different ages and social classes. As we have seen from her diaries she had obviously expected to feel immediate empathy with women in India but felt repelled, initially at least, by customs that she did not understand or approve of. Her failure to influence her pupils' behaviour must have been an added incentive to giving up the school.

This comparison is certainly not meant to be conclusive, but rather a vehicle for exploring some of the different and often contradictory ways that feminists tried to comprehend the connections between domination by gender and domination by race. They lived at a time when Britain was struggling to maintain its economic and military position in the world, in a culture obsessed with questions of nationhood, patriotism and race. As potential mothers, women of all classes were affected to some degree by imperialist ideology, as Anna Davin, whose classic study of motherhood and Empire, which discusses the connections between social policy towards women and racist ideologies, has shown.[66] And as another historian, Pat Thane, has argued, 'Earlier in the century good mothering was proposed as woman's contribution to stability *within* a rapidly changing British society – a stable home was expected to produce secure, responsible citizens. Later, its additional role was to help secure Britain's *international* position'.[67] But it was not just as mothers that British women performed a central role in maintaining the Empire: the ideology of white womanhood, structured by class and race, embraced women in all their familial roles. Whether as Mothers of the Empire or Britannia's Daughters, women were able to symbolize the idea of moral strength that bound the great imperial family together. In their name, men could defend that family in the same spirit as they would defend their own wives, daughters or sisters if they were under attack. Faced by this ideological burden, the writings of many feminists like Annette Ackroyd and Josephine Butler show a fundamental tension in their attitudes to the idea of Empire. They might challenge or contest reactionary images of womanhood on which the imperialist project depended for support, but in doing so they expressed a lack of patriotism. Or they could adhere to their feminist principles, and effectively condone racist and imperialist policies which suppressed the freedom and independence of other people.

For many women, the geographical extent of the Empire allowed them potential knowledge of and contact with their 'sisters' in other lands. This immediately created the possibility of totally unequal and dependent relationships in which women from the 'Mother Country' helped to define and describe the conditions under which the colonized women lived, as well as the nature of those women themselves. Both the grotesque imagery of the suffering Indian female, halfway between dog and saint, and the earlier portrait of women whose situation provoked shame and sorrow are examples of ways in which British women have been instrumental in reinforcing the image of 'Oriental' or 'Eastern' women as passive, quiescent victims of male power, whose subordination was sometimes connected with, but always relative to, that of Western women. Some felt morally obliged to help non-European women improve their lives and to throw off the shackles of male domination, which was generally seen as a direct result of religions and customs they saw as heathen and marking a lack of civilization. Feminism could thus be seen as part of the civilizing process, along with English civil law, education and Christianity. Meanwhile at the heart of that civilization feminists set themselves in opposition to the laws and institutions that they disliked so much in their own society.

The broad question I set out to address in this chapter concerned the extent to which feminism offered an alternative view of popular imperialism in this period. In my conclusion I find myself asking another question, this time more specific. Was it possible to be a feminist and simultaneously to have an alternative view of popular imperialism? The tensions and contradictions involved in the politics of Annette Ackroyd and Josephine Butler suggest that it was not yet possible to comprehend what feminism's most effective response to different forms of imperialism should be, by which I mean feminism's contribution to the downfall of Empire and the liberation of colonized people. What was lacking was a vision of liberatory politics that connected the struggle against masculinist ideology and power with the struggle against racist domination in the colonies. Yet, in

Butler's analysis it is possible to see a glimmer of light on this question. By the turn of the century, there was a significant number of British women who did effectively support Indian feminism and who were able to see that any demand for change in women's status had to be linked to the emerging nationalist movement. It was not until the issue of women's suffrage had transformed feminism in the Mother Country that women there could really begin to take part in the political emancipation of the colonies.

## Notes

1 Patrick Brantlinger, *Rule of Darkness: British Literature and Imperialism, 1830–1914*, Cornell University Press, Ithaca/London 1988, p. 19.

2 John M. Mackenzie, ed., *Imperialism and Popular Culture*, Manchester University Press, Manchester 1986, p. 3.

3 John M. Mackenzie, *Propaganda and Empire*, Manchester University Press, Manchester 1984, p. 2.

4 Brantlinger, p. 35.

5 For a summary of nineteenth-century evolutionist arguments about sex roles see Janet Sayers, *Biological Politics – Feminist and Anti-Feminist Perspectives*, Tavistock Publications, London/New York 1982, ch. 3. (Also fn 38 in Part two).

6 Philippa Levine, *Victorian Feminism, 1850–1900*, Hutchinson, London 1987, p. 23.

7 Sen gave this invitation at a women's meeting of the Victorian Discussion Society, 1 August 1870. Sophia Dobson Collett ed., *Keshub Chunder Sen's English Visits*, Strahan, London 1871, pp. 474–5.

8 William Beveridge, *India Called Them*, London 1947, p. 220. Annette Ackroyd's son and biographer was Lord Beveridge, chairman of the Unemployment Insurance Statutory Committee, 1935–44, who produced the Beveridge Report, blueprint for the welfare state. *India Called Them* is an account of the lives of his parents.

9 Sophia Dobson Collett, *An Historical Sketch of the Brahmo Somaj*, Calcutta 1940. See also Sophia Dobson Collett, ed., *Keshub Chunder Sen's English Visits*, and *The Life and Letters of the Raja Rammohun Roy*, London 1900.

10 Mary Carpenter, *Last Days in England of Rajah Rammohun Roy*, Calcutta 1915.

11 Ibid., p. 77.

12 Ibid., p. 87.

13 See Lata Mani's discussion of *sati* and the influence of Rammohun Roy on nineteenth-century debates on the position of women in India in 'Contentious Traditions: The Debate on SATI in Colonial India', *Cultural Critique*, no. 7, Fall 1987, pp. 119–56.

14 Carpenter, p. 106.

15 Ibid., pp. 103–4.

16 Ibid., p. 125.

17 Sophia Dobson Collett, ed., *Keshub Chunder Sen's English Visits*, p. 199.

18 *English Woman's Journal*, vol. IV, November 1860, p. 170.

19 A. J. Hammerton, 'Feminism and Female Emigration 1861–1886', in Martha

Vicinus, ed., *A Widening Sphere: Changing Roles of Victorian Women*, Methuen, London 1980, pp. 53, 70.

20 A. J. Hammerton, *Emigrant Gentlewomen*, Croom Helm, London 1979, quoted in Jane Mackay and Pat Thane, 'The Englishwoman', in Robert Colls and Philip Dodd, eds, *Englishness: Politics and Culture 1880–1920*, Croom Helm, London/Sydney/Dover, NH 1986, pp. 203–4.

21 Jane Rendall, *The Origins of Modern Feminism: Women in Britain, France and the United States, 1780–1860*, Macmillan, London 1985, p. 66. See also Joanna Liddle and Rama Joshi, *Daughters of Independence: Gender Class and Caste in India*, Zed Books/Kali for Women, London/New Delhi 1986, pp. 28–9.

22 Eliza Fay, *Original Letter from India*, E. M. Forster, ed., Hogarth, London 1986, pp. 203, 207. I have not been able to find much evidence of writings by British women about Indian women during the late eighteenth and early nineteenth centuries.

23 Annie van Sommer and Samuel M. Zwemer, *Our Moslim Sisters (A cry of need from lands of darkness interpreted by those who heard it)*, Fleming H. Revell, London and Edinburgh 1907, p. 254. Though published a little later, the tone of the title and of the book itself provides a good illustration of this evangelism directed especially towards saving women, and of Islam existing in a state of darkness needing Western 'light'.

24 *Englishwoman's Review*, July 1868, pp. 472–82, p. 482.

25 *Englishwoman's Review*, April 1873, p. 119.

26 *Englishwoman's Review*, April 1870, p. 87.

27 Cited in Christine Bolt, *Victorian Attitudes to Race*, Routledge & Kegan Paul, London/Toronto 1971, p. 159.

28 Brantlinger, pp. 76–85.

29 Brantlinger, pp. 82–3.

30 Geoffrey Moorhouse, *India Britannica*, Paladin, London 1984, p. 96.

31 Moorhouse, p. 96.

32 For example, in the last ten years of her life she worried her political advisers by her closeness to a Muslim servant, Abdul Karim, who worked at the palace and whom she promoted to being her *munshi* (teacher) of Hindustani. This story can be found in Rozina Visram, *Ayahs, Lascars and Princes*, Pluto, London 1986, pp. 30–3. See also Michael Alexander and Sushila Anand, *Queen Victoria's Maharajah: Duleep Singh 1838–93*, Weidenfeld & Nicolson, London 1980.

33 Sophia Dobson Collett, ed., *Keshub Chunder Sen's English Visits*, pp. 481–2.

34 Ibid., p. 471.

35 Annette Ackroyd's diary, letters and notebook are all unpublished manuscripts contained in the Annette and Henry Beveridge Collection in the Oriental and India Office of the British Library (Mss.Eur. C.176). Unless otherwise indicated, all extracts are from this collection catalogued under A (correspondence between Henry and Annette Beveridge), B (Annette's diaries) and D (correspondence with others, including her sister, Fanny Mowett).

36 Notebook entry for 27 March 1873.

37 Collett, *Life and Letters of Raja Rammohun Roy*, p. 130.

38 *Englishwoman's Review*, April 1871, p. 90.

39 'Race Prejudice in India', *Daily News*, 22 May 1888, reprinted from *Anti-Caste*, vol. 1, no. 4, June 1888. See Part 4 for a detailed discussion of *Anti-Caste*.

40 Letter to Henry Beveridge, 21 March 1875.

41 Letter to Fanny Mowatt, January 1875.

42 Cited in Pat Barr, *The Memsahibs: The Women of Victorian India*, Secker, London 1976, p. 167.

43 Cited in Beveridge, *India Called Them*, p. 91.

44 Ibid., p. 90.

45 Notebook, 26 January 1873.

46 Cited in Beveridge, p. 220.

47 As a result of opposition to the Bill the viceroy amended it so that a jury of at least 50 per cent Europeans would be required in any case where an Indian judge faced a European in the dock.

48 Thane and Mackay, p. 191.

49 Levine, p. 18.

50 Olive Banks, *Faces of Feminism: A Study of Feminism as a Social Movement*, Martin Robertson, Oxford 1981, p. 90.

51 Extracted in *The Storm Bell*, April 1900, p. 297.

52 Judith R. Walkowitz, *Prostitution and Victorian Society: Women Class and the State*, Cambridge University Press, Cambridge 1980.

53 Kenneth Ballhatchet, *Race, Sex and Class under the Raj: Imperial Attitudes and Policies and their Critics, 1793–1905*, Weidenfeld and Nicolson, London 1980.

54 E. Moberly Bell, *Josephine Butler: A Biography*, Constable, London, 1962, pp. 227–8.

55 Nancy Boyd, *Josephine Butler, Octavia Hill, Florence Nightingale: Three Victorian Women Who Changed their World*, Macmillan, London 1982, p. 75.

56 Boyd, p. 76.

57 Jenny Uglow, 'Josephine Butler, from Sympathy to Theory (1826–1906)', in Dale Spender, ed., *Feminist Theorists: Three Centuries of Women's Intellectual Traditions*, The Women's Press, London 1983, p. 158.

58 *The Storm Bell*, June 1898, p. 59.

59 *The Dawn*, no. 22, December 1893.

60 Josephine Butler *Native Races and The War*, London 1900 (Fawcett Library, London).

61 Diary, 1 January 1873.

62 Boyd, p. 91.

63 *Native Races and The War.*

64 Levine, p. 21.

65 Brantlinger, p. 21.

66 Anna Davin, 'Imperialism and Motherhood', *History Workshop Journal*, 5 Spring 1978, pp. 9–65.

67 Pat Thane, 'Late Victorian Women', in T. R. Gourvish and Alan Day, eds, *Later Victorian Britain 1867–1900*, Macmillan Education, London 1988, p. 183.

Part Four

# 'To Make the Facts Known'

## Racial Terror and the Construction of White Femininity

Women of the Klu Klux Klan, North Carolina 1964–5

You see, the white man has never allowed his women to hold the sentiment 'black but comely', on which he has so freely acted himself. Libertinism apart, white men constantly express an open preference for the society of black women. But it is a sacred convention that white women can never feel passion of any sort, high or low, for a black man. Unfortunately facts don't always square with convention; and then, if the guilty pair are found out, the thing is christened an outrage at once and the woman is practically forced to join in hounding down the partner of her shame.

Ida B. Wells, 1894[1]

A vital project awaits any historian interested in exploring the social and political dynamics of race, class and gender in nineteenth-century Britain: quite simply, to identify and describe the anti-colonial movement that was formed in opposition to the rapacious growth of Empire. While there are separate studies of anti-imperialist campaigns, organizations and individuals, I do not believe there has been a single work that attempts either to document or to analyse the early formation of anti-imperialism as a movement. It would be an enormous task as it would require a study of the nascent nationalist groupings in the different colonies, their supporters in England, Scotland, Ireland and Wales, and the network of various philanthropic organizations that campaigned at the heart of Empire. Yet a single account would never be enough; the history of anti-imperialism would benefit from endless debate and reframing, from being scrutinized from different points of view, and from being constantly referred back to other social and political movements of that period. Just as the history of abolitionism has both added to and been influenced by an understanding of the early women's rights movement, so a compendium of anti-imperialist thought and practice would enrich current perceptions of nineteenth-century feminism.

Feminist history has credited individual women with expressing criticism of Empire: women like Annie Besant, for example, who immersed herself in the Indian nationalist movement, or Olive Schreiner, who wrote about colonial relations in her native South Africa. It would be possible to list many other extraordinary women whose names have arisen in the context of particular struggles – women like Lady Florence Dixie and Harriet Colenso, who each played a decisive role in negotiations between the Zulu people and the British government, or Daisy Bates, who left her husband and son in Australia to live with aborigines. Their individual stories are always highly intriguing, and in most cases require far greater study than has so far been given to them. However, when they are added together, the existing accounts immediately suggest the need for an analysis of the role that women played in the anti-imperialist movement in late Victorian Britain – an analysis which considers, at the same time, their relationship to feminism.

There has been an enormous amount of useful feminist research on the different strands of feminism that competed with each other during the late nineteenth century. In *Faces of Feminism*, Olive Banks has described the development of different political agendas among feminists in Britain and America, showing how, by the end of the nineteenth century they were involved in 'contradictions between different definitions of feminism and different and indeed opposing concepts of femininity'.[2] In this essay I want to bring this interpretation to bear on a study of a particular episode in the history of anti-imperialism. It centres on the formation of a political grouping which came together in England to campaign against lynching in America, and its relevance for this project of connecting race, class and gender stems from three main sources. First, the campaign was initiated and largely sustained by women; second, it was a product of collaboration between white English women and a black American woman who galvanized the campaign with a coherent political analysis based on her own research and experience; and finally, through addressing issues of sexuality and femininity, the short-lived anti-lynching movement not only forced a division between different kinds of feminism, but actually made possible a radical politics that acknowledged the connection between the domination of black people and the subordination of women.

## Lynch Law

'Lynching is a peculiarly American tradition', wrote Manning Marable in his book *How Capitalism Underdeveloped Black America*.[3] The word is now used so carelessly that its meaning has lost much of its association with racial terror. It was first used to describe the system devised during the American Revolution by a Quaker political leader called Charles Lynch to curb criminal behaviour in a community which was two hundred miles away from the nearest court of law. The accused man was given the opportunity to defend himself, but if convicted, was sentenced to a punishment deemed appropriate to the crime. This practice, started in a town in Virginia, known today as Lynchburg and famous for Jack Daniels whisky, was fairly common in the Southern states until the end of the eighteenth century, when it came to mean the actual execution of the allegedly guilty person.

It was not until twenty years after the end of the Civil War that the murder of untried suspects became a means of political administration in the South, one which particularly affected black people. By the late 1880s a new generation of blacks and whites had grown up without any direct experience of slavery. Southern society had seen enormous social and economic disintegration, and where ideas about black behaviour and pathology were once governed by the institution of slavery, they were now informed by theories of race and biological difference. As the decade moved from prosperity to recession, racist diatribes on black criminality and bestiality came to be accepted by whites as the observable truth, and in 1889 there began an orgy of lynching. From then on the practice became a specific form of racial terror: the great majority of those who were lynched in the years from 1882 to 1930 were black: of the 4,761 recorded deaths by lynching, 1,375 were of whites.[4] In the period 1889–93, which saw an unprecedented number, 579 blacks and 260 whites were lynched – and 134 of the total 839 took place outside the South. By the turn of the century, from 1899 to 1903, only 27 of the total 543 recorded lynchings were of whites.

The statistics themselves reveal nothing of what lynching actually involved. With the tolerance, and usually the participation of the local establishment, suspects were sometimes taken from gaols after their arrest; at other times the mere rumour of a crime was enough to send out a lynch mob in search of a victim and in such cases people were seized without any evidence whatsoever. Far from being a spontaneous act of revenge, a lynching was frequently publicized a day or two in advance, sometimes even beyond the area in which it was to take place. Public transport might be organized for those wishing to watch and tickets were sold in advance. The event itself often became a mass spectacle involving ritual torture – usually castration – and execution, watched by thousands of people, including children. Photographs and eyewitness accounts describe how families flocked to witness lynchings and then fought to get a souvenir from the victim's charred and dismembered remains. On one occasion a gramophone record was said to have been made of the victim's screams.[5] The event was usually written up in detail by the local press.[6]

The fact that the local law-enforcement officers were often directly involved in these practices meant that when they began to spread in the late 1880s there was almost no opposition from white institutions in the South. In the North, which had by then withdrawn its occupying army, lynchings came to be seen as a natural outcome of abolition; it was thought inevitable that former slaves would wish to take revenge on whites, who would feel threatened by their liberty. It was also assumed that the crimes which precipitated lynchings were invariably of a sexual nature – in other words, that black men were assaulting white women. It was this assumption that made millions of people throughout the United States condone the behaviour of the lynch mobs, either through silence or by voicing approval. Lynching was certainly 'the ultimate of historical white justice and black death'[7] – and it was carried out in the name of defending the honour of white women. Few thought to question this apparent justification, and to relate the pattern of lynching to the political and economic fate of black Southerners after Reconstruction.

By 1892, when the number of lynchings reached a peak, the laws that guaranteed black citizens legal and constitutional equality with whites had been dismantled or overridden by state legislation in most of the Southern states. Segregation was enforced on public transport, in places of entertainment, hotels and schools, and voting rights were in the process of being removed either by law or by intimidation of black voters at the polling booths. The old anti-slavery movement had fallen apart after emancipation, and although there was a great deal of protest and opposition, this made little impact on the federal government which had already sanctioned these developments.

The British anti-slavery movement had also disintegrated, although many former activists retained an interest in conditions in both the Caribbean and America. However, it was in Britain that the first concerted public campaign against lynching took place. 1893 saw a resurgence of activity in support of African-Americans, inspired and largely maintained by the efforts of a few British women who were determined to organize a protest movement. Against a background of Empire mania in their own country, these women, who came from different political and social backgrounds, were briefly united in an alliance with black people across the Atlantic. Their motivation came partly from the horror they felt when reading about lynching; but it was their understanding of the role of white women in justifying the practice that made their involvement so important. This essay will begin by looking at the background to the campaign, before moving on to discuss the arguments and conflicts that came up during its course.

## Support from Britain

In 1894 the Anti-Lynching Committee was set up in London sponsored by an impressive list of editors, politicians and public figures.[8] Its aim was

> to obtain reliable information on the subject of lynching and mob outrages in America, to make the facts known, and to give expression to public opinion in condemnation of such outrages in whatever way might best seem calculated to assist the cause of humanity and civilization.[9]

The catalyst for this group of people was the young African-American journalist, Ida B. Wells, who had spent several months in 1893 and again in the following year touring Britain in an attempt to draw attention to the way blacks in the United States were being systematically denied the legal justice and equality guaranteed them in the constitution.

Ida. B. Wells's lecture tours were not particularly unusual, as an increasing number of African-Americans had visited Britain from the 1830s onwards to campaign against slavery and to raise money for black projects. The networks, both personal and organizational, which had invited and received American abolitionists were still very much in existence following the Civil War and many of the friendships that had resulted were carried on by the younger generations on both sides. When Frederick Douglass made his last visit to Britain in 1886–87 it was primarily to see his friends rather than to make new political contacts; however, he was often called upon at social gatherings to make speeches about the situation in post-war America.[10] In the course of one of these meetings in London he met Catherine Impey, who was ultimately to be responsible for the anti-lynching campaign on the British side of the Atlantic. They met again a few weeks later at the home of Helen Bright Clark, daughter of the radical MP John Bright, who had met Douglass as a child when he was befriended by her father. Catherine Impey described her second meeting with Frederick Douglass in her diary:

> During the evening . . . Mr Douglass gave us a luminous half hour's address

> on the present condition of the coloured population in America, speaking of the caste barriers that everywhere blocked their way, of the iniquitous truck system, their oppression, and their total inability to protect themselves without the ballot of which they had been deprived by cruel persecution and the fraudulent manipulation of the ballot box.[11]

Shortly after this encounter, in 1888, Catherine Impey launched a magazine called *Anti-Caste* which was 'devoted to the interests of the coloured race'. She wrote a substantial part of it herself, but relied on correspondents in America and different parts of the British Empire to supply her with first-hand information and newspaper cuttings about the maltreatment of black people by white. When Frederick Douglass invited her to visit his home in Washington, Catherine was overjoyed and three years later, while in America on family business, spent several days with him learning about the realities of life for black people after emancipation.[12] It was during the same trip that she arranged to meet Ida B. Wells, whose outspoken condemnation of lynching had brought her to the attention of Frederick Douglass.

Shortly after her return, Catherine Impey was sent a report of a lynching in Alabama that had appeared in a local newspaper, complete with graphic photograph. She published the picture on the front page of *Anti-Caste* with a caption that drew attention to the children posing by the body of the hanged man.[13] In doing so she was risking her own reputation, not so much because of the explicit nature of the photograph, but because she was raising the forbidden subject of rape, and even worse, defending the perpetrators of a particularly terrible crime. It would have required very strong convictions for a woman to have brought it to public attention anyway, let alone as a white woman defending black men against charges of assaulting her fellow white women. At that time the circulation of the journal was small, but those who saw it were horrified. A newspaper editor in Liverpool criticized her strongly in his own paper, assuming that the picture was a drawing and had been embellished by the artist. When, however, he was told that it was a photograph sent out by the lynchers themselves, his disapproval of Catherine turned to outrage at what the photograph depicted, and he became one of Catherine's most influential supporters.

Only days after this edition of *Anti-Caste* was published, Catherine Impey read an account of a lynching so sadistic that it had reached even the pages of the British press. A black man in Paris, Texas, was arrested and charged with raping and murdering a five-year-old girl. While he was in prison but before any semblance of a trial, preparations were made to burn him alive with the full consent of the authorities. Schoolchildren were given a day's holiday and trains carried people from the surrounding countryside to watch the event which was carried out in broad daylight. The local papers described in detail how the prisoner was tortured with red-hot irons for hours before the flames were eventually lit; after it was over the mob fought over the ashes for souvenirs in the form of bones, buttons and teeth.

Catherine Impey wrote the same day to Frederick Douglass asking him to arrange for someone, preferably Ida. B. Wells, to come to Britain to help influence public opinion and campaign against lynching from outside the United States. She was encouraged to do so by an acquaintance, Isabella Fyvie Mayo, a Scottish widow whose own philanthropic tendencies had led her to take in lodgers from different parts of the world.[14] Isabella Mayo's reaction to the lynching question was at first cautious as, like most people, she assumed that there must have been evidence of some dreadful crime, presumably of a sexual nature, to justify the revenge of the lynch mob. Catherine's account of her meeting with Ida B. Wells the previous year intrigued Mayo enough to want to meet the outspoken American woman, and plans were immediately made for a speaking tour. Two months later, in April 1893, Ida B.Wells disembarked at Liverpool and after a brief trip to Somerset to recover from the journey, the three women set to work in Mayo's house in Aberdeen planning the tour.

Through Catherine Impey's contacts in the newspaper world and her membership of the Society of Friends, and through Mayo's Scottish connections, meetings and publicity were quickly arranged and Ida B. Wells was accompanied on a rigorous circuit of engagements. A new organization was set up, called the Society for the Recognition of the Universal Brotherhood of Man (SRUBM), which declared itself

> fundamentally opposed to the system of race separation by which the despised members of a community are cut off from the social, civil and religious life of their fellow man. It regards lynchings and other forms of brutal justice inflicted on the weaker communities of the world as having their root in race prejudice, which is directly fostered by the estrangement, and lack of sympathy consequent on race separation.

Ida B. Wells (1862–1931), taken *c.* 1893

Years later, Ida B. Wells wrote down the details of her trips to Britain in her autobiography, *Crusade for Justice*. She quoted numerous press reports and the interviews she gave, in addition to comments on the places she visited and the reactions of the people who met her. She also wrote regular dispatches for the Chicago paper *Inter-Ocean*, becoming the first black overseas columnist for any paper in America. In an interview with *The Sun*, a sympathetic American paper, Ida B. Wells described the reaction to her lectures while she was in England:

> Well, you know that the English people are very undemonstrative. At first everything I said was received in absolute silence, but I saw that their interest was intense. . . . What I told them about the negro lynchings in the South was received with incredulity. It was new to them, and they could not believe that human beings were hanged, shot, and burned in broad daylight, the legal authorities sometimes looking on. . . . They could not believe that these acts were done, not by savages, not by cannibals who at least would have had the excuse of providing themselves with something to eat, but by people calling themselves Christian, civilized American citizens.[15]

Ida B. Wells had anticipated a sceptical reaction and came well armed with evidence to support her argument that black people in the South were being systematically denied access to the same processes of law that were available to whites. All her examples came from Southern newspaper reports, so that no one could accuse her of exaggerating the details, and she had carefully recorded the circumstances of each incident to demonstrate that the lynch mobs were prepared to murder without a shred of evidence of any 'crime' committed.

Her audiences consisted 'of all classes, from the highest to the lowest' as she travelled round churches, social clubs, political and social reform gatherings, and even drawing-room meetings requested by 'fashionable ladies'. Like many of the African-American lecturers who had preceded her in the years before the Civil War, she was surprised to find that many white people in Britain, whatever their class background, were prepared to be receptive and sympathetic to her cause, in contrast to her experience at home. In the same interview in *The Sun*, Ida B. Wells was asked whether she encountered any race prejudice in Britain. According to the report she replied 'enthusiastically':

> No, it was like being born again in a new condition. Everywhere I was received on a perfect equality with the ladies who did so much for me and my cause. In fact, my color gave me some agreeable prominence which I might not otherwise have had. Fancy my feeling when in London I saw the Lady Mayoress taking a negro African Prince about at a garden party and evidently displaying him as the lion of the occasion.

In her autobiography Ida B. Wells expanded on the subject, describing her acquaintance with Ogontula Sapara, a young African medical student who volunteered to help with the campaign in 1894. He once visited her at her hotel in London, accompanied by six fellow-students, also from Africa: 'Such excitement you never saw, and several of the residents of the hotel said that they had never seen that many black people in their lives before'.[16] Sapara entertained Ida with stories of how some of his patients, who had never seen a black man, refused to let him touch them. But she was convinced that this was nothing compared to the hatred and prejudice she was accustomed to in America. Her enthusiasm, however, must be read as an index of the racism in the South rather than of the lack of it in Britain, where resident black people were all too aware of what Catherine Impey called 'the dark spirit of Caste, which so often lurks hidden behind the scenes'.[17]

## Ida B. Wells's Analysis

The press reports of Ida B. Wells's lectures and interviews during both her visits are witness to her remarkable ability to move her audiences to condemn racism. She evidently spoke quietly, which many found impressive, and was ready to draw on personal experience as well as presenting a carefully argued analysis of the failure of the American legal system to protect black people. Born into slavery in Mississippi in 1862, Ida grew up in the early days of the post-emancipation South, receiving an unusually comprehensive education in a college set up by the Freedmen's Aid. However, by the time she was twenty-two years old she had already been disillusioned of any ideals of equality for blacks under the law when she became the first person to contest newly introduced legislation permitting segregation on the railways. When she went to sit in the women's compartment of a first-class carriage she was ordered by the guard to remove herself to the smoking carriage. After a physical struggle in which she was virtually dragged out of the compartment, much to the delight of the white passengers, she left the train with her ticket intact and returned to Memphis to bring a suit against the railway company.

Her argument was that under the law, black people were permitted separate but equal accommodation on the trains, and that as there had been only one first-class carriage, she was entitled to sit in it. She won the first round and was awarded $500 damages, but the railway company appealed and the case was decided against Ida on the grounds that she had intended all along to harass the company and 'her persistence was not in good faith to obtain a comfortable seat for a short ride'.[18]

Ida B. Wells wrote in her diary:

> I felt so disappointed because I had hoped such great things for my people generally. I have firmly believed that the law was on our side and would, when we appealed to it, give us justice. I feel shorn of that belief and utterly discouraged, and just now, if it were possible, would gather my race in my arms and fly away with them.[19]

However disappointed Ida felt with the power of the law to protect black people in the South, she never lost her commitment to fighting for legal justice. Her politics became more sharply focused when she abandoned her career as a teacher and took over as editor of *Free Speech*, a black newspaper in Memphis. It was at this point in her life that she first turned her attention to lynching and its function in Southern society. In her autobiography she wrote that once she too had 'accepted the idea . . . that although lynching was irregular and contrary to law and order, unreasoning anger over the terrible crime of rape led to the lynching; that perhaps the brute deserved death anyhow and the mob was justified in taking his life'.[20] When, however, one of her best friends was murdered in cold blood with the sanction of the white establishment, she realized that the lynch law was becoming a primary means of controlling black social and economic life.

In her autobiography, Ida gives a detailed account of this incident, which was to change her life dramatically. Three black businessmen, Thomas Moss, Calvin MacDowell and Henry Stewart, were arrested after some white men were wounded in a street fight. Fearing more violence, the black community organized a guard outside the gaol where they were held for two nights. On the third night, a crowd of armed white men entered the police prison, took the three prisoners out and shot them a mile outside the town. One of the daily newspapers delayed its appearance in order to give full details of the lynching.

The men who died had opened a grocery shop in a crowded black suburb, threatening the custom of a white grocer who had until then had a monopoly in the neighbourhood. They were well known and liked in the community and news of their murder came as a terrible shock. A crowd gathered outside their shop, the People's Grocery Company, to talk about the incident, but there was no violence. However, when word came back to the courts that 'Negroes were massing', orders were given to the sheriff to take a hundred men and 'shoot down on sight any Negro who appears to be making trouble'. The white mob swarmed into the grocery, destroying what they could not eat or drink, while the black onlookers were forced to submit to all kinds of insults. A few days later the shop was closed by the creditors and the white grocer was able to continue his business without competition.

It was reported in the newspaper that the last words of Thomas Moss, a close friend of Ida B. Wells, who had pleaded with the murderers to spare him for the sake of his wife and unborn child, were, 'Tell my people to go West – there is no justice for them here.' Ida B. Wells's paper, *Free Speech*, urged people to take this advice, arguing that there was no protection for black people in Memphis if they dared to compete in business with whites. Within a few weeks there was a great exodus of black families from the city. White business was practically at a standstill as it relied heavily on black custom. Even the transport system was affected as people preferred to walk in order to save their money for the journey west. When anxious executives from the City Railway Company came to the offices of *Free Speech* to ask them to use their influence, Ida B. Wells wrote up the interview with them and urged readers to continue to keep their money for themselves. She then travelled out west herself, spending three weeks in Oklahoma reporting on the successes of the new settlers in order to counteract the fabrications of white newspapers in Memphis, which were now urging blacks to stay in the city. Immediately after this she accepted an invitation to speak at a conference in Philadelphia, and from there she intended to make a short trip to New York before returning to Memphis. On her arrival in New York she was greeted by the news that the white establishment in Memphis was out for her blood. Her paper had been closed down and orders had been given to punish with death anyone who tried to start it again. Her friends wrote to her warning her not even to consider returning as there were white men watching every train ready to kill her on sight. Ida knew that it was her support of the economic boycott that had driven the white authorities to try and suppress her paper, but it was the final editorial, published while she was in Philadelphia, that had provoked the mob to destroy her offices and to attempt to lynch her as well.

In the three months following the death of her friend, Ida B. Wells had thought a great deal about the way in which the white establishment was able to prevent black businesses from competing successfully. The law was totally inadequate in protecting blacks from intimidation and murder and, more than this, the highest figures of authority were frequently implicated in organizing this violence. Meanwhile the rest of the country condoned lynching because of a readiness to believe that it was a spontaneous outburst of revenge against black rapists and child molesters. Ida began to investigate reports of lynchings and discovered that in every incident in which white women were said to have been assaulted, the facts had actually been distorted out of recognition. There was almost no evidence to support the rape theory, except that in each case there was a white woman who had been found to have been associating with a black man of her own free will. In one example, the sheriff's seventeen-year-old daughter was traced to the cabin of one of her father's farm-hands, who was then lynched by the mob in order to salvage the young woman's reputation. The press reported that 'The big burly brute was lynched because he had raped the seven-year-old daughter of the sheriff.'

The final editorial of *Free Speech* was direct in its denunciation of this example of the notorious Southern chivalry:

> Eight Negroes lynched since last issue of *Free Speech*. Three were charged with killing white men and five with raping white women. Nobody in this section believes the old thread-bare lie that Negroes assault white women. If Southern white men are not careful they will over-reach themselves and a conclusion will be reached which will be very damaging to the moral reputation of their women.[21]

Following her exile to the North, Ida B. Wells expanded her theoretical observations, comparing the widespread rape and abuse of black women and girls by white men under slavery with the savagery they showed towards any white woman suspected of intimacy with a black man. She had become convinced that the Southerner had not recovered from the shock of losing his slaves and of seeing free black men and women working for themselves and enjoying their constitutional rights to education, voting and holding public office. The racism of the whites, constantly refined and developed as the economy of the South went into a severe depression following Reconstruction, invoked a hysterical fear of black male sexuality which made any contact between black men and white women a danger. If a black man so much as looked a white woman in the eye he risked being accused of lechery or insolence, and in some cases this was as good as committing an actual assault. As long as white women were seen to be the property of white men, without power or a voice of their own, their 'protectors' could claim to be justified in taking revenge for any alleged insult or attack on them. Whenever the reputation of white women was 'tainted' by the suggestion of immoral behaviour, it could always be saved by the charge that they had been victims of black lust.

Lynching was a way of reinforcing white supremacy by rule of terror. Black people had learned that any action that might cause annoyance to whites, however trivial, could provoke a violent reaction for which there was no redress in law; and the most plausible justification for this kind of violence was the prospect of the sexual assault of a white female by a black male. The young black woman's instigation of an economic boycott had been damaging enough to the white authorities in Memphis; her slur against the white womanhood of the South, implied in her last editorial, made her own lynching an inevitability if she dared to return home.

Ida B. Wells's analysis of the economic and political treatment of blacks in the post-Reconstruction South was received cautiously in the North, which prided itself on its comparative liberalism. The complacency which followed from abolishing slavery had led to a general apathy on matters of race while attitudes and behaviour towards black people had scarcely changed. However, she had just begun to make a name for herself when she was invited, through Frederick Douglass, to go to Britain in the hope of gaining a more sympathetic hearing.

## British Responses

In many ways, Ida B. Wells's audiences outside America were more shocked than those at home by her portrayal of Southern justice. The main hostility that she encountered came from those who thought that the British had no right to criticize Americans, especially over what appeared to be a complicated internal issue of law and order. *The Times* expressed this view in a scathing denunciation of the Anti-Lynching Committee, which had written to the governor of Alabama asking him to verify certain reports of lynching in that state. *The Times* had obtained a copy of the governor's reply which it used to illustrate its point. In a familiar tone, the paper's editorial professed to have no sympathy with lynching, and none with 'anti-lynching' either, portraying the committee as a 'large number of well-known Dissenters' who were meddling in affairs that had nothing to do with them:

> Nor do we suppose that those who are responsible for the unfortunate letter have the least suspicion that it was likely to be represented as a piece of officious impertinence. Burning with sympathy for the much trampled on negro, they betray no consciousness of the magnitude and delicacy of the problem in which they are intervening. We should not be surprised if the Anti-Lynching Committee's well-meant letter multiplied the number of negroes who are hanged, shot, and burnt by paraffin, not only in Alabama, but throughout the Southern states. This would be a bitter stroke of irony. But it is the fate which frequently attends a fanatical anxiety to impose our own canons of civilisation upon people differently circumstanced.[22]

In an attempt to be humorous the editorial paid almost as much attention to the grammar of both letters as to the content, even to the extent of suggesting that the committee's secretary, Florence Balgarnie, was in danger of being 'lynched by a mob of enraged grammarians'. It gave far greater space and weight to the governor's reply, and after proposing that this was not the occasion to discuss lynching itself, went on to display the very attitudes that condoned it. While condemning it as a form of race hatred, since it was only blacks who were being lynched, the writer then felt compelled to point out:

> . . . although the negro, it must be acknowledged, does something to justify such differential treatment by the frequency and atrocity of his outrages on white women. That is a circumstance which ought to weigh with Miss Balgarnie and the numerous ladies upon the Anti-Lynching Committee.

The Anti-Lynching Committee would not have been at all surprised by this reaction from *The Times* as it represented the most conservative sections of the ruling class. However, the facetious tone and arrogant racism that lay behind it could not obscure the point that it was hypocritical to criticize other countries for their standards of behaviour when comparable atrocities were being carried out nearer home. Just as pro-slavery agitators had claimed that the terrible conditions in Britain's growing industrial centres were far worse than those on most slave plantations, so the protagonists of American racism could point to the treatment of many of Britain's colonial subjects. The savage repression of the 1857 uprising in India, for example, was a case in point. British criticism of the handling of the 'race problem' in the South must have seemed continuous with their condemnation of slavery in the decade before the Civil War, and many resented both the interference and the tone of moral superiority that often accompanied it. In Britain it was indeed relatively easy to express horror at the way white Americans turned illegal executions into mass spectacles, but this outrage did not necessarily have the effect of challenging forms of racism that existed within the country and throughout the colonies.

On the other hand, as far as commentators like *The Times* were concerned, those who defended black people in America might as well be defending all blacks, whether in the Caribbean, India or Africa. By the late nineteenth century, theories of so-called scientific racism had sought to prove that all people with darker skin were biologically different from and inferior to whites. Serious uprisings in the Caribbean and in India had made these theories more attractive to those who supported the idea of the British Empire, which by now had been extended throughout Africa, Australia and the Indian subcontinent. Those who actively supported organizations like the Anti-Lynching Committee or the Society for the Recognition of the Universal Brotherhood of Man earned themselves the epithet 'nigger philanthropists' among those who believed in white supremacy. It was not surprising then that the anti-lynching campaign launched by Ida B. Wells brought together individuals from different backgrounds who were prepared to make connections between racism at home and abroad, and who realized their own responsibility to challenge it.

At the centre of this group of people, including the 'numerous ladies' referred to in *The Times* editorial, was the journal *Anti-Caste* and its editor, Catherine Impey. The name 'Anti-Caste' itself meant virtually the same as 'anti-racism', which might seem strangely modern for a period more commonly associated with jingoism. The paper was produced from Catherine Impey's house in Street, Somerset, on a monthly basis, with the help of her mother and sister, and sold for a nominal sum of a halfpenny to cover the cost of postage. It relied on subscriptions and donations for immediate support, though the main costs were borne personally by the editor.

Catherine Impey (1847–1923), on the right, with her sister Nellie

Catherine Impey's family and many of her subscribers belonged to the Society of Friends: Street was one of the largest Quaker communities in southern England. At its centre was the Clark shoe factory which was run by William Clark, also from a Quaker family. He was married to Helen Bright, who had retained many of her father's radical connections after he died, and who was part of a network of English feminists and philanthropists. Yet although Catherine Impey received a great deal of support from local Friends, little evidence of her work has survived and all her papers have disappeared without trace. The loss of her diaries is tragic as they would have contained so much information about the networks of anti-racist sympathizers, as well as more insights into Catherine herself. Apart from a few surviving letters and essays and invaluable personal recollections from friends and more distant relatives in Street who remember her towards the end of her life, the main sources of information about her are to be found in Ida B. Wells's autobiography and in *Anti-Caste*.

Catherine was an unusual woman, not just because of her commitment to what we would now call anti-racism, but because she made a conscious decision to remain independent and devote her life to various social and political causes. Her father, who ran a small business selling agricultural equipment, died when she was thirty-eight and Catherine was given the opportunity to carry on the family business. In a letter to a friend, however, she wrote that her sister had taken over the business, which allowed her to continue with her 'social reform' work, as she called it: 'I am very glad not to be obliged to work for my living, but it is a more serious matter than it seems to some – to deliberately choose a life of independence.'[23]

It is hard to do more than speculate on Catherine's early political influences. Judging from the support her mother gave her, and the number of local names and addresses on her early subscription lists, she seems to have been part of a network of politically sympathetic families, many of whom were Quakers who had been active in the anti-slavery movement. In the first issue of *Anti-Caste* she wrote that she believed all arbitrary distinctions between people to be 'contrary to the mind of Christ', and that 'of all such distinctions the meanest and most cruelly irritating to the victims are those which are based purely upon *physical* characteristics – sex, race, complexion, nationality – in fact, form or deformity of any kind'. In the tradition of most Victorian philanthropists she relied on the power of religious language to express her own views on what she felt to be right and wrong, and biblical references and quotations permeated her writing. But although she referred to all kinds of discrimination and oppression as 'evil', she was also quite specific about what she meant. At the beginning of her fourth year as editor she wrote:

> While Religion teaches men that God is the Father of *all*, that we are all 'brethren', that of 'one blood hath He made all nations of men for to *dwell together*', the 'Father of Lies' goes up and down in the world, teaching that the God of Heaven created separate races of men, to dwell apart – separated

> from each other, that a fair skin is always superior to a dark one, that fellowship between differing races is contrary to man's nature, that the strong should *compel* the submission of the weak, crushing and if necessary, exterminating those who resist. From such a doctrine spring the horrors, whose echoes reach us from all quarters of the Globe, from Central Africa, to ice-bound Siberia, from the United States with her slaughtered Indian babes and women and her down-trodden millions of dark-hued workers, to thoughtful cultured India under the heel of British militarism, from the Australian forests, to the islands of the Southern Seas.[24]

Apart from equality between the races, Catherine Impey's ideal of human brotherhood included the abolition of the alcohol traffic, an end to militarism, a respect for the environment and the humane treatment of animals – she was also a strict vegetarian. She often wrote about these issues in the 'Village Album', a monthly collection of essays and correspondence kept by the Quaker community in Street. In the last twenty years of her life she became a Poor Law Guardian, though sadly very little is known about this period of her life. Her obituary in the Quaker journal, *The Friend*, remembered how her 'warm and generous sympathies had ever been at the service of the many interests to which she was wholeheartedly devoted'. 'Nevertheless,' it continued, it was 'the colour question, which enlisted her closest sympathy, and on which she held deep convictions in her consistent advocacy of equal rights for the white and coloured people.'[25]

By the time she founded *Anti-Caste*, Catherine Impey had already visited the USA three times, and had made important contacts with black writers, clergy and teachers. Among those she listed as her personal acquaintances in the first issue of her journal were Frederick Douglass, Amanda Smith (a preacher who passed through England on her way to Africa), Judge Albion Tourgee, author of the first novel to deal with Reconstruction, Thomas Fortune, editor of the *New York Freeman* and an influential figure in black politics, Fanny Jackson Coppin, President of the Institute of Coloured Youth In Philadelphia, and Frances E. Harper, head of the black women's section of the Women's Christian Temperance Union, and with Coppin and four other black women, a speaker at the World's Congress of Representative Women, which was held as part of the Colombian Exposition in Chicago in 1893.[26] Many of these friends kept up a correspondence with Catherine which must have given her great encouragement: 'My friend and sister,' wrote Frances E. Harper, 'permit me to say go on with your work in the name of Him who honoured our common humanity by respecting it.'[27]

Catherine Impey also relied upon friends and contacts throughout the Empire to supply her with information. She was particularly concerned about the situation in India – both the exploitation of workers on tea plantations and of the state of the nationalist movement. In one issue she wrote: 'We are sure the comfortable tea-drinking public little knows at what a cost of human lives their cheap tea is procured.'[28] She went on to describe the conditions under which the coolies of the Assam tea gardens were forced to work, comparing the abuse of the system to slavery in America and the West Indies. Quoting an article in the *Indian Messenger* which claimed that many of the British did not regard Indians 'as in any way superior to lower animals', Catherine agreed: 'This is strongly put, but it is undoubtedly the feeling of many of our Indian fellow-subjects. And what wonder! when race prejudice is manifested towards their converts even by the men to whom has been entrusted the solemn responsibility of introducing the Christian religion in the East.' She then cited a new book that exposed the corrupt behaviour of missionaries in India, given to her by a 'Christian working man'. His own verdict of the book had been that 'if this is the state of affairs . . . I feel I should be doing God's service more by circulating this work, than by contributing to the Missionary Society.'[29]

Reports from Australia, the Caribbean, South America, Africa, China – wherever the British or white Americans were responsible for injustices – appeared regularly, although Catherine Impey was careful to keep her journal short ' so that it may be read even by busy people'. She was also quick to condemn racism in England itself, most notably when Lord Salisbury, the prime minister, referred to Indians as 'black men'. Although his remarks were given wide publicity in the press, and he was forced to apologize by Queen Victoria, Salisbury had evidently felt he was expressing a view held privately by many others. Catherine pointed out that it was this underlying racism which was as much a problem as its open manifestation: 'On the whole we feel somewhat glad that the dark spirit of Caste, which so often lurks hidden behind the scenes – the prompter of so many a cowardly and bloody act on the part of our rulers – for once allowed his face to be openly seen.' This was followed by a long extract from another paper, the *Pall Mall Gazette*, which attributed Salisbury's use of the phrase to a 'certain mental defect . . . which is probably the direct result of his aristocratic training'. His sneer at darker-skinned people would not have been felt as much if whites had not dominated them: 'The white man is the aristocrat of the world, and he sums up his superiority in his own estimation when he sneers at the blackamoor, and the taunt goes all the more surely home because the darker-skinned man is more or less in subjection.'[30]

Apart from providing her readers with information, Catherine Impey was also adamant that *Anti-Caste* should be a space for black writers to 'present their case'.[31] She advertised and often supplied pamphlets written by black men and women, and reprinted extracts from black newspapers or even letters sent to her personally. Educational achievements were of particular interest and when visitors like Hallie Quinn Brown came to Britain to raise funds for schools and universities for black children in America, she gave them her full support.

From reading *Anti-Caste* over the eight years it was published, it is clear that Catherine Impey's own political vision was continually developing, particularly as a result of her contact with black activists such as Ida B. Wells and Frederick Douglass. This is illustrated most forcefully by the alterations she made to the subtitle of her paper. *Anti-Caste* began life as a journal 'devoted to the interests of coloured races'. Some eighteen months later this masthead was amended to: 'Advocates the brotherhood of mankind irrespective of colour or descent'. The editorial explained the reasons for the change:

> True, it has been, as it said from the first: 'devoted to the interests of coloured races' but that declaration of its object imperfectly indicated the standpoint from which those interests were treated. Among the aristocracy of Europe, thousands are 'devoted to the interests of' the working classes. Alas! few are there who 'advocate the *brotherhood*' of rich and poor as the basis of their 'devotion'. 'Anti-Caste' advocates the brotherhood of Mankind irrespective of colour or descent. Its purpose, however feebly fulfilled, is to awaken in the breasts of others some of that aching sense of wounded love that should stir a brother's or sister's heart, in view of the shameless cruelty under which the most defenseless of God's family on earth are being helplessly crushed. Our money they do not need, though they are poor; nor our patronage, nor cheap condescension . . .[32]

Six years later, in the final year of its publication, the subtitle changed again. As a result of a personal rift between Isabella Mayo and herself,

Catherine Impey may have felt obliged to clarify her aims still further. She wrote that *Anti-Caste* now 'Assumes the brotherhood of the entire human family, and claims for the dark races of Mankind their equal right to protection, personal liberty, equality of opportunity and human fellowship'.[33]

Shortly after this the journal ceased publication altogether, and we can only speculate on the reasons for this. One, almost certainly, was that Hannah Impey, Catherine' s mother, became ill in 1895 and died within a few months. She had always been supportive of her daughter's activities and it is likely that Catherine would have missed her intensely, especially because her sister Nellie suffered from ill-health as well. But there was another reason for *Anti-Caste*'s demise – one which accounted also for a gap in publication the previous year. Catherine's passionate belief in the equality of black and white led to a situation that jeopardized the whole anti-lynching campaign in Britain, and exposed a range of different attitudes towards questions of race, gender and sexuality.

## Femininity and the 'Female Accusation'

Scarcely one month after she had arrived in Britain, Ida B. Wells witnessed what she later described as one of the most painful scenes of her life.[34] During the two weeks which she had spent in Aberdeen with Isabella Mayo and Catherine Impey preparing for the campaign, she wrote that she had very much enjoyed the 'atmosphere of equality, culture, refinement, and devotion to the cause of the oppressed darker races'. The three women were helped by Isabella's lodgers, one of whom was George Ferdinands, a dental student from Ceylon, as it was known then, who had trained and qualified while in Aberdeen under his host's patronage. The tour began when Ida accompanied Isabella Mayo on a visit of Scottish towns and cities while Catherine went ahead to prepare the way in northern England. Soon after she had left Scotland, Catherine wrote to George Ferdinands proposing marriage, and he professed to be so shocked by her letter that he forwarded it immediately to his benefactor. Ida was shown the letter by a scandalized Isabella Mayo, who more or less ordered her to denounce Catherine at once. Catherine was summoned and asked to explain herself.

In the offending letter, Catherine had declared that she 'returned the affection' that she was sure Ferdinands felt for her and that she was taking the initiative because she knew he hesitated to do so, being 'of a darker race'. She had already written to her family announcing her intention of marrying him and saying that she 'rejoiced to give this proof to the world of the theories she had approved – the equality of the brotherhood of man'. Catherine was at this time forty-five years old, an age at which hopes of marriage for a single Victorian woman would have receded. According to a cousin she was once engaged to a member of the Clark family in her home town, but the marriage was called off, possibly for financial reasons.[35] However, there is no evidence that she ever expressed regret at not having a husband and, as we have seen, was positive about the independent life she felt she had chosen. George Ferdinands, about whom we know next to nothing, apparently 'revered' Catherine for her work on India, but never dreamed of her in any romantic connection. It is hard to believe that Catherine would have made the proposal without any encouragement, and the whole episode remains a mystery. However, what is very clear is that for Isabella Mayo, her colleague's behaviour was completely unacceptable. She insisted that Catherine was a disgrace to the movement and that she was 'the type of maiden lady who used such work as an opportunity to meet and make advances to men'. Ida recalled that Mayo even called Catherine a nymphomaniac, and demanded the destruction of the edition of *Anti-Caste* which had their name as joint editors. Catherine, who was devastated, was evidently no match for the older woman's 'scorn and withering sarcasm'.

Having been forced by Isabella to choose between them, Ida spent a sleepless night 'praying for guidance'. Although she felt that Catherine had been mistaken in acting so impulsively, she had not committed any crime by falling in love and was certainly not likely to do it again. Moreover, she had already proved by her work that she was genuinely concerned about equality and justice for black people and Ida was not prepared to desert her just to appease Isabella Mayo. She also knew it would be impossible to explain to people at home, who had immense respect for Catherine Impey and her work, why she had abandoned her. She begged Mayo to change her mind, but, 'stern upright Calvinistic Scotchwoman that she was', she cast the two women 'into outer darkness' and Ida never saw her again.

In spite of being humiliated by Isabella Mayo, Catherine refused to withdraw from the work. She accompanied Ida on a tour of Newcastle, Birmingham and Manchester, arranging interviews with newspapers to obtain maximum publicity. They then returned to Street to plan the next stage of the itinerary. Isabella Mayo, who had tried to prevent Ida from continuing with her engagements, insisted that if she went to London she must at least be escorted by a more 'suitable' companion. The alternative was presumably that Mayo would publish scurrilous reports of Catherine's behaviour which would cast a bad light on Ida. Mayo had already sent details to her friends in America, criticizing Ida's behaviour and denouncing Catherine. Ida attended a few meetings in London in May of that year and then returned home, leaving her friend full of bitterness and self-reproach that the tour had ended without more success.

In her autobiography, Ida B. Wells explained that she had only written about the episode to remove any misunderstandings that might have arisen. She remained friends with Catherine for several years, inviting her to her wedding in 1895 and having her pamphlets distributed from Catherine's home address. In subsequent meetings she often referred to Catherine's work, expressing 'the gratitude of the colored races' to her for her efforts.[36] It seems that the quarrel, which, as I shall explain shortly, continued to disrupt the unity of the campaign, also affected Ida's relationship with Frederick Douglass, to whom Mayo wrote complaining about Ida's ingratitude towards her English hosts. But however difficult it is to piece together the narrative, the subject matter of the dispute raises intriguing questions about the politics of race, gender and sexuality. What exactly was the nature of the crime that Catherine Impey had committed in Isabella Mayo's eyes? Was it that she dared to proposition a man, or that she was attracted to a black man? In other words, did she transgress the accepted bounds of her gender or was it her racial identity that she betrayed? The evidence suggests that it was probably both. And what was the significance of Ida, a black woman, supporting Catherine, and what does this imply about her sexual politics? Possible answers to these questions emerged more clearly as the anti-lynching campaign gathered pace.

Shortly after Ida B.Wells returned to America, the anti-lynching campaign was relaunched, a feat which Mayo credited to her own efforts. She enlisted the help of a Caribbean writer and editor called Celestine Edwards who agreed to take over the leadership of the newly formed Society for the Recognition of the Universal Brotherhood of Man. In July 1893, Edwards launched a new paper called *Fraternity*, which was to be its mouthpiece. The aim of the society, which Edwards explained in his first editorial, was 'to direct its attention to the work of removing inequality and wrongs from races, whom we feel sure will, with greater opportunity and freedom, do as much credit to themselves as any nation in Europe'. *Fraternity*'s format was very similar to that of *Anti-Caste*, with editorials, letters, information about events in India, Africa or America, prayers, poems – anything thought to be relevant to the cause of abolishing racism.

If Mayo hoped that Catherine would be snubbed by the revitalized society, she was mistaken, for Edwards had clearly been an admirer of *Anti-Caste* for some time and knew its editor personally. His attitude towards Catherine Impey bears out her reputation in Britain and America as a serious political crusader. The first sentence of his new paper read:

> For years one has been longing for the opportunity to plead the cause of the oppressed and helpless, and when we first came into contact with *Anti-Caste* years ago, we thought that there was at least a prospect of helping those who were actually doing a work which our own experience (in all the countries in which the work of this Society will extend) convinced us was very much indeed. For more than six years *Anti-Caste* has been doing a quiet work in England, slowly but surely permeating society, and winning the hearts of good men and true women to the cause of the struggling helpless races in America, India, Africa, and Australia, and wherever tribes, races, and nations have been oppressed by the accursed enemy of mankind – Caste.[37]

Edwards was born in Dominica, the youngest of nine children, but had settled in England in the 1870s when he was in his late teens. By that time he had become a convinced Christian and a champion of the temperance movement. He quickly made a name for himself, campaigning first in Scotland and then all over England. He was a popular speaker, and used to draw crowds of over a thousand at his public meetings. At the time when he was approached by Mayo to front the SRUBM he was editing another magazine, *Lux*, which was a 'weekly Christian Evidence Newspaper' that frequently expressed the same anti-imperialist views as *Fraternity*. In one editorial Edwards wrote that 'the British Empire will come to grief unless it changes its methods of dealing with the aboriginal races.' He went on to warn that 'the day is coming when Africans will speak for themselves. . . . The day is breaking and . . . the despised African, whose only crime is his colour, will yet give an account of himself.'[38]

Whether or not Edwards knew what had caused the rift between Catherine Impey and Isabella Mayo, we shall never know, but he obviously attempted to steer a middle course between them. He relied heavily on

Catherine's help with contributions for *Fraternity*; for a few months both editors continued to publish their own journals, until *Anti-Caste* temporarily suspended publication in 1894 and Catherine donated all her material to Edwards. Another example of Catherine's continuing involvement, and of her undamaged reputation, was given during the weeks that followed Ida B. Wells's visit. The second edition of *Fraternity*, published in August 1893, carried a report of a meeting in Newcastle where 'thousands' gathered to hear Edwards lecture on 'Black and White in America'. The chairman, who had been a missionary in Jamaica, opened the proceedings by giving a 'high testimony to the earnest zeal of Miss C. Impey . . . the originator of the society, who, almost unaided, has carried on the work up to the present time'.

Isabella Mayo was continually frustrated in her attempts to dissociate the campaign from Catherine Impey. When Edwards died of illness and exhaustion in 1894, she took the opportunity in writing his obituary of giving a revised version of his leadership. She explained how he had been

> hampered by a small clique, who had gained some footing in the society, even in the brief interval which necessarily elapsed between the first startling appearance of difficulty and Mr Celestine Edwards' obtaining power to grapple with it. The object of this clique has been to force upon the society's councils a person of admitted mental instability – the victim of 'hallucination' – one, too, who on being expostulated with on the matter, had given promises of absolute withdrawal from active and official relations with the society, which promises were immediately afterwards broken.[39]

This 'clique' to which Mayo referred consisted of Catherine and her friends and supporters who had apparently taken control of the society by unconstitutional means soon after Edwards left the country in a desperate attempt to recover his health. They had been helped by the fact that Edwards had not managed to find time to record the preliminary sessions, according to Mayo, who resolved to keep control of the journal until the society was again in the hands of a properly elected council.

Edwards's greatest achievement as leader of the SRUBM was to organize a second tour for Ida B. Wells, who returned in March 1894 and stayed for several months. Mayo still refused to have anything to do with her, so it is quite likely that Catherine Impey instigated the tour, even if she was to keep a lower profile this time. During Ida's visit, which was followed closely in the pages of *Fraternity*, Mayo took the opportunity to publish her most damning indictment of Catherine's behaviour in order to humiliate her into silence. It was deliberately published next to Ida's final report, shortly after Edwards had been forced to give up work as editor. Headed 'The Female Accusation', it is worth quoting at length, partly because it reveals more about its writer than its intended victim, but mainly because it throws more light on the nature of the quarrel between the two women:

> Seeing the frequency of 'female accusation' in the case of the lynched negroes, too little attention seems to have been given to certain morbid peculiarities well known to medical men and matrons of experience. There are women who will 'fancy' anything which will give them a sensation and a little passing notoriety. In wild countries, where terrible crimes will occasionally occur, such diseased imaginations will fasten upon these, and imagine a criminal and an attempted crime in any innocent stranger. Under happier social circumstances the morbid egotists may only imagine that 'men fall in love with them'. Be it remembered that even this 'imagination', if indulged in by a 'white woman', regarding a 'nigger' in some of the States, would mean *the death of the man*, perhaps the more ignominious death, if he ventured to say in self-defence that the 'imagination' was wholly baseless, or must have been derived from some of the natural and proper civilities paid by youth and strength to age and manifest infirmity. For it must be noted that female sufferers from this diseased egotism are not necessarily young and flighty. They are often elderly, dowdy, and disappointed. Nor are they invariably recognised by their nearest connections as fit objects for pity and care. Their friends often leave them to wander among unsuspecting strangers, heedless of the annoyance and hindrance they give. Such kinsfolk are ready enough to crave for mercy and to plead hereditary mental affliction and general weakness, and instability, if even from this unfortunate woman's own statements they think she is likely to get *herself* into serious trouble; but they are prepared to recall all their words *when only the interests of others, or even of great public causes, are concerned*!
>
> We have just risen from perusal of the documents in a strikingly typical case of this kind, in which all the points of diseased vanity, prurient insinuation, and the self-contradictory selfishness of 'kinsfolk' are strongly brought out.[40]

Isabella Mayo's continued assertion that Catherine had behaved in a way that would have caused a lynching in the Southern states must have been extraordinarily wounding – it was intended to be so. After a plea to all sensible men and women to avoid 'these poor creatures', Mayo suggested that the sufferer should retire for the sake of her mental health: 'And can anything be more wholesome for this complaint (which in its earliest stages is, as the best lunacy authorities assert, simply vanity and the basest egotism), that the knowledge that the active outbreak of these symptoms will leave the sufferer to "go softly" all her days'.

Mayo's parting shot gives an interesting slant on her understanding of the lynching question:

> If the women in the South were all 'pure in heart and sound in head', we should hear of fewer lynchings; and if British philanthropy, whenever forewarned gently set aside the dubious help of these diseased imaginations . . . many good works which now flag and falter, would go on apace.

This suggests a conservative approach both to women's sexuality and to the question of race. Her use of the phrase 'pure in heart' implies that it was not acceptable for women to take an active role in relations with men. This was a conventional attitude towards female sexuality which was shared by many women – feminists and non-feminists alike. The idea that madness contributed to white women's attraction to black men is harder to interpret. Possibly Mayo meant that in a climate hostile to interracial relationships a woman would have to be 'unsound in head' to risk the consequences both to herself and to her lover. I find it strange that her argument is at odds with Ida B. Wells's analysis of the situtation in the South, and this suggests to me that her motives for backing the anti-lynching campaign had been different from Catherine's from the start.[41]

Isabella Mayo wrote as though it was the immoral and irresponsible behaviour of white women which contributed to the increase of lynching, taking a moralistic view of the activities of actual women. It was true, as Ida frequently pointed out, that friendships between black men and white women were often initiated by the woman, and that it was invariably the man who was punished as a result. Instead of blaming white women for immorality, her demand was that such voluntary relationships should be allowed to exist in the open, just as they were between white men and white women, and that if there was any element of coercion, the guilty party should be brought to trial according to the law of the land. In other words, Ida B. Wells was not interested in criticizing the behaviour of the white women who were implicated in lynchings; her argument was based on a perception of white womanhood as an ideological component of American racism. The 'sacred convention that white women can never feel passion of any sort, high or low, for a black man' was, in her eyes, incompatible with the evidence she had collected during her research. This conviction helps to explain her decision to support Catherine who, she thought, had made a mistake but not committed a crime. The ultimate significance of this episode is that it dramatized important aspects of Ida B. Wells's analysis of lynching. By exposing Isabella Mayo's conservative views on female sexuality which were expressed in response to Catherine Impey's unorthodox feminine behaviour, it forced a division between the two women who had made the campaign possible in the first place.

By the time Ida B. Wells returned to Britain in 1894, she had collected even more statistics and had sharpened her arguments to show that whites were deceiving only themselves in their efforts to 'protect' their women. Much of this information was contained in a pamphlet called *United States Atrocities* which was published in Britain during her second trip. Celestine Edwards wrote an introduction in which he tried to explain the reasons for Southern racism:

> The *real* cause lies, not in the Negro's fondness to outrage white women, but in the fact that slavery was abolished by force – physical force, and without compensation to the slaveholder. . . . Besides, the white man, who boasts of superior mental power, must know that the immoral tendencies which he attributes to the Negro of today is greatly due to himself, because for three hundred years he kept him like a horse and bred him as a pig.[42]

During Ida B. Wells's second visit, her forthright speeches on Southern hypocrisy – in particular her insistence on the active participation of white women in sexual relationships with black men – led her into another controversy, which, involving other women as well, eclipsed the one between Catherine Impey and Isabella Mayo. What began as a personal dispute between Ida B. Wells and Frances Willard, a famous American women's rights campaigner, soon emerged as a bitter confusion of ideas about female sexuality and race. Although the argument took place in the context of American politics, it was significant that it was first publicly aired in Britain. This next section will explain how the controversy came about and explore its implications for women's politics on both sides of the Atlantic.

## The Dispute between Ida B. Wells and Frances Willard

It was pure coincidence that Frances Willard, the world-famous leader of the Women's Christian Temperance Union (WCTU), was staying in England at the same time as Ida B. Wells. She was an extremely charismatic speaker and an astute organizer, who left her home in the United States in order to rest from the relentless campaigning that had begun to undermine her health. She stayed as a permanent guest of Lady Henry Somerset, the aristocratic leader of the British Women's Temperance Association, and the two women shared a close friendship and a mutual influence which earned them criticism from their respective organizations. Their alliance was further proof of the close political exchanges between different movements in Britain and America.

Frances Willard held a complex and contradictory set of political ideas which reflected many of the changing beliefs about women's place in the nineteenth-century Western world, and her influential life and work has been studied by several historians of this period.[43] In accordance with the dominant theory of gender relations, she believed that women were by nature more moral than men, which meant that their influence within the public world was both necessary and desirable. Like many of her contemporaries she attributed women's subordination to their childbearing role and general sexual subservience, aggravated by men's propensity for alcohol. She summed up her philosophy in the phrase 'a white life for two', a symbolic crusade for sexual abstinence between married couples, which would give women time and energy to become independent while allowing men to become more acquainted with domestic roles. However, this critique of masculinity did not involve rejecting the traditional male-dominated family structure which continued to be one of the mainstays of society.

According to Barbara Leslie Epstein, the WCTU was not strictly a feminist organization, because its aim was to reform society through promoting higher morality, rather than to raise women to equal status with men. As she documents in her book *The Politics of Domesticity*, however, the temperance movement overlapped with many other social reform movements of the time, including feminism and socialism. Many women who belonged to suffrage organizations shared the conviction of WCTU members that women were naturally better equipped than men to reform society. It was thought that only by allowing women access to the vote and to public office would the interests of the family be represented and a relative balance between the sexes restored. Frances Willard was also committed to the labour movement in the United States, which supported the idea of equal pay and employment for men and women. During her stay in England, she was introduced to the Fabian Society by Lady Henry Somerset, and became a member. She is reported to have said that if she were ten years younger she would have devoted her life to socialism.

In the view of the WCTU, all social evils could be linked to the consumption of alcohol, a view which enabled its members to sympathize with other social reform movements. Under the leadership of Frances Willard the organization's horizons expanded significantly. She considered that the temperance movement was the appropriate place to develop her arguments for greater political power for women; using her platform at the head of the WCTU, she persuaded members to link the demand for women's suffrage to the campaign for 'Home Protection' and social purity.

In Britain the concerns of the temperance movement were much narrower. It was not a cause particularly associated with feminism, although many feminists felt strongly about the prohibition of alcohol. However, Lady Henry Somerset was entirely won over by Frances Willard's strategies, and together the two women attempted to force the suffrage issue on to a most unwilling membership. The majority were not only conservative in their beliefs and not interested in participating in public life to any extent, they also greatly resented interference from an American. Even those who were involved in more progressive women's politics, such as Helen Bright Clark, who was also a friend of Susan B. Anthony and Elizabeth Cady Stanton, tried to suggest to Frances Willard that she restrict her influence. In reply to a letter from Helen Bright Clark, Frances Willard wrote:

> Thank you for your kind letter and suggestions. Be assured that I have not meant to intrude. . . . My reception from the religious, temperance, and philanthropic guilds in the beloved 'mother country' has been so generous that I may have overestimated the friendliness of temperance women but 'in the long run' I am quite sure we shall be warmly appreciative, mutually, and misunderstandings will be cleared away.[44]

Frances Willard was in England for nearly two years, much to the annoyance of the members of the WCTU in America. During this time she gave many lectures throughout the country, captivating audiences by her brilliant performances. When Ida B. Wells arrived in Britain on her first tour in 1893, many of those who came to hear her talk were anxious to know if Frances Willard, as a prominent American speaking on moral issues, had condemned lynching. Ida B. Wells, who always made the point that silence amounted to consent, felt particularly angry about Frances Willard, having read an interview with her in the New York *Voice* in which she practically condoned lynching. Not having a copy of the paper, she was unable to substantiate this charge, but she never mentioned the temperance organizer's name unless asked specifically about her. On her second visit, however, she came prepared with the evidence because she felt it was an example of the way that lynching was continually misunderstood by Northern liberals. The interview, given in October 1890, was printed under the heading: 'The Race Problem: Frances Willard on the Political Puzzle of the South'. It began with Willard claiming not to have 'an atom of race prejudice', having been born an abolitionist and believing that it was the colour of the heart, not of the skin, that settled a human being's status. Her argument was that whites in the South would never consent to real equality with blacks, and that the best way for black people to develop themselves freely was to return to Africa:

> If I were black and young, no steamer could revolve its wheels fast enough to convey me to the dark continent. I should go where my color was the correct thing, and leave these pale faces to work out their own destiny.[45]

However, it was not the idea of repatriation which annoyed Ida B. Wells – though she had fundamental political disagreements with those who proposed it, black and white – but the reasons that Frances Willard gave for the 'race problem'. It was her belief that rather than giving all men the vote after emancipation, there should have been an educational qualification. In the interview she portrayed the majority of blacks as illiterate, ignorant alcoholics who multiply 'like the locusts of Egypt'. Her sympathy was for the Southerner who was mostly 'kindly intentioned towards the coloured man', but who had an 'immeasurable' problem on his hands. Willard also managed to convey the idea that white women were particularly at risk from marauding drunk black men – which was the very point that was always made to justify lynching.

The opinions expressed in the interview were not at all unusual, as they represented the standard white Northern American attitude towards what they perceived to be the social problems of the South. Many of those who thought of themselves as progressive shared the same views. Frances Willard's politics are of particular interest to us because her beliefs about women's safety and black sexuality which she revealed in the *Voice* interview overlapped with claims made by some leading American feminists. The early women's rights movement, which had developed out of and alongside the anti-slavery campaigns, moved sharply away from alliances with black men and women almost immediately after slavery was abolished. Whereas at one time the rights of black slaves and of women had been seen to be interconnected, political pressures forced abolitionists, black and white, male and female, to narrow their objectives in the struggle for the vote.[46] This brought about bitter divisions between those who supported universal suffrage and those who saw the necessity for enfranchising black men to protect them from the repercussions of abolition and who feared that too broad a demand would jeopardize all their chances. Within a short space of time, many younger white women who became involved in the movement for women's suffrage in the second half of the nineteenth century had become convinced that their rights should come before those of former slaves, and that women's interests would only be hindered by being linked to the demands of black people. At the heart of this belief was the fear that white women needed protection from black men. Elizabeth Cady Stanton, formerly a passionate abolitionist, made this very argument when the debates over the strategy of demanding votes for both women and blacks came to a head after emancipation. In an article that railed against male abolitionists for their failure to support universal suffrage, Stanton declared that just as women had had no protection from the laws and institutions made by 'Saxon' men, it was even more likely that when black men were enfranchised they would be victims of even worse treatment. Quoting a case of child abuse in which a young white girl gave birth to a black child and then strangled it herself, she asked:

> With judges and jurors of negroes, remembering the generations of wrong and injustice their daughters have suffered at white men's hands, how will Saxon girls fare in the courts for crimes like this?[47]

By 1890 this quite specific fear of black men's desire for revenge after years of subjugation had become a fundamental aspect of American racism.

With the increasing numbers of European, non-English-speaking immigrants into the United States, many middle-class, urban feminists extended this hostility towards black men to a general mistrust and hatred of 'aliens'. As we have already seen, those who believed that women were morally superior were antagonistic towards men generally. But while all male sexuality was potentially threatening to all women, it was black and working-class men who represented the threat at its most uncontrollable and frightening.

Frances Willard was merely repeating conventional Northern prejudices in her interview, and like thousands of others was probably unaware that she was supporting the torture and murder of innocent black men in the name of protecting white women. As far as she was concerned, the threatening behaviour of the 'ignorant and illiterate' was due to their consumption of alcohol, and she portrayed them as victims of the liquor trade, the source of most social problems. While on the one hand she attempted to cover herself in the *Voice* interview by saying that 'neither by voice or by pen have I ever condoned, much less defended any injustice towards the coloured people', on the other she insisted that it was wrong to give the vote to black people and to 'alien illiterates, who rule our cities today with the saloon as their palace, and the toddy stick as their scepter'. Under her leadership the WCTU established numerous departments to deal with specific areas of work, and one of the least contentious was that for Temperance Work among Negroes and Foreigners. But the views she expressed in her interview and the way she was to defend herself against the charge that she condoned lynching only served to illustrate Ida B. Wells's point that most white Americans were quite indifferent to the fate of black people in the South.

On her return to Britain in 1894, Ida B. Wells was soon obliged to produce her evidence against Frances Willard, and so she took the opportunity of publishing part of the New York interview in *Fraternity* together with an explanation. As a result she came up against the combined anger of both Willard and Lady Henry Somerset, and the latter threatened to use her influence to stop Ida from giving any more public lectures in Britain. Ida found herself in a very vulnerable position, which she later described in her autobiography:

> Here were two prominent white women, each in her own country at the head of a great national organisation, with undisputed power and influence in

> every section of their respective countries, seeming to have joined hands in the effort to crush an insignificant coloured woman who had neither money nor influence nor following – nothing but the power of truth to fight her battles.[48]

Two weeks after the edition of *Fraternity* appeared, the *Westminster Gazette* which called itself the 'leading London afternoon daily', carried a lengthy interview of Frances Willard by none other than her close friend Lady Henry Somerset. Rather than retracting or apologizing for her remarks made in the American paper, Frances Willard went on to repeat the same assertions:

> I ought to add that which I had been told by the best people I knew in the South – and I knew a great many ministers, editors and home people – that the safety of women, of children, is menaced in a thousand localities so that the men dare not go beyond the sight of their own roof trees.[49]

This time, however, Frances Willard was careful to add that there was 'no crime however heinous (that) can by any possibility excuse the commission of any act of cruelty or the taking of any human life without due course of law'.

One of the most remarkable things about the interview between the two temperance leaders in the *Westminster Gazette* was the patronizing tone in which they spoke about their adversary. In the introduction, Lady Henry Somerset presented Ida B. Wells as a victim of her own race prejudice by using, out of context, a remark she had made in another newspaper interview. On that occasion Ida had been asked by the editor about her own racial origins; her reply had been characteristically direct:

> Taint, indeed! I tell you, if I have any taint to be ashamed of in myself, it is the taint of *white* blood![50]

The editor, who published a sympathetic piece condemning lynching on the front and inside pages, began his interview with Ida's retort, though it was clear it was made in response to a question. Somerset, however, quoted it as an example of Ida B. Wells's racism towards whites, and then set it against her statement in *Fraternity* that 'There was no movement being made by American white Christians toward aiding public sentiment against lynch law in the United States.' After this attempt to portray the black American woman as a troublemaker, she then explained how she decided to hear Frances Willard's point of view: 'I therefore sought the first opportunity of a quiet hour with her under the trees of my garden at Reigate.' The conversation began with an attempt to be humorous, a point to which Ida B. Wells was quick to draw attention in her reply. Frances Willard adopted a slightly aggrieved tone when asked about Ida's accusations, adding that when she had first heard that she was in the country, she had tried to help her, 'for I believe in the fraternity of nations and that we ought to help each other to a higher plane by mutual influence'. The interview ended with both women agreeing that it was most unfair for Ida B. Wells to have 'misconstrued' remarks made by Willard in an interview that had 'nothing to do with lynching', and it appealed to British justice to trust her reputation.

As it happened, Ida B. Wells believed that the way the two influential women joined forces publicly to denounce her only served to her advantage. She wrote later that the attack was a 'boomerang' to Frances Willard and that it seemed to appeal to the British sense of fair play. Her reply to the interview, which sliced through its condescending and complacent tone, was published in the same paper the following day:

> The interview published in your columns yesterday hardly merits a reply, because of the indifference to suffering manifested. Two ladies are represented sitting under a tree at Reigate, and, after some preliminary remarks on the terrible subject of lynching, Miss Willard laughingly replies by cracking a joke. And the concluding sentence of the interview shows the object is not to determine best how they may help the Negro who is being hanged, shot and burned, but 'to guard Miss Willard's reputation'.[51]

Ida B. Wells's letter showed no mercy to the famous American woman. She ignored the personal attacks made on her own integrity, pointing out that it was not her reputation at stake, but the life of her people. The additional evidence that she gave of Frances Willard's supposed commitment to black people was particularly damning. Why, she asked, had Willard sat in silence when she had placed a resolution condemning lynching in front of two national meetings of the British Women's Temperance Association? In suggesting an answer to her question, Ida B. Wells introduced ammunition against Willard which was probably more damaging to her in the eyes of her British followers:

> I should say it was because as president of the Women's Christian Temperance Union of America she is timid, because all these unions in the South emphasise the hatred of the negro by excluding him. There is not a single coloured woman admitted to the Southern WCTU, but still Miss Willard blames the negro for the defeat of prohibition in the South!

Frances Willard had no defence against this charge of segregation practised by her organization. Ida B. Wells later called it a 'staggering revelation' which 'stunned the British people', and although this was something of an overstatement, she certainly appeared to gain support as a result of exposing Frances Willard's apparent hypocrisy. The editor of the *Westminster Gazette* defended Ida by denying that she had expressed any race hatred in his interview with her, and shortly afterwards she was invited to both breakfast and dinner in the House of Commons. Finally the Anti-Lynching Committee, set up on her last evening in the country, proved to be Ida B. Wells's greatest triumph. In her autobiography she printed a list of the names of all the influential and prestigious members. Among them were MPs such as William Woodall, Dadabhai Naoroji and Alfred Webb; labour leaders like Keir Hardie and the American Samuel Gompers; the editors of the *Manchester Guardian*, the *Liverpool Daily Post*, the London *Daily News*, the *Bradford Observer* and the *Contemporary Review*; and leading clergy, including the Archbishop of York. The names of both Lady Henry Somerset and Frances Willard were on the list as well, which Ida B. Wells remarked on as one of her greatest achievements.

But the antagonism between the two American women did not end while they were both in London; and it continued to draw in many others on both sides of the Atlantic.

## Race and Gender in Temperance Politics

The dispute was to prove as long as it was bitter. At the heart of it were several issues which were all interconnected. First, there was straightforward racial prejudice promoting the belief that it was indeed unsafe for white women in the South because of the licentious and drunken nature of black men; as far as most members of the WCTU were concerned, all men could be dangerous to women after taking alcohol, but black men were thought to be especially prone to drunkenness, because of their class as well as their race. From the 1880s on, there was a proliferation of books and articles claiming that there were marked biological differences between blacks and whites. These all identified immorality and bestiality as race traits to be found overwhelmingly among the black population, now freed from the restraining influence of slavery. Frances Willard's claims not to have 'an atom of race prejudice' looked less convincing when she repeated 'what she had been told in the South' – that blacks multiplied like locusts and threatened the safety of good white women. The very language in which she expressed these opinions echoed the words of one of the South's most well-known academic racists, Phillip Alexander Bruce. In a book called *The Plantation Negro as Freeman* published in 1889, Bruce expounded his theory of 'regression'. For him the most striking example of the return to black savagery was the increasing frequency of 'that most frightful crime', the rape of white women by black men. He wrote:

> There is something strangely alluring and seductive to them in the appearance of a white woman; they are aroused and stimulated by its foreignness to their experience of sexual pleasure, and it moves them to gratify their lust at any cost and in spite of every obstacle. This proneness of the negro is so well understood that the white women of every class, from the highest to the lowest are afraid to venture any distance alone, or even wander unprotected in the immediate vicinity of their homes.[52]

Second, there was the issue of segregation practised by white women's organizations. Whether or not Frances Willard personally approved of it, the fact was the WCTU permitted segregated sections in some Southern states. Some of their leading white members, women such as Rebecca Felton, who had been loyal Confederates during the war, were fiercely opposed to the idea of working together with black women.[53] The fear of losing Southern members was too great to prevent the WCTU leadership from outlawing separate organizations for black and white women throughout America. Like many liberals in the North, Frances Willard was able to profess and believe in the theoretical equality of the 'races' while at the same time turning a blind eye to the reality of segregation and discrimination in more distant parts of the country. By 1897 the racist climate had so degenerated that Rebecca Felton won huge popular support by declaring, 'If it takes lynching to protect women's dearest possession from drunken, ravening beasts, then I say lynch a thousand a week if it becomes necessary.' Encouraged by friends and supporters she then embarked on a crusade for the salvation of white women from the 'black fiend'.[54]

The third element of the quarrel between Frances Willard and Ida B. Wells was the fact that it was a black woman who was publicly challenging the dominant view of white women's sexuality. Ida's insistence that it was white women who often initiated illicit relationships with black men did not accord with the belief held by many in the WCTU, including Frances Willard, that women were invariably victims of male lust. The scenario of drunken black men – and those who were 'ignorant and illiterate' and could become doubly dangerous through drink – preying on white women accorded entirely with WCTU philosophy, while the possibility of willingness on the part of the so-called victims was viewed as an outrageous suggestion. But it was not just the idea of women being actively interested in sex that scandalized so many American women; Ida B. Wells had also raised the forbidden topic of miscegenation. It was common knowledge that black women had suffered sexual abuse at the hands of white men during slavery, a fact that was often described in abolitionist propaganda, particularly in works of fiction. The idea, however, that white women might find black men desirable was altogether a different issue. In 1856, the well-known abolitionist campaigner Lydia Maria Child lost much of her popular support when she wrote an appeal against miscegenation laws, citing several happy unions between white women and black men. Even though she dared to speak out, risking 'the world's mockery', she still felt obliged to distance herself from any such possible desires by claiming that it was only the lowest class of white women who would consider such a union, the difference between them and middle-class women being 'a matter of taste'.[55] Although it was almost forty years later, the racism that Ida B. Wells encountered both in Britain and in the United States contained the idea that black men had long held suppressed desires for white women. She constantly refuted this by citing the example of plantation owners who spent extended periods away from home, leaving a wife and family in the hands of trusted slaves:

> Do you remember when the American negro had his great opportunity? When his master went into the field openly to fight against his – the negro's – freedom, and left his wife and children in the negro's charge? What wrongs those negroes had to avenge! And what a temptation to vengeance! Yet not a man of them betrayed his master's trust.[56]

Frances Willard, whose contacts in the South had assured her of the problems caused by the behaviour of the former slave population, also had to think of her standing among the white women members of the WCTU. Speaking at the 1894 WCTU convention in Cleveland, Ohio, Frances Willard attacked Ida B. Wells in her opening address, hoping to silence her on this issue for once and for all:

> The zeal for her race of Miss Ida B. Wells, a bright young colored woman, has, it seems to me, clouded her perception as to who were her friends and well-wishers in all high-minded and legitimate efforts to banish the abomination of lynching and torture from the land of the free and home of the brave. It is my firm belief that in the statements made by Miss Wells concerning white women having taken the initiative in nameless acts between the races she has put an imputation upon half the white race in this country that is unjust, and, save in the rarest exceptional circumstances, wholly without foundation.[57]

Willard referred to herself as a 'friend and well-wisher' and urged Ida to 'banish from her vocabulary all such allusions as a source of weakness to the cause she has at heart'. She also accused her of misrepresenting the WCTU while she was in England. After her speech there was not one resolution offered that mentioned lynching, even though one had been passed unanimously the previous year. Ida B. Wells, who was present at the convention, recalled in her pamphlet, *A Red Record*, that she worked with sympathetic WCTU members to produce one, but it was not adopted. After the conference the WCTU paper, the *Union Signal*, reported a far milder and clearly ambiguous resolution. It spoke generally about the need to ban all kinds of lawless acts, but looked forward to the time when

> the unspeakable outrages which have so often provoked such lawlessness shall be banished from the world, and childhood, maidenhood and womanhood shall no more be the victims of atrocities worse than death.

Ida B. Wells finally met Frances Willard during this convention, after the president had attacked her in her speech. In a chapter of *A Red Record*, called 'Miss Willard's Attitude', Ida gave an account of their conversation and conclusively demonstrated the way that white women were able to silence and attempt to dominate their 'coloured sisters'. She asked Frances

Willard to correct her statement that she had misrepresented the WCTU or that she had 'put an imputation upon one-half the white race in this country'. Willard's reply was that 'somebody in England told her it was a pity that I [Ida] attacked the white women of America'. When Ida demanded to know why she had gone out of her way to distort what she had said, not because of what she heard herself but because of what someone else had told her, Willard merely answered that Ida should not blame her for her rhetorical expressions – that she had her way of expressing things and Ida had hers. She made no attempt to retract her speech during the rest of the convention, although a few words appeared in the next edition of *Union Signal*. Instead of withdrawing the attack made on Ida, the editorial announced that Miss Willard had not intended a literal interpretation to the language used, but 'employed it to express a tendency that might ensue on public thought as a result of utterances so sweeping as some that have been made by Miss Wells'. Ida B. Wells's final comment was bitterly angry: 'It is little less than criminal to apologise for the butchers today and tomorrow to repudiate the apology by declaring it a figure of speech'.

Meanwhile in England a similar debate was held in the women's temperance movement. In early 1895, almost a year after Ida B. Wells had returned home, Lady Henry Somerset referred to Ida's 'injudicious speech' in her address to the British Women's and World Women's Temperance Convention in London. Although the British women passed a resolution against lynching, it was followed by another supporting the position of the WCTU in America. Florence Balgarnie, secretary of the Anti-Lynching Committee and an active temperance organizer, rose to Ida's defence in an 'eloquent and impassioned speech', according to Catherine Impey's report in *Anti-Caste*.[58] The editor of the London *Daily News*, with whose family Ida had stayed while in London, was also quick to pour scorn on the temperance organization's equivocating: 'The American ladies, led by Miss Willard, appear to complain that Miss Wells had not sufficiently minced her words in telling of these shocking outbursts of lawlessness.'[59]

A further sign that Frances Willard felt threatened by Ida B. Wells's campaign was provided the same year. Early in 1895 a declaration was published in America, signed by leading radicals and former abolitionists, absolving Frances Willard of any blame in what she had said or not said about lynching. Having first established her abolitionist ancestry, the statement announced that 'as President of the WCTU, and founder of the World's WCTU, Miss Willard has always maintained the position that no colour line could be drawn by either society'. It went on to explain that the WCTU was organized on the basis that each state had the right to manage its own internal affairs, and that in 'some of the Southern states coloured unions had been formed with the hearty concurrence of leading coloured women'. Assurance was then given that black women delegates were received 'on terms of perfect equality with white women' at national meetings.[60] Frederick Douglass and William Lloyd Garrison both put their names to the document, which was republished by Lady Henry Somerset in an English newspaper in an effort to clear her friend's name. It was a dishonest attempt though, as Ida B. Wells's English supporters quickly tried to prove.

One of these was Florence Balgarnie, who was also an active member of the BWTA and editor of their journal, *Women's Signal*. When Ida B. Wells decided to publish her attack on Frances Willard in *Fraternity*, Florence Balgarnie, who was a journalist herself, had counselled her to act more cautiously. She persuaded her to wait until she had spoken to Lady Henry Somerset on the telephone in order to arrange a meeting to discuss the matter before the journal was distributed. Ida did so, but was insulted and threatened by the aristocratic English woman, who then hung up before Ida could reply. Convinced of the need to support the anti-lynching cause wholeheartedly against the temperance leaders' hypocritical claims, Florence Balgarnie threw herself into the argument. She challenged the declaration published by Somerset, declaring that she was in possession of a letter from Garrison proving that he had given his signature before he was informed of what had happened at the annual conference of the WCTU three months earlier. On this occasion, as we have already seen, a strongly worded resolution against lynching was withdrawn in favour of an ambiguous one which repeated the charge that it was 'unspeakable acts' that had provoked such lawless behaviour. Garrison was horrified at this 'apology for Southern outrages', as Florence Balgarnie pointed out, but Somerset chose to ignore her and printed the document exonerating Frances Willard again, this time in the annual address of the BWTA. Balgarnie challenged her publicly from the platform of the City Temple, but received such an unsatisfactory reply that it made her determined to expose the truth. In the November edition of *Fraternity* she asked two straight questions: first, how could Lady Henry Somerset reconcile her original statement that the people who had put their names to the document had also worded it, with her subsequent admittance that it was she herself with Frances Willard who had drafted and circulated it? Second, how was it possible that Frederick Douglass, who had signed the declaration the day before his death, could claim that the WCTU had 'put themselves squarely on record against lynching' if he had known what had taken place at the convention several weeks earlier?

Lady Henry Somerset never replied to these questions in public. Florence Balgarnie was sacked from her job at the *Women's Signal* without receiving any compensation, censured by the BWTA executive committee and boycotted as a temperance lecturer. The following month she was vindicated when Frederick Douglass's widow, Helen, wrote to her confirming that her husband had certainly not been aware of the WCTU's resolution when he gave his public support to Frances Willard, and that 'any impeachment of his integrity in this or any other matter' was an insult to his memory. In the same letter Helen Douglass, who was white, recalled another incident which showed the influence of the South on Northern women's organizations:

> It is not two years since, at the great annual convention in Washington DC of the National Woman Suffrage Association, an Afro-American woman of exceptional cultivation and refinement, a college graduate, a fine Greek and Latin scholar, and a writer of ability called at the Riggs House, the headquarters of the suffragists, to see one of the officers of the Association on business, and was ejected from the elevator, and not one word of protest from the Association, which hushed the matter up, and thereby lost this grand opportunity of embodying its principles, obliterating caste distinction, securing justice, and putting itself on record in a way not to be misunderstood. To conciliate the white Southern sisterhood it paid the price, its own stultification, and the degradation of the coloured Southern sisterhood.[61]

This exclusion of black women would have been particularly hateful to Frederick Douglass as he was the first man to support women's suffrage publicly. The last day of his life was spent attending a women's suffrage convention in Washington. In the third issue of *Anti-Caste* Catherine Impey had reported how Douglass refused to co-operate with women from the National Suffrage Movement who were trying to form black women's suffrage societies. He was obliged to make his reasons public to avoid any misunderstanding. In a letter to the press he wrote: 'My appreciation of the moral and intellectual worth of the coloured woman was the ground of my opposition to having them pushed off into separate organisation in defence to a prejudice which belongs to the barbarism of slavery, and which I trust is fast dying out and against which my whole life has been a protest.'[62]

Catherine Impey, who by March 1895 had reluctantly, in response to Isabella Mayo's efforts to silence her, taken up the editorship of *Anti-Caste* once more, added her voice to the criticism of the American women's organization. She first examined the infamous document absolving Frances Willard, focusing her attack on its references to the 'colour line'. By allowing separate organizations on the grounds that it suited both black and white women to work independently, she contended, the leaders of the WCTU were bowing to the demands of the white members to exclude their black 'sisters'. Their claim to welcome black women on equal terms as officers and delegates to the national organization glossed over the fact that it was extremely intimidating for the few who were selected to attend their 'monster assemblies'. Catherine Impey concluded that the Southern conscience was 'too blunted by the effects of slavery to be trusted where the rights of coloured women are concerned', and if the North did not realize the significance of this concession, then pressure would have to come from elsewhere – 'from English protest, where feelings and conscience are less benumbed'.[63]

## The Significance of Anti-Lynching Politics for White Women's Feminism

The detail of this controversy is important, I think, because it illustrates the range of positions that different women took in their attempts to formulate a political outlook that acknowledged both gender and race. It is also significant that the public quarrel between Frances Willard and Ida B. Wells first surfaced in England and was carried back to the United States where it had originated. This was partly due to circumstance, in that Frances Willard happened to be in Britain when the Society for the Brotherhood of Man was being set up. But as a young, unknown black woman in her own country, Ida B. Wells would never have been able to attract public support for her criticism of a figure of Frances Willard's calibre. Yet in London her relative obscurity seemed to add weight to her argument; she believed that the British public felt more sympathy for her after the two temperance leaders threatened to use their influence to silence her. It would be wrong, however, to attribute Ida's moral victory solely to what she perceived as the British sense of fair play. The support that she was shown indicates that there was a substantial current of anti-imperialist thought in Britain at that time, which was able to make sense of and accept her political analysis of racial terror in America with all its implications for the social and political relations of race and gender elsewhere. But this makes me wonder whether this analysis was acceptable because it was made in an American context, or whether it was also seen to hold good in British colonial societies, where segregation and racial subordination were also part of everyday life. Why did Ida B. Wells not face more opposition in Britain than she did, since her description of social relations in the South were often uncomfortably close to those in parts of the Empire? As she herself frequently pointed out, the hardest part of her work in Britain was to convince people that black men were not 'wild beasts after white women'.[64] When *The Times* drew the attention of Florence Balgarnie and 'the numerous ladies upon the Anti-Lynching Committee' to the 'frequency and atrocity of his outrages on white women', it was not just referring to the black man in America, but to everywhere where a man with a darker skin could come into contact with whites.

This belief, which lurked in the recesses of the imperial imagination, had been more widely expressed, not in the context of the British experience of slavery and abolition, but in reaction to uprisings of black colonial subjects in India and the Caribbean – in particular the Indian 'Mutiny' of 1857 and the Morant Bay uprising of 1865, both discussed in Part 1.[65] Although responses to the uprisings were part of a much more complex debate about the nature of democracy at home and the legitimation of imperial rule abroad, these rebellions and the manner in which they were suppressed occupied an indelible place in the memory of racial dominance. Yet it does not appear that the British anti-lynching campaigners saw useful analogies between the situation in the Empire and conditions in the Southern states of America. Their opponents in the South, however, were quick to cite the cruel suppression of the Sepoy rebellion as an example of barbarity committed by the hypocritical British. While the 'ladies' involved in the Anti-Lynching Committee would have been too young to remember the actual events surrounding the insurrections, they would have been familiar with the mythologies that developed as a result. Not being American, they might have been less sensitive to the outrage caused by Ida B. Wells's remarks about Southern white women enjoying intimate friendships with former slaves, but they would certainly have been aware of the impact of such arguments had they been made in the context of British colonial society. The way that Isabella Mayo reacted to Catherine Impey's proposal to her lodger was evidence that even when friendship between black men and white women was possible, marriage was an entirely different matter.

I shall now consider what motivated the women who rallied behind Frances Willard and Lady Henry Somerset to defend the name of white women in America. The details of the controversy belie the simple conclusion that it was a conflict between middle-class white women who saw themselves as representing what they understood to be women's interests and middle-class white women who were more concerned with the idea of helping oppressed people than fighting for their own rights as women. By focusing on the writings of Frances Willard, Catherine Impey and Florence Balgarnie, it is possible to explore the political beliefs that these white women shared as well as where they disagreed with each other.

Frances Willard belonged to a body of women who believed that society needed moral reform, and that woman's equality was justified by her ability to provide moral and spiritual guidance rather than as an end in itself. Ultimately, the WCTU was a conservative organization, although many of its actual policies suggested some degree of radicalism, intersecting with both socialism and feminism. There was a constant tension within the network around its identification with feminist aims – the demand for 'rights for women' was considered 'too strident', for example.[66] However, by the beginning of the twentieth century, the movement for social purity was in decline, as Victorian ideas on morality became outdated. Frances Willard died in 1896, and her life and her philosophy – summed up by the call for 'a white life' – were very soon identified with an era that had passed.

It is no coincidence that Willard's views on race were also more appropriate to an earlier historical period. She was, as she claimed so proudly on many occasions, a child of the abolitionist movement, and it is significant that in the 1890s she still felt this was sufficient proof of her freedom from racial prejudice. 'I was born an abolitionist, taught to read out of the "Slave's Friend", she announced at the beginning of her interview in the New York *Voice*. The propaganda of abolitionism was often directed at women in their capacity as guardians of a superior morality, and it appealed to many because of its support for basic domestic values, the most important one being the defence of the family. For thousands of women, campaigning against slavery was entirely compatible with demanding equal rights for women outside the home, as long as they still accepted that women were basically responsible for the moral and spiritual welfare of the family. As we have already seen, Willard's views on the liberation of black people *beyond* emancipation appear to have been confined to a general sympathy for educated blacks and support for the policy of repatriation.

Catherine Impey, whose views on racism were expressed through her columns in *Anti-Caste*, was also born into an anti-slavery tradition. However, the changes she made to the masthead of *Anti-Caste* from 1888 to 1895 revealed that she was more in touch with the aspirations and achievements of black people than Frances Willard was. As we have already seen, the aim of her journal moved from being 'devoted to the interests of coloured races' to claiming black peoples' equal right 'to protection, personal liberty, equality of opportunity and human fellowship'. This change reflected a shift from a conventional philanthropic stance, in keeping with her Quaker background, to a more active recognition of the autonomy of black struggles for racial justice.

Like Frances Willard, Catherine Impey, who lived in a household of women, was in no way dependent on a man for her upkeep. Although this does not necessarily mean that she believed women should be active in a wider sphere, her writings and involvement in the anti-imperialist network all take for granted an assumption that women should be as free as men in expressing their political opinions. She recognized that women had a particular role to play in the anti-lynching campaign, though whether this was due to a sense of women's philanthropic mission is not clear. Her first issue of *Anti-Caste* stated her belief that purely physical differences between people, such as those arising from 'sex, race, complexion, nationality', were arbitrary. However, as far as we know she did not campaign specifically for women's rights, nor was she a member of any campaign for women's suffrage during this period. Superficially – and there is so little evidence to take it further – her views on suffrage and women's role in the public sphere were entirely compatible with Willard's.

In the only surviving writing by Catherine on this subject – an article written for the Street 'Village Album' – she tried to address the arguments that were frequently raised against women's demand for the vote.[67] Her reasoning was not without its own contradictions. She first pointed out the dangers of women achieving political power at the expense of losing their influence at home. This was not the conventional line that it was women's job to raise the children while the men took care of life outside, but an attempt to understand the basic objection to women's suffrage expressed by its opponents – that it was 'unnatural'. Her theory was that 'very few political or social arrangements of permanence have originated solely in evil' and therefore it was vital to the success of the reform movement to understand why those arrangements evolved. People, she suggested, were generally very slow to realize that as society changed so these old systems became inappropriate and 'obnoxious'. But it was a mistake to think that everything about the outdated system was automatically wrong and override it by 'the iron wheels of modern theory-in-action'.

Catherine's argument was that the time was right for women to vote and take part in political life because the family – 'historically the unit of all our political systems' – had changed radically. She explained how the 'Division of Labour principle' accounted for the greater involvement of men in certain activities, but this was for immutable physical reasons rather than ideological ones. It is significant that she turned to examples of 'primitive "village communities" in parts of the East' to demonstrate the influence that women had in the absence of their men. It was more often the case that proponents of women's rights throughout the nineteenth century tried to distance themselves from 'primitive' society by arguing that women's subordination was an index of lack of civilization.

Apart from the fact that the family unit had changed so that women were now often heads of households just as men were, the importance of that 'external life', which men traditionally saw as their domain, had altered as well. She wrote: 'We must realise a state of things where national life and organisation (in which men ruled) was, compared with today, feeble and of small account and where local, even family life and organisation, where women ruled, was full of life, importance and variety'. The loss, in modern 'artificial' society, was that women's influence and responsibility were diminished at the expense of society as a whole. Now that the public political sphere was so much more pervasive and accessible to both men and women, it made sense for women to be equally involved. At the same time Catherine made it clear that she still believed that it was women who were primarily responsible for maintaining family life. It was wrong to place too much hope on endowing women with political power:

> Even at present there are too many instances that women when suffered to

> enter the professions, the political positions which have been formerly men's alone, have adopted some of the very modes of thought and feeling which it was hoped women's influence in these spheres would correct. Especially we have to guard in the present days of this movement against anything that tends to the undervaluing of family life which is the basis, humanly speaking, of the religion and true civilisation of the world.

Clearly there are important overlaps between the politics of Frances Willard and Catherine Impey, illustrated by this last sentence. Catherine was also an active member of her local temperance organization and was very likely to have been an admirer of the WCTU leader before the campaign against lynching began.

By the time that Catherine Impey wrote her article, the suffrage issue was just beginning to attract greater popular support from women in Britain. The trade union movement was rapidly expanding, and many middle-class women involved themselves in employment issues with or on behalf of working-class women. In 1885, Florence Balgarnie was appointed secretary of the Central Committee of the National Society for Women's Suffrage. She had already made a name for herself by her skills in both organizing and public speaking, and she was widely respected for her commitment to women's rights. In 1889 she was one of a group of women who founded the Women's Trade Union Association, and she was also, through her work as a journalist, closely involved in the British Women's Temperance Association. An interview with Balgarnie in the *Women's Penny Paper* revealed that she felt most at home when addressing meetings of working people, particularly men.[68] Born and brought up in Scarborough, Yorkshire, daughter of a Scottish Congregational Minister, her favourite book as a child had been *Uncle Tom's Cabin*. Education was another cause that interested her and she helped set up the Scarborough branch of the University Extension Scheme; for two years she sat on the school board there, having been elected alongside men. In the same interview she named Ruskin, John Stuart Mill and Mazzini as writers who had influenced her greatly, although she also lectured on the life and works of her other favourite author, Charlotte Brontë.

Florence Balgarnie was, like Catherine Impey, an independent woman engaged in reform work. More of a 'conventional' feminist by virtue of the fact that she belonged to suffrage and women's rights organizations, she encountered the anti-lynching campaign through her work as a journalist and was not able to pass it by without becoming deeply involved. After being elected secretary of the Anti-Lynching Committee in 1894, she wrote an article about Ida B. Wells in a popular magazine called *Great Thoughts*. It began:

> The age of chivalry is not dead nor dying. It is gloriously real and present with us. This so-called prosaic nineteenth century thrills with romance, the very air palpitates with deeds of daring and heroism. We have brave knight-errants in many a field, and, better still, women, the Jeanne d'Arcs of today, are not wanting.[69]

Despite the purple prose, Florence Balgarnie's account of her young life and her analysis of lynching accords completely with Ida's own version. For instance, she contrasted the treatment of white women by black men with that of black women by white men, and drew attention, using Ida's own words, to the fact that black men were being lynched for rape when the relationship between the victim lynched and the alleged victim of the assault was 'voluntary, clandestine, and illicit'. The article went on to describe Ida's success in Britain and its effect on her work back in America, where at last an anti-lynching campaign seemed to be gathering momentum. Balgarnie was aware that Great Britain 'should be the last to condemn another nation' when it came to race prejudice, but that it was in the spirit of '*goodwill, brotherly kindness, and large human affection*' that they were pressing for equality between black and white in America.

The key to the connection between Florence Balgarnie and Catherine Impey can be found in their use of language. It was this concept of 'human brotherhood' that inspired many of those who actively supported anti-racist causes. Throughout the nineteenth century the word 'brotherhood' had been an ideal most often expressed in religious language, but as the socialist movement gathered pace, it acquired more secular and literal connotations. The development of *Fraternity* into an overtly socialist publication illustrates this process perfectly. In 1895 the SRUBM became the International Society for the Recognition of the Brotherhood of Man, and the motto 'Fellow-Workers' was adopted. A statement in the magazine declared: 'We are endeavouring to widen the scope of our work in order the better to serve the interests of the weak and oppressed in all lands'. The revised aims of the new society were:

> To declare the Unity of the Human Race and to further the Brotherhood of Mankind.

> To influence public opinion in the promotion of Justice and Sympathy between all Races, Classes, Creeds, and Communities.
>
> To discourage and denounce Race Separation, Race Animosity, and Race Arrogance wheresoever displayed.
>
> To assert the Inter-dependence of Nations and the Responsibilities and Reciprocities, and especially to insist upon the duty of the strong (Nation) to protect the weak (Nation).[70]

These aims have a significantly different tone to the opening editorial in *Anti-Caste*, which had renounced all forms of inequality, including those between men and women. Women continued to be involved in *Fraternity*, however. Isabella Mayo claimed to be the founder of the new society, and her own politics were radically influenced by the new socialist spirit. Introducing Caroline Martin as the new editor, she wrote that 'brighter days are now dawning for our work! For we have at last gained a firm standpoint in that very section of society which we dared to enlist with us, *the workers of the world*, all of whom we long to see banded together as *fellow-workers*, since only they can stand against the world's forces of wrong and robbery.'[71] Caroline Martin, who died only weeks after taking up her post, was about to become trade union organizer for the north of Scotland, having written and lectured extensively on 'Labour matters'. She too was a Christian, as Mayo was at pains to point out, and 'was led on to her most advanced standpoints, not by "revolutionary" pamphlets, nor even by "economic" considerations . . . but by the earnest study of the New Testament itself'.[72]

*Fraternity* was evolving during a period of popular imperialism, which demanded new arguments and new tactics. In the 1896 annual meeting of the ISRBM, a resolution was put forward which lamented 'the present outbreak of "Jingoism"' and condemned the policy which had led to attempts by different European countries to divide up Africa. The man who proposed the motion argued that the society should try to educate the working man in the true principles of fraternity and persuade him that the notion that trade follows the flag was all 'nonsense'.[73] This emphasis on the working man dominated the magazine in the last few months of its life under the editorship of Frank Smith, who succeeded Caroline Martin in 1896. In one of its last editions he published an article in favour of women's suffrage in an attempt to redress the imbalance of language. The writer began by saying that he – or she – had never considered the fact that 'fraternity' was a masculine word until asked to write for the paper. The argument was the familiar one that 'the world wants mothering, and it can't get it until women are free and have their full share in the management of it'.[74] Readers were exhorted to think of the 'national home, of the great human home of the race, denied even the participation of women in the management of its affairs, and say if you can wonder that it falls so far short of being ideal'.

The changing language of *Fraternity* expressed perfectly the transition of the anti-lynching campaign from a generally middle-class philanthropic concern to a more concerted attempt to involve the working class in a protest against imperialism in general. As the movement became more infused with socialist ideas and dedicated to the task of converting workers to its cause, so the concept of 'fraternity' became more literal. Despite the attempts of women workers to form and join trade unions, the ethic of labour politics was predominantly masculine and the word 'fraternity' inevitably came to be associated with men, losing its previous humanitarian meaning. The vision of 'human brotherhood' shared by Catherine Impey and Florence Balgarnie had included justice and equality for all, regardless of sex, race, nationality or class. At that time there was no language to express the particular connections between women and black people, beyond the vocabulary of slavery and emancipation, yet it was through the anti-lynching campaign that those connections were made explicit.

This was ultimately the significance of the short-lived movement. It showed the possibility of an alliance between black and white women in which white women went beyond sisterly support for black women; by confronting the racist ideology that justified lynching, these white women also began to develop a radical analysis of gender relations that intersected with class and race. Whether or not they were 'feminist' can be judged perhaps by the way they lived their lives and identified themselves with social and political issues – the implications of their own independence were that they believed women should be free to choose how and with whom they lived or associated themselves. By refusing to accept the portrait of innocent and vulnerable white women painted by those who supported or ignored lynchings in the United States, they were not only defending the rights of the black population but also claiming a different and more active version of femininity. As a result, they threw into relief a range of conservative beliefs about both women and black people, not just those held by their opponents but also the beliefs of those who considered themselves progressive.

There was not a clear cut division between the politics of the women who supported Ida B. Wells and those who tried to silence her, but there were two main differences. Where Frances Willard and others in the temperance movement saw themselves as largely representing women's interests, both Catherine Impey and Florence Balgarnie declared themselves to be advocates of human brotherhood, which expressed, as we have just seen, a desire for universal equality across race, class and gender. The second difference was that those who were offended by Ida B. Wells failed to see the centrality of racism which worked both to oppress black people and, in the case of lynching, to undermine more radical ideas about women as well.

## Notes

1 Interview with Ida B. Wells in the *Westminster Gazette*, 10 May 1894; also quoted in David M. Tucker, 'A Memphis Lynching', *Phylon: Atlanta University Review of Race and Culture*, vol. XXXII, no 2, Summer 1971, p. 120.

2 Olive Banks, *Faces of Feminism: A Study of Feminism as a Social Movement*, Martin Robertson, Oxford 1981, p. 102.

3 Manning Marable, *How Capitalism Underdeveloped Black America: Problems in Race Political Economy and Society*, South End Press, Boston, 1983, p. 15.

4 Jacqueline Dowd Hall, *Revolt Against Chivalry: Jesse Daniel Ames and the Women's Campaign Against Lynching*, Columbia University Press, New York 1979, pp. 134–5.

5 R. M. Brown, *Strain of Violence: Historical Studies of American Violence and Vigilantism*, Oxford University Press, New York 1975; H. A. Bulhan, *Frantz Fanon and the Psychology of Oppression*, Plenum Press, New York 1985, ch. 8.

6 See, for example, Ralph Ginzburg, *100 Years of Lynchings*, Black Classic Press, Baltimore 1962/1988, a book compiled entirely from press reports during the period 1880–1961.

7 Bulhan, p. 157.

8 The source of information for much of this part of the book is Alfreda M. Duster ed., *Crusade for Justice: The Autobiography of Ida B. Wells*, University of Chicago Press, Chicago 1970. For further reading about the life and political influence of Ida B. Wells, who is now being acknowledged as one of the most important black figures of her generation, see Joanne M. Braxton, *Black Women Writing Autobiography: A Tradition Within a Tradition*, Temple University Press, Philadelphia 1989, pp. 102–38; Hazel V. Carby, *Reconstructing Womanhood: The Emergence of the Afro-American Woman Novelist*, Oxford University Press, New York/Oxford 1987, pp. 108–16; Angela Y. Davis, *Women, Race, and Class*, Random House, New York 1981; Paula Giddings, *When and Where I Enter: The Impact of Black Women on Race and Sex in America*, William Morrow, New York 1984; Dorothy Sterling, *Black Foremothers*, The Feminist Press, New York 1988, pp. 61–118.

9 *The Times*, 1 August 1894.

10 Douglass made the trip to Europe with his second wife; he also achieved a long-held ambition to visit Egypt before he grew too old.

11 *Anti-Caste*, vol. VII, April 1895.

12 Ibid.

13 *Anti-Caste*, vol. VI, January 1893.

14 Isabella Mayo was also a novelist who wrote under the pseudonym of Edward Garrett. She later wrote an autobiography called *Recollections of What I Saw, What I Lived Through and What I Learned during More than Fifty Years of Social and Literary Experience* (John Murray, London 1910) which unfortunately contains almost no reference to her political activities.

15 *The Sun*, 26 August 1894.

16 Duster, p. 214.

17 *Anti-Caste*, vol. VII, January 1889. For more information on racism in Britain at this time see Douglas A. Lorimer, *Colour, Class and the Victorians: English Attitudes to the Negro in the Mid-Nineteenth Century*, Leicester University Press 1978; James Walvin, *Black and White: The Negro and English Society, 1855–1945*, Allen Lane, London 1973; Peter Fryer, *Staying Power: The History of Black People in Britain*, Pluto, London 1984.

18 Duster, p. 20.

19 Duster, p. xvii.

20 Duster, p. 64. See chapters 6 to 8 for Ida B. Wells's own acount of her realization that lynching was a form of political and economic terror.

21 Duster, p. 65.

22 *The Times*, 6 November 1894.

23 Letter to Frederick Chesson 1886, Rhodes House Library, Oxford (Ref: c138/163–74).

24 *Anti-Caste*, vol. IV, January 1891 (supplement).

25 *The Friend*, 4 January 1924.

26 For a discussion of this occasion see Carby, pp. 3–19.

27 *Anti-Caste*, vol. IV (supplement) January 1891.

28 *Anti-Caste*, vol. III, January 1890.

29 *Anti-Caste*, vol. III, June 1890.

30 *Anti-Caste*, vol. II, January 1889.

31 Her actual words were: 'We hope little by little to give some insight into the evils of Caste as it prevails in countries where our white race habitually ostracises those who are even partially descended from darker races; and by circulating in our pages the current writings of prominent and thoughtful persons of coloured races hope to give them fresh opportunities of presenting their case before white races.' *Anti-Caste*, vol. I, March 1888.

32 *Anti-Caste*, vol. II, August 1989.

33 *Anti-Caste*, vol. VII, March 1895.

34 For Ida B. Wells's account of this, see Duster, ch. 14, 'An Indiscreet Letter'. The only account that remains of this incident is in Ida B. Wells's autobiography, compiled years later after Ida had lost touch with Catherine. However, assuming that she kept a diary and that her memory was good, there is no reason to suspect Ida of embroidering on the affair, especially as she was implicated in it as well.

35 I am indebted to Stephen Morland for his help and interest in remembering Catherine Impey, or Katie, as she was known, as an elderly relative – one of the pleasanter ones – who visited his family when he was young, and for suggesting further contacts.

36 *The Friend*, 1 June 1894.

37 *Fraternity*, vol. I, July 1893. See Fryer (p. 278) who puts forward the interesting theory that *Fraternity* was a large step towards the production in Britain of a politically-committed Pan-African press. In fact Edwards was editor for only a short period due to his bad health, and subsequent editors were white socialists, which affected the orientation of the journal considerably.

38 Fryer, pp. 278–9.

39 *Fraternity*, vol. II, September 1894.

40 *Fraternity*, vol. II, August 1894.

41 This suggestion is supported by Ida B. Wells's account of Catherine Impey's first conversation with Isabella Mayo about lynching: in response to Mayo's question about why 'the United States of America was burning human beings alive in the nineteenth century . . . Miss Impey's reply was evidently not satisfactory' (Duster, p. 85).

42 Ida. B. Wells, *United States Atrocities*, London 1893.

43 Barbara Leslie Epstein, *The Politics of Domesticity: Women, Evangelism, and Temperance in Nineteenth-Century America*, Wesleyan University Press, Middletown, CT 1981; Mary Earhart, *Frances Willard: From Prayers to Politics*, University of Chicago Press, Chicago 1944; Ruth Bordin, *Frances Willard: A Biography*, University of North Carolina Press, Chapel Hill/London 1986.

44 Correspondence of Helen Bright Clark, Clark family archives, Street, Somerset. Helen Bright Clark was an interesting figure in her own right. Daughter of the Liberal MP John Bright, she married into the Clark shoe family at a time when the industry began to be very profitable. She maintained many of her father's contacts after his death, and was in close contact with American feminists such as Susan B. Anthony and Elizabeth Cady Stanton, as well as black and white abolitionists from America. Much of her correspondence with women reveals the class nexus of transatlantic radicals, from which Catherine Impey would have been excluded, possibly on account of her slightly inferior class background. Her previous engagement to a member of the less well-off branch of the Clark family may also have explained why she was not in the same social circle as Helen Bright Clark.

45 *Voice*, New York, 23 October 1890.

46 See Part 5, pp. 240–41.

47 Ellen Carol Dubois, ed., *Elizabeth Cady Stanton, Susan B. Anthony: Correspondence, Writings, Speeches*, Schocken Books, New York 1981, p. 123.

48 Duster, p. 210. For an account of the dispute see Duster, ch. 25, 'A Regrettable Interview'.

49 *Westminster Gazette*, 21 May 1894. See also Duster, pp. 204–8.

50 *Westminster Gazette*, 10 May 1894.

51 *Westminster Gazette*, 22 May 1894. See also Duster, pp. 208–9.

52 Joel Williamson, *The Crucible of Race: Black–White Relations in the American South since Emancipation*, Oxford University Press, New York/Oxford 1984, p. 121.

53 Williamson, pp. 124–30, Felton is an interesting example of a white Southern women's rights campaigner who actively supported lynching. She became known through her association with her husband who was a congressman, but by 1893 was a national figure in her own right, working as a politician, journalist, prohibitionist and feminist. From 1890 to 1893 she was a member of the all-white Board of Lady Managers of the Chicago World's Fair, which refused to allow black women to have a representative. In response to an exhibition at the Fair organized by Harriet Beecher Stowe around the life of Uncle Tom, she arranged an exhibit depicting 'the actual life of the slave', with 'real coloured folks'

spinning and carding cotton, playing the banjo and presenting a non-threatening display of domesticity, ignorance and contentment.

54 Williamson, p. 128.

55 Karen Sanchez-Eppler, 'Bodily Bonds: The Intersecting Rhetorics of Feminism and Abolition', *Representations*, 24, Fall 1988, p. 44. This article contains an interesting discussion of the theme of miscegenation in anti-slavery fiction. See also James Kinney, *Amalgamation: Race, Sex, and Rhetoric in the Nineteenth-Century American Novel*, Greenwood Press, Westport, CT/London 1985.

56 *Westminster Gazette*, 10 May 1894.

57 Ida B. Wells, *A Red Record: Tabulated Statistics and Alleged Causes of Lynchings in the United States 1892–1893–1894*, Chicago, 1895, p. 80. See ch. VIII, 'Miss Willard's Attitude', for her account of the meeting between Frances Willard and Ida B. Wells.

58 *Anti-Caste*, vol. VII, June/July 1895.

59 Ibid.

60 Lady Henry Somerset's Annual Address to the British Women's Temperance Association, May/June 1895, in BWTA Archives/Collection.

61 *Fraternity*, vol. IV, July 1896.

62 *Anti-Caste*, vol. I, May 1888.

63 *Anti-Caste*, vol. VII, March 1895.

64 Duster, p. 220.

65 Lurid accounts of slave violence in the Caribbean dating back to the eighteenth century were also used to stoke up opposition to the abolition of slavery in America. See Forrest G. Wood, *Black Scare: The Racist Response to Emancipation and Reconstruction*, University of California Press, Berkeley, CA 1970, p. 28.

66 Epstein, p. 147.

67 Catherine Impey, 'Some Thoughts on the Women's Suffrage Question', Street 'Village Album', c. 1887.

68 *Women's Penny Paper*, vol. 1, no 21, 16 March 1889.

69 *Great Thoughts*, 1894, p. 384.

70 *Fraternity*, vol. IV, January 1897.

71 *Fraternity*, vol. III, July 1896.

72 Ibid.

73 *Fraternity*, vol. III, June 1896.

74 *Fraternity*, vol. IV, January 1897.

Part Five

# Taking the Veil

## Towards a Partnership for Change

Methinks I see beside the camp fire sitting
Many an Empire Mother at her knitting,
Take heart! The bonds of friendship draw us close –
Soon we shall be one family – who knows?

The Mothers of the Empire are mothers of us all,
From humble cot or palace they hear Britannia's call.
On Baffin's icy margin or Africa's sultry shores,
They hear the call to duty and answer it by scores.

See them trooping to the standard, hear them answer to the cry
Across our far-flung frontiers (Theirs not to reason why).
The hand that rocks the cradle is the hand that rocks the world,
And it waves above each infant head a Union Jack unfurled.

(chorus)
They are the Mothers of the Empire,
The Sisters of the Free –
Hands across the sea;
Girls of the Bulldog breed!
From New Zealand and Australia, Ceylon and Wai-hai Wei,
Bermuda, Malta and Bangkok,
Chips of the Grand Old Block.[1]

This song was written and performed in the late 1940s, in our mothers' lifetimes if not in our own. Today it seems ludicrous to have still been celebrating a brand of patriotism more appropriate to the turn of the century at a time when Britain was rapidly losing her colonial possessions, but it does serve as a reminder of how recent that history is. For many white women in Britain the immediate memory of Empire was overshadowed by the 1939–45 war which dominated the early lives of those born or growing up in the 1950s. Since then there have been various attempts, both in foreign policy and at home, to revive the idea of the once 'Great' British Empire and restore a sense of that identity to the national collective. As most people were aware at the time, the war with Argentina over the Falkland Islands in 1982 provided a convenient symbol of Britain's capacity to become the Mother Country once again, sending forth troops to protect a remote colony threatened by aliens.

Post-war feminism developed as a political and cultural movement during a period of continuous reconstruction of colonial memory, which has been shaped by specific forms of racism operating within the shifting boundaries of British society.[2] One symptom of feminism's uneasy awareness of its own historical context has been the apparent lack of engagement with this process. For instance, until recently there seems to have been a resounding silence concerning any personal connections to the people who were involved in the colonizing process, particularly the 'Mothers of the Empire'. The women's liberation movement that emerged in the late 1960s was full of women whose mothers, aunts or grandmothers were affected in some way by the emigration of British people to different parts of the Empire – there can certainly be few white middle-class families who did not have colonial connections in some form or other over the last eighty years. Wealth acquired in the colonies provided for many sons and daughters to attend private schools, for example, and later universities. There must have been a significant number of feminists – and post-war radicals generally – whose education was paid for by money earned through the labour of Indian tea pickers, Malaysian rubber workers or Kenyan coffee farmers. The point is not to devalue anything about feminism in the 1960s or 1970s by drawing attention to this, but to emphasize the connections with Empire that have been played down, even if in the interests of solidarity with the anti-imperialist struggles of those same workers' descendants.

Apart from a few outstanding anthropological essays, I have been unable to find many attempts to analyse, rather than describe, the roles of white women in pre-1945 colonial society.[3] While white feminists with colonial backgrounds may not feel it is necessary or desirable to talk about this aspect of their personal histories, the majority of black women living in Britain are in an entirely different position. Depending on the specific history of their country of origin, they are visibly and personally connected to the British Empire whether they wish to recognize this fact or not. Women from South Asia, from the Caribbean, from East and West Africa, are largely descended from former colonial subjects whose lives were bound up in different ways with white British administrators, soldiers, businessmen, missionaries, doctors, nurses or teachers. The feminism of those black women who began to immigrate to Britain in the 1950s has consequently been derived from a network of political concerns and priorities quite different than those that influenced white women during this same period. It is probably even true that black women's insistence that racism and imperialism be included on a feminist agenda has made many white feminists even more reluctant to come to terms with colonial skeletons in the family cupboard. Adrienne Rich identified a similar situation in the USA where black and white women's histories are less inescapably connected to one another:

> A great deal of white feminist thinking and writing, where it has attempted to address black women's experience, has done so labouring under a massive burden of guilt feelings and false consciousness, the products of deeply inculcated self-blame, and of a history we have insufficiently explored.[4]

In each of the essays in this book I have looked at different aspects of this history, or histories – those that take full account of race as well as gender and class – in order to raise questions that are relevant to contemporary feminism. In my conclusion I want to look at some of the problems and questions involved in interpreting the immediate reconstruction of historical memory. Post-war feminism has uncovered an enormous amount of information about women's lives in the past and their resistance to different forms of oppression, and in doing so has identified central questions of power and knowledge relating to the very concept of history. There has, however, been less emphasis on the role of historical memory in the development of contemporary forms of domination. Whether or not there are personal reasons for overlooking it, one of the problems that arises from insufficiently exploring this recent history of Empire is the lack of critical, feminist reaction to the way that the memory of colonialism is constantly being recycled and reconstructed. I have already mentioned the way that this memory is evoked in relation to Britain's changed political status in the international world, but there has been a corresponding cultural retrospection of Empire as well. It is as though enough time has elapsed for the former Empire to look back nostalgically at the raw imperialism that belonged to another era. Such reflection is guided by contemporary ideologies of race, class and gender which make sense of that past in politically charged ways that range from self-criticism to celebration. I think that by overlooking this important cultural phenomenon feminism loses invaluable opportunities to contribute to this process of reinterpretation; as a result, feminism is less effective in understanding and changing oppressive ideologies of race, class and gender today.

I used the words 'recycled' and 'reconstructed' to convey two levels of producing historical memory. The first refers to cultural material that came directly out of the colonial experience, but which continues to be absorbed and enjoyed for a variety of reasons. Conventional documentary accounts of life in the Empire, whether in books or on film, tend to give an impression of 'that's how it was', where everyone knew their place and the consequences of stepping outside it. Fiction seems to have offered a far more complex view in which both the mechanics and the ethics of Empire are explored from varied perspectives – and in this context I am talking specifically about literature produced by the colonizers.[5] Leaving aside the classic works of male writers like Rudyard Kipling, Rider Haggard, and E. M. Forster, there is a genre of colonial novels written by or predominantly for women, including M. M. Kaye's *Far Pavilions* or some of Rumer Godden's works, which has rarely been studied despite the continuing popularity of these types of books today. After all, the colonial world provided an ideal setting for romantic fiction, full of possibilities for transgression, adventure and exoticism. Nor is it just adults who continue to enjoy literature produced in the colonial period. Many classics in children's literature contain references to Empire which contribute both directly and indirectly to a memory of a national imperial past, recycled in the cultural education of each successive generation.[6]

The second idea, which concerns the reconstruction of historical memory, relates to the way that colonial experience is represented in more recent times, whether it involves the reworking of old materials or the creation of new ones. The 1980s, for example, witnessed the production of lavish television serials such as *Jewel in the Crown* and *The Flame Trees of Thika*, and elaborately made films like *A Passage to India*, *Out of Africa* and *White Mischief* proved extremely popular at the box-office. While some writers have made serious attempts to examine the dynamics of colonialism with fresh perspective, the act of fictionalizing or romanticizing the past through film or television inevitably helps to revise the sense of national history associated with Empire. For those who have experience either of colonial life abroad or of growing up in Britain as the centre of Empire, these representations may or may not connect with something familiar; for those born later, the representations of colonialism in popular cultural forms are likely to have a very different resonance. There has been little feminist cultural criticism or comment on these kinds of films which is surprising considering the high profile of female characters in so many tales of imperial adventure. I suspect this has partly to do with a sense that films made by British directors with largely British actors set in colonial society are bound to be racist, and so they are dismissed. When teaching a mixed group of women whom I had not met before, I showed a ten-minute extract depicting a particularly obnoxious garden party from the film, *A Passage to India*.[7] It was quite unnerving to feel how the atmosphere dropped several degrees, but this tension only supported my point about the reasons why feminists had overlooked this popular cultural phenomenon.

I had decided to discuss this particular episode in the film because I felt it neatly illustrated the importance of fictional female characters in conveying British attitudes towards race and class. The official garden party provided the backdrop against which a range of positions were highlighted both towards Indians and the Raj itself. Two newcomers to British India, the protagonist, Adela Quested, and her prospective mother-in-law, Mrs Moore, were horrified by the disdainful way in which the Indian guests were being treated. Since the party was arranged mainly for their benefit, having voiced a desire to meet 'real Indians', the two English women could not understand why their hosts were being so unfriendly. The older woman, Mrs Moore, remonstrated with her son, an up-and-coming colonial official, that the occasion was just an excuse for flaunting power. Adela Quested remained incredulously naive – she was fascinated by her own idea of what India was really like and terrified of becoming like the other memsahibs who had settled there. A third Englishwoman, Mrs Turton, represented the unselfconsciously racist official's wife – the stereotypical memsahib, in fact – who revelled in the reflected glory of her husband, the most important man in the district.

The English men, by comparison, were either unquestioning of their own power, or downright cynical, both towards the Raj and towards any possibility of change. The Indian women, who were assembled in a group waiting for the white women to make the first move, were seen through British eyes. Assumed at first to be friendly, if shy and non-comprehending, they turned out to be fluent in English, well travelled throughout Europe and highly amused by the attempts of Mrs Turton to speak down to them in their own language. The sequence finished with a rendering of 'God Save the King', played by an Indian brass band, during which Mrs Moore argued with her son about the morality of British rule in India.

This extract gives some idea of how female characters are able to signify both distance and difference between black and white, rulers and ruled. But equally interesting is the suggestion that the three positions occupied by Mrs Moore, Mrs Turton and Adela Quested – the Good, the Bad and the Foolhardy – occur again and again throughout British colonial fiction, particularly when it is set in India. The first – the Good – illustrates a spiritual opposition to all forms of oppression and unfairness: the character who conveys this is destined to suffer because she feels deeply about the injustice of a political system which she is powerless to change. The second – the Bad – shows the apparently uncomplicated attitude of the wife who enjoys the trappings of power and superiority that accompany her class position in the Raj; she may resent the climate and the people, but she knows her place and performs her imperial duty with enthusiasm. The third example – the Foolhardy – is perhaps harder to define. For a start she usually displays feminist inclinations, which is part of her unwillingness to conform. India represents for her untold exotic mysteries, which in turn fascinate and repel her: her fate is to 'dabble' in things she knows nothing about, and to break the taboos of colonial society, usually with disastrous consequences both for herself and for her racial community.

The three types of characters that I have described articulate contrasting modes of white femininity, which in this example are defined in relation to particular constructions of black femininity and white masculinity. They each express different aspects of Englishness, conveying the complexity of social, political and economic relations in colonial society. Their recurrence in the fiction of this period confirms that gender as well as race and class is an important component of key ideological symbols. During my own research into this area, I became particularly fascinated by the Adela Questeds of colonial fiction, and by the way that their transgressive behaviour threatens to upset the whole system, revealing interlocking structures not just of race and class domination but of gender as well.

An episode in Paul Scott's *Jewel in the Crown*, also set in India but published in 1975, fifty years after Forster's novel, provides a further illustration of the theme of proto-feminist transgression. Daphne Manners, a young white woman with a similarly inquiring mind, was raped while meeting her Indian lover secretly one evening in a park. Despite her lack of co-operation – she refused to identify anyone, claiming that it could just as easily have been British soldiers blacked up – the authorities acted with swift repression, arresting and imprisoning several Indians, including her lover. The injustice of this response and its effect on the nationalist movement formed one of the main themes of Scott's quartet. These powerful images of white female vulnerability set against black male sexual aggression recur repeatedly in the imaginary world of the Raj, and are usually implicated in the legitimation of colonial authority. Like authority itself, these images are best subverted when the white women who are supposed to be passive victims refuse to behave as such and thereby challenge the whole system of racist and masculinist domination which is being defended in their name. As a result of their transgression, neither Adela nor Daphne were allowed to remain in their colonial communities. Daphne's punishment was particularly severe as she not only lost her lover but actually died as a result of giving birth to his child. This specifically female form of suffering can be read as a consequence of love 'across the colour line', another theme of so much colonial literature but one which often has an independence from issues of political repression and resistance. In Kipling's story, 'Beyond the Pale', it was the Indian woman who was punished for breaking the unwritten laws while her white lover, who disguised himself as a woman in order to visit her, learned the old colonial maxim too late:

> A man should, whatever happens, keep to his own caste, race, and breed. Let the White go to the White and the Black to the Black. Then, whatever trouble falls is in the ordinary course of things – neither sudden, alien, nor unexpected.[8]

Interracial sex frequently leads to death in colonial fiction, and it is important to ask what this means. Is it a discourse on the impossibility of love between a man and woman from entirely different cultures? If it is, then there would be little substance to the romance that invariably leads to such dramatic resolution. In Louis Bromfield's novel, *The Rains Came*, the wealthy white American who falls helplessly in love with an Indian surgeon acquires a humanity and humility she has hitherto lacked; but in her desire to convince her lover of her sincerity she falls victim to the outbreak of cholera which they are both involved in treating. Where white women are concerned, it would be useful to study the configuration of plots and characterizations that both lead to and result from their involvement in such dangerous territory.

Moving between fiction and history (what 'really' happened) is a difficult and often delicate process, but I think the idea of historical memory forms an important link between them. The recycling of literature helps to revise this memory, while an awareness of history can be useful in making sense of the imaginary or semi-fictional worlds. The clearest example of this relationship between fiction and history is provided by the theme which I have just discussed: the imagery of white female vulnerability threatened by black male aggression. This spectre, which was invariably enhanced by reports and rumours of actual events, was used effectively in the 1857 uprising in India to fuel desire for British revenge against the mutinous Sepoys. As I suggested in Part 1, this episode of colonial history helps to explain both how and why the safety of white women in the Empire became an ongoing ideological question, linked inextricably to the legitimation of colonial power. Most of the literature of colonialism that draws on the imagery of threatened white women refers back not necessarily to the uprising itself but to its historical memory, passed from one generation to another. In Forster's novel the panic that erupted among the British community at the thought of interracial rape was clearly connected to their terror of nationalist fervour and the loss of control by the authorities. To put it simply, the historical memory forms a familiar backdrop in the novel, while Forster's own narrative allows a closer examination of the ideological processes involved in the revision of that memory. As Jenny Sharpe writes in an essay called 'The Unspeakable Limits of Rape: Colonial Violence and Counter-Insurgency':

> If we are to read literature for its disruption of an ideological production that prevents social change, we can no longer afford to restrict our readings to the limits of the literary text. Rather we should regard the literature as working within, and sometimes against, the historical limits of representation. *A Passage to India* contends with a discourse of power capable of reducing anti-colonial struggle to the pathological lust of dark-skinned men for white women. Adela serves the narrative function of undermining such racial assumptions but then, having served her purpose, she is no longer of interest in the novel. The 'girl's sacrifice' . . . remains just that, a sacrifice for advancing a plot centered on the impossibility of a friendship between men across the colonial divide. As feminists, we should not reverse the terms of the 'sacrifice' but rather, negotiate between the sexual and racial constructions of the colonial female and native male without reducing one to the other.[9]

It is also important to try to connect this discussion of the relationship between colonial fiction and colonial history to the dynamics of race, class and gender in contemporary Britain.

Another urgent task for feminism is to deconstruct the symbolism of white womanhood in imperialist ideologies in relation to the actual experiences of those who lived in colonial societies in order to provide historical accounts that give a more complex view of the social relations entailed in colonialism. However, there are several problems that flow from this objective, which form the main concerns of my book: first, how is the relevant information about colonial society actually collected; second, the historical perspective needed to disentangle the complicated web of social relations relies on a knowledge and understanding of the interrelation of race, class and gender in history that has yet to be written; finally, there needs to be more detailed discussion of theoretical issues which analyse the connections between different systems of social domination, for example, or the way that categories like 'woman' or 'femininity' are to be used. As a way of combining some of the themes in all these essays, I want to turn to this question of theory.

## Common Ground

> Coherent theories in an obviously incoherent world are either silly and uninteresting or oppressive and problematic, depending on the degree of hegemony they manage to achieve. Coherent theories in an *apparently* coherent world are even more dangerous, for the world is always more complex than such unfortunately hegemonous theories can grasp.
>
> Sandra Harding[10]

To say that the British histories of black people and women have been interconnected is just another way of underlining the fact that race, class and sex continually intersect. It is at the more abstract level of theory that I feel that feminism in Britain is lacking a coherent account of these deceptively straightforward questions: why have black people *and* white women been dominated in different ways as a result of racist and masculinist hierarchies in British/European history? What are the connections between racism and the subordination of women, black and white? What, then, are the connections between the politics of black liberation, whether from slavery, colonialism or the racism of post-industrial society, and those of the different strands of feminism? Like most questions of theory, it is not the answers that are important so much as interesting and fruitful lines of inquiry. I want to look first at common ground shared by some black people and some women, as this might also help to explain similarities in how the two sets of oppression have been made to work. Although class is an essential factor in all these equations, for the sake of clarity I shall concentrate on race and gender for this part of my argument. To get straight to the point, here is a set of very simple questions which can all be answered in the negative.[11]

*Is it the way we are made?*

First, there is the question of biology. Whereas there are certain significant physical differences between the male and female body, the same cannot be said about people categorized as 'white' and 'non-white'. At the same time, there is still relatively little understanding about the relationship of biology to culture, which remains highly disputed territory.

It is when we look at *perceptions* of biological difference that there begin to be connections between race and gender domination. Nineteenth-century European evolutionism tried to rationalize the supposedly innate superiority of 'white' males by categorizing humans according to perceptible difference: both gender and 'racial' features such as skin colour have been the supposedly natural lines of differentiation. Other physical characteristics such as brain size, skull shape and size and genitals were used to justify and explain culturally determined social divisions, both along race lines and those of sex. As Sandra Harding says in *The Science Question in Feminism:* 'The division of humans into races is a cultural act, and how the division is made is extremely variable historically. Similarly,' she continues, 'the division of humans into two or more sexes depends upon a culture's interest in and ability to perceive sex differences at all, as well as upon what they are taken to consist in.' This statement offers a useful insight into colonial society where race interrupted the apparently simple division between men and women. It could be said that where a colonial elite presided over an indigenous population the differences between the lives of white women and black women and between the ways in which they perceived each other were so great that it is less useful to view them as a single category – women – rather than each as a compound of sex and race. The same would apply to black and white men, creating at least four different categories of difference.

*Is it the way we think?*

This question concerns the development of European scientific, rational thought which has legitimized theories of biological difference and defined both blacks and women as Other. White, masculinist science and epistemology – that is, the basis of Western thought – has been constructed within a set of conceptual dichotomies that gives 'man' dominance over the natural world: mind is separated from body, culture from nature, reason from emotion, knowing from being, self from others, objectivity from subjectivity. In each pair, to quote Sandra Harding again, 'the former is set to control the latter, lest the latter threaten to overwhelm the former, and the threatening "latter" in each case appears to be associated with the "feminine" in social hierarchies of masculine dominance, or with non-Europeans in the case of racial dominance.' However, the dichotomies are seemingly endless, and gender, race and class do not always fit so neatly on one or other side of the dividing line. Civilization, for example, is the other side of the coin to savagery. In some contexts, white women might indeed be associated with the idea that female nature is inherently uncivilized, primitive when compared to men, and lacking self-control. In the context of imperialism or modern racism, the dominant ideology would place white women firmly in the civilized camp, in opposition to non-European women whose lack of social and political rights are to be read as a mark of cultural savagery. This means that white women can occupy both sides of a binary opposition, which surely accounts for much of the confusion and ambivalence to be found in the ideology of gender relations.

The conceptual basis of European thought has been attacked by the development of postmodernist philosophy.[12] The definition of logical and rational thinking is itself shown to be an ethno-historically specific artefact that has changed even within the history of Western thought. The ways in which a society sees itself and its relationship to nature or other societies, for example, affects how it constructs theories of logic and rationality. The history of Western science, premised on the idea of continual technological progress, has shown clearly how beliefs about the origins of the universe or the properties of gravity, for example, discredit previous claims and therefore shift the ground of what appears to be logical explanation.

One of the clearest examples of this is the shifting boundaries of scientific culture that defines how 'man' himself is constituted. Donna Haraway explains this in her essay, 'A Manifesto for Cyborgs'.[13] What made 'man' human and special was partly his distinction from animals. In the late twentieth century, 'the last beachheads of uniqueness have been polluted, if not turned into amusement parks – language, tool use, social behaviour, mental events. Nothing really convincingly settles the separation of human and animals.' The biological and evolutionary theories which emphasized the lines between different categories of organisms have now reduced them to 'a faint trace re-etched in ideological struggle or professional disputes between life and social sciences'.

A second way that 'man' was defined was through his ability to create machines, which possessed no autonomy of their own, to work for him. But, as Haraway so convincingly puts it: 'Late-twentieth-century machines have made thoroughly ambiguous the difference betwen natural and artificial, mind and body, self-developing and externally designed, and many other distinctions that used to apply to organisms and machines. Our machines are disturbingly lively, and we ourselves frighteningly inert.'

An obvious question that arises from this: if there is no such thing as 'man', can there be 'woman'?

*Is it what we do?*

The final seam of inquiry relates to the social division of labour. It is generally agreed that the domination of women by men provided the first model of the human division of labour but as yet very little is known about how and when gender, class and race became interlocking systems. In the meantime, the short answer to the above question is that the life of each member of society today is determined to some extent by the division of labour – a division which affects individuals' psychological development and education, and therefore often their economic prospects in adulthood as well.

In other words, women do not perform domestic labour because this type of work demands skills that are essentially feminine, but because of historically and culturally specific meanings attached to being female. Black people do not occupy the low-paid sector because they are intrinsically less able, but because racism systematically denies them opportunities to qualify for better paid jobs. However, women's role as primary carer for the very young is more complicated because of their experience of pregnancy, childbirth and breastfeeding. Feminist theorists continue to contest the ground between the two poles of essentialism and constructivism – how we are and how we are made to be.

The answers to these three questions may not tell us why systems of race and gender subordination have existed for so long, but at least they help to explain how they have been maintained. The set of theoretical questions that I suggested earlier lines the route to the very heart of feminist knowledge and understanding, a heart which is inevitably claimed and wooed by theorists of many different persuasions. Feminist epistemology has never been under such intense scrutiny, and there is still little consensus over the definition of the concept of gender or indeed whether it is useful to separate sex from gender as an analytic category. My own interest in treading this path is to develop more solid ground for opposing all forms of domination, and I now want to return to the themes that emerged from each of the historical sections in order to assess their relevance to feminist political action today.

## Themes through History

> When the true history of the Anti-Slavery cause shall be written, women will occupy a large space in its pages; for the cause of the slave has been peculiarly women's cause.
>
> Frederick Douglass

One of the themes that runs through the histories of women and black people is the extent to which their various struggles for emancipation relate to each other. I took slavery as the first example of the ways in which white women turned to the situation of enslaved black people in order to understand, interpret or sympathize with the experiences of another social group. Having made these connections, it is important not to idealize them, and to recognize that they emerged or disappeared depending on whether or not they were useful to the women making them at the time. But this was very much the beginning of a process that continues today, and that has implications for defining what we want in future.

This kind of political empathy or affinity may be a preliminary stage towards but is not a substitute for making actual alliances. It is more a question of one group of people being able to see parallels between their own subordination and that of another set of people, not necessarily of the same class, gender or racial group, and possibly living hundreds of miles away. The connections may not be mutual, or even welcome, but the act of making them is a vital stage in developing an awareness of the nature of domination, or possibly even of the process of revolution itself. There are pragmatic aspects of this kind of relationship, however one-sided or idealistic it is, which might be more easily recognizable. In Part 1 I described how American feminists in the 1960s began organizing as a result of social and political upheaval stemming largely from the civil rights movement. Some of the language from this movement and tactics such as sit-ins and other forms of non-violent protest were borrowed directly from black activists to become an integral part of political campaigns waged by other groups, especially feminists. This is not simply because women preferred non-violence on practical grounds; there was also a recognizable element of anti-militarism and hence anti-masculinism in that form of 'peaceful' protest, whoever was carrying it out. Another more recent example is the way some environmental groups have adopted beliefs and practices formerly associated with Native Americans to affirm their relationship to the earth.

The extent to which this borrowing, or appropriating, is acknowledged obviously varies a great deal, but I think it can potentially provide an important link between different types of struggles. As I argued in Part 1, having an awareness of the genealogy of a particular political struggle can be a way of recognizing the intersection of race, class and gender that gives it its momentum. In practical terms, however, it is important to move beyond sympathy and self-recognition to forming alliances that give a different weight to the politics being expressed. For example, many people in Britain, black or white, might feel strongly about apartheid or famine because they identify in different ways with the victims of these kinds of oppression. At what point, if at all, does donating money or wearing T-shirts and badges become effective in challenging global and local networks of power?

It is also important to recognize that there is no necessary or automatic connection between people just because they feel oppressed, and that shared oppression often works to distance different groups of people from each other, particularly if there is an element of competition. Turning to the example of suffrage and slavery in the USA, some of the leading feminists who had been so active in the abolitionist movement became positively hostile to black suffrage when they split from the Equal Rights Association. Similarly there were tensions within the British suffrage movement over the question of class: many women feared that their cause would be dragged down by the prospect of working-class people becoming enfranchised and tried to dissociate themselves from demands for universal suffrage in the interests of votes for particular categories of women.

Sometimes this empathy deepens to form the basis of alliances. The early history of feminism in the USA provides one of the most celebrated examples of an alliance that fell awkwardly apart when different sets of political priorities became counterposed. It is important to return to the minutes of the Equal Rights Association meeting, at which black and white men and women argued their different priorities, in order to understand how bitter the split was. So eloquent and heartfelt were the speeches it is hard at times not to be swayed by both sides, and subsequent accounts are inevitably weighted according to the political standpoints of their authors.[14]

In Britain, where the suffrage issue was fought on entirely different grounds, it was the question of lynching, discussed in Part 4, that best illustrates the complexities of political alliance between black people and white women. The women who supported Ida B. Wells in the campaign against lynching were, whether they meant to or not, actually challenging certain ideas about women and femininity which were contributing to their own subordination. This made their solidarity and political work all the more effective and radical. On the other hand, Frances Willard and her followers were unable to match their beliefs about women's rights with their ideas about race and the behaviour of black men in particular. Although at one level they declared that they had no problem with the demand for racial equality, in practice they were unable to face up to the implications of their own political doctrines on the oppression of women. In other words they insisted that black men were still higher than white women in the hierarchy of gender dominance, and were reluctant to admit that white women dominated black men as well as black women in the hierarchy of race relations. Their anger came in part from the fact that it was a black woman, whose social position was at the bottom of both systems of dominance, who was challenging them most insistently.

This pattern has been repeated throughout Europe, North America and wherever whites have colonized non-European peoples. It has shown itself consistently around the spectre of black male violence against white women, which continues to haunt racist societies, although there are other types of situation that produce similar configurations of alliance and conflict. In order to build solid political alliances in the future there has to be some awareness of the historical processes that have brought different groups together and kept them apart.

The contradiction between the unifying category of women and the particularities of race and class is another theme that emerges very strongly. Annette Ackroyd provides a perfect example of a feminist who was ill equipped and unable to deal with the differences between women across race and culture. The spectacle of a middle-class white feminist setting out to help educate Indian women, only to find that she could not tolerate the way that most of them dressed, sat or ate, might give some people sufficient reason for dismissing her, but her life symbolizes the perpetual crisis within women's politics over the negotiation of race and class differences which has everything to do with racism and imperialism. Feminism has battled with the problem of representing the experiences of all women, while the social hierarchies of race and class ensure that the complexities and contradictions of women's lives cannot be easily articulated or contained. The influence of nineteenth-century imperialism on British feminism since Annette Ackroyd's futile attempts to work with Indian women needs to be explored in more detail, but the main problem seems to stem from the belief that 'women' were a universal category in a way 'men' were not. Historically, ideas about what constituted 'womanhood' were culturally defined within a masculinist social structure; the fact of difference itself was rarely disputed while the main area of struggle was the significance given to various types of difference, whether physical, mental or spiritual, and the relevance it had to equality. In the same way, ideas about femininity – what was acceptable, deviant, exotic – were constructed as part of a complex system of control and resistance. Both race and class were important factors that determined how these constructs were developed, maintained and perceived. Although I have only dealt with the history of the nineteenth century there is enough evidence to assert that the deconstruction of concepts like 'woman', 'women' and 'femininity' in any period will yield important clues about the links between race, gender and class domination.

The final theme of this book, and in a way the most problematic, is the need for a political language that will express the differences between people without losing sight of the aims and ideals that we have in common. During the early nineteenth century it was religion that provided the main source of imagery for emancipation of any kind, just as it was the institution of racial slavery that gave it its urgency. The concept of brotherhood used by Catherine Impey represented one strand of politics that crossed the line between liberal and religious activity, but it was not able to withstand the emerging secular language of socialism. One hundred years later the vocabularies of socialism and communism no longer function to inspire radical political action. Ecology may be able to provide the basis of a new language, as it questions the relationship of humans to their environments and demands a new basis on which societies can be built and maintained, but on its own it is not enough. There is a search going on for new reference points, new concepts with which to describe exciting and visionary futures for all those who have been marginalized by the dominating structures of race, class and gender. Trying to talk about race, and gender, without forgetting class, is constantly a struggle against the urge to over-simplify and generalize without over-stressing particularity; against the urge to speak for others without ignoring them entirely; against the urge to run away from complicated and contradictory desires and feelings, without losing sight of the way identities are interconnected. Feminism and the politics of black liberation share the goal of redefining language and of ridding the ways in which we speak and understand each other of negative and oppressive meaning.

## Femininity and Nature – A Clean Break?

In the course of writing this I came across a most bizarre feature in a glossy women's magazine which, I felt, demonstrated some of the problems of trying to articulate a radical viewpoint without seeing connections between race and gender. On the front cover of the journal (winner of the Women's Magazine of the Year) was the heading 'Group Sex, False Wives in Brazil'. Flicking through I was startled to find a double-page spread showing a row of Kayapo women, semi-naked with painted faces, who were described as women who are 'strong, resilient and love to dance'. The article in question was entitled 'Mystics and Magic' and took the form of a travel diary written by Anita Roddick on two recent trips abroad, first to Nepal and shortly after to the Brazilian rainforest. The introduction to the article read:

> In parts of Nepal people live on roof-tops, women have several husbands, and mystics make love to corpses. In the Brazilian rainforest, people decorate themselves to look like parrots, and natural medicines include plant extracts to stop menstruation. This is what Anita Roddick discovered on two journeys she made last year in search of recipes and ingredients for Body Shop products, and ways to help protect these peoples' increasingly fragile environments.[15]

The first picture showed, as one might expect after such a lead-in, a robust-looking Anita Roddick, founder of the mega-successful Body Shop enterprise, surrounded by a group of Nepalese children who were described in a caption as 'inhabitants of a hostile natural environment who suffer from serious vitamin deficiency and a lack of hygiene and medication'. I could not help being struck by the similarity of this image to early photos of the white female missionary sitting amid a group of pupils or converts. Skimming through the text my eye caught the sentence: 'This may seem abhorrent, but what is extreme and odd to us they consider natural.' I turned the page. 'The last thing in the world I'd ever want to be in this society is a woman or a dog.' And two columns later: 'With the women, on the other hand, there is a great sense of camaraderie. I find it wonderful therapy to be able to touch and stroke these women. It is a great release to be in a society where one is able to be tactile and show affection without being regarded as odd.' In Brazil, where Roddick visited the Kayapo on her second foraging trip, the atmosphere was altogether different: 'Sexual activity among the Kayapo is "extremely natural" . . . a lot of horniness goes on. The men are forever lusting after the women and the women teasing and playing with the men, but there is none of the squealing and hiding that you notice in our society.' In the concluding paragraph I learned that the Kayapo are to be idealized/idolized because they live 'in complete harmony with their environment'. This was in contrast to Nepal where Roddick found the 'absolutely natural' way of life of the Sadhus, the 'crazy holy men', unthinkable.

What I found most extraordinary was the insidious way that the female reader was being invited to share this vision of heaven and hell through an assumption of shared interests in Body Shop products and a prurience relating to the sex lives of 'natural' peoples. Throughout the feature – and no doubt this was due entirely to the efforts of the editorial staff – captions for the images managed to mention 'penis' in connection with both societies. Details of Roddick's own health and hang-ups ('going to the lavatory within sight or earshot of anyone else') increased the sense of intimate revelations, while the uninhibited use of 'we', meaning 'First World', and 'they', meaning 'Third World' (that is, underdeveloped), gave a very familiar perspective to the undoubtedly well-meant endeavour. The images of exotic peoples, some of them posed and self-conscious, some ethnographical, told their own story. Interestingly, the advertisement on the very next page showed a sleek white couple, entirely naked and entwined round each other, the product being Calvin Klein's perfume 'Obsession' for men. In this context the idea of 'naturalness' was being constructed through very different reference points.

As the introduction to the article stated, the aim of the two trips east and west was to combine a search for new recipes and raw ingredients for cosmetics with attempts to set up environmental projects that would benefit the local people. Anita Roddick is an important figure in environmental politics: she has been described as 'the originator of the movement that allowed us to consume, with a nod to conscience, cosmetics and then petrol, washing up liquid, investments, and still campaign for Amnesty International and the rain forests.'[16] As I read the article, I felt that it raised some pertinent questions about the current state of green consumerism. In short, it was implying that we girls in the West can have smooth and fragrant skin and hair in return for subsidizing ecologically sound agricultural products in places where being a female is comparable to being a dog, because life is so arduous. Yet, 'we' are told, as long as this is 'natural' then it is all right.

At the centre of this proposition is the connection between femininity – that is, what it means to be female – and nature, a subject of intense debate among feminists and their opponents that goes back centuries. The category of women in this article is itself problematic. Roddick described aspects of their lives as they appeared engaging or remarkable to her, but she found very little that she had in common with them and generally seemed to feel more comfortable with the men in both societies. This impression had the effect of sharpening the reader's focus on the brand of feminism which ran seductively through Roddick's monologue. It was there in her interest in women's lives and the sexual division of labour, her independence and her readiness to admit her own physical weakness, her hard-headed business sense as she pursued a new source of raw materials, combined with an unconvincing aside that she was brought up to think that capitalism was evil. One of the 200 richest people in Britain, Roddick embodies a kind of green, feminist capitalism which was made possible by the political and economic conditions of the 1980s.

On the other hand she did enjoy a brief experience of a shared female identity when she went to wash in the river with the women in Nepal: 'It was a beautiful ritual – they gave me ground-up herbs to use on my hair.' This anecdote highlighted a particular version of femininity – a positively natural way of being female – which Body Shop products are designed to encourage. There is a suggestion here that activities like this, which involve real herbs and traditional rituals, allow us to get closer to 'nature', and temporarily dissolve our differences with women from entirely different cultures.

It is relatively easy to see how ideas about 'nature' are central to the environmental movement, even if people disagree as to the meaning of the word. At the same time, green consumerism – that is, the creation of a new economic market in response to a perceived demand – has made many women feel uneasy about the way that environmentalism can often confirm woman's traditional roles as mother, carer and cleaner by portraying them as an aspect of the 'natural' world. Ideas about femininity and 'nature' have long been important concerns of feminism too: for over a century feminists in different parts of the world have been divided over the connections between women and nature, and over the nature of women's nature, in fact, and these tensions are still rife today. Eco-feminism, for example, is often associated with ideas about women that were prevalent in the nineteenth century: that women's biology gives them a special relationship to nature, and that women are essentially superior to men, both morally and spiritually. Socialist feminists, and those who look for materialist causes of male domination, have tended to reject suggestions that biology gives women a privileged connection to nature, arguing instead that it is the division of labour which stems from women's reproductive role that has configured women's subordination.

As the world approaches the end of the twentieth century each of these two positions begins to look outdated. The very concept of 'knowledge' is under attack, primarily from postmodernist critiques of philosophy, which have enormous implications for how concepts like 'nature' are understood. In this society, for example, the study of the so-called natural sciences was created, developed and given social significance at particular moments in history. For quite specific reasons 'nature' became something that had to be dominated in order for it not to overwhelm 'culture', which was thought to distinguish humans from the rest of the natural world.

Because of women's capacity for childbirth, the line separating 'natural' processes from 'cultural' has never been so clearly drawn as it has with men. But the division of labour in Western societies has been organized according to where this line appears to fall. Why is it that so many so-called green products are connected to housework and why has so much advertising focused on women's role in cleaning up the environment in the home? Possibly because it is women who are charged with the tasks of cleaning toilets and baths, handling food, changing nappies, in other words, trying to keep the 'natural' world at bay in order for men to carry on reproducing 'culture'.

The world of the Body Shop and the connections between women and nature that it seeks to encourage – cleanliness, fragrance, ideas about bodily hygiene – are all associated with a particular kind of femininity which dates back to the sanitary reform campaigns of Victorian Britain. In 1859 women officially joined the crusade for improving public and private health with the founding of the Ladies Association for the Diffusion of Sanitary Knowledge (LADSK). This was an organization of middle-class women who saw it as their moral duty to visit the poor and teach them about the virtues of fresh air, good diet, clean clothes and houses, and clean living. Since it was women who prepared food and who were responsible for negotiating dirt and disease in the private sphere, they were prime targets for health education. A precursor of the health visitors' movement formed nearly fifty years later, the network of local groups provided opportunities for women to move into a highly important area of social reform. However, there was another aspect to the proliferation of pamphlets with sensible titles like *The Power of Soap and Water*. As cleanliness was next to godliness, it was also part of racial hygiene. In a speech made at the inaugural ceremony of the LADSK , Charles Kingsley, who identified sanitary reform with 'the will of God', urged women to recognize that 'one of the noblest duties' was 'to help the increase of the English race as much as possible' in order to colonize the Empire. Personal cleanliness had become an index of class difference within Britain. It also provided another measure of civilization in the colonies.[17]

In her account of her travels abroad, Roddick was reaffirming the connection between femininity and personal hygiene in her role as provider of a particular branch of cleaning materials and cosmetics. Yet after finishing 'Mystics and Magic' I was left with the question: Why does it make me so sick? I am as eager for effective face creams as the next woman, I admit to being a green consumer, and I am also interested to know how women in other societies live. I decided that there were two main problems.

First, I was disturbed by the absence of any kind of explanation for the way that the world has been degraded, environmentally, politically, economically. There was no sense that colonialism or racism might have been a factor in anyone's lives, including Roddick's own. In fact, her diary of impressions and experiences replicated the ready assumption of superiority which is the familiar cultural baggage of the white Western traveller, male or female. Second, the article raised the problem inherent in many types of green consumerism, where the act of purchasing something is offered to the consumer as a substitute for other forms of political action. In this case, it suggests the possibility that choosing a particular brand of cosmetics becomes instrumental in saving the Brazilian rainforest; and that by buying 'natural' products women are embracing a supposedly natural way of being female that will somehow ensure the protection of the planet.

## Non-Innocent Categories

> It has become difficult to name one's feminism by a single adjective – or even to insist in every circumstance upon the noun. Consciousness of exclusion through naming is acute. Identities seem contradictory, partial, and strategic.
>
> Donna Haraway[18]

Travel writing is an obvious place to explore ideas about what is essentially female, or essentially anything human in fact. In another article, a million miles from Anita Roddick's, June Jordan concentrated on her relationship to black domestic servants whom she met while on holiday in the Bahamas. Her discomfort in the contrast between her own situation as holiday-maker and that of the woman cleaning her hotel room led her to conclude that:

> Race and class and gender remain as real as the weather. But what they must mean about the contact between two individuals is less obvious and, like the weather, unpredictable. . . . When these factors of race and class and gender absolutely collapse is whenever you try to use them as automatic concepts of connection. They may serve well as indicators of commonly felt conflict, but as elements of connection they seem about as reliable as precipitation probability for the day after the night before the day.[19]

Immediately on her return to the USA she found herself involved in supporting a white woman seeking refuge from a violent husband. What might have seemed a more unlikely connection to another woman's predicament was given meaning through an understanding and shared experience of male violence – 'commonly felt conflict'.

In an interview given on her first expedition to Britain, June Jordan explained further what she meant:

> We have been organising on the basis of identity, around immutable attributes of gender, race and class for a long time and it doesn't seem to have worked. . . . I think there is something deficient in the thinking on the part of anybody who proposes either gender identity politics or race identity politics as sufficient, because every single one of us is more than whatever race we represent or embody and more than whatever gender category we fall into.[20]

There was a time when it was a heresy to suggest that there was nothing about being a woman, or being working class, or being black or being a lesbian that necessarily guaranteed anything about a person's political orientation. At best this meant that women were able to deal honestly with differences between them, and to use them as a basis for a shared politics. At worst, this inevitably produced a certain amount of tokenism, particularly in the field of employment, where many black women found that they were given jobs in predominantly white organizations and then expected to deal with matters of race, often without the support of white colleagues. There was also a belief in the hierarchy of oppressions, however much people argued against it and tried to resist it, a belief that allocated credentials to women on the basis of race, ethnicity, class or sexuality. Despite the problems and difficulties involved in allowing different feminist viewpoints to co-exist, there was at least a recognition, at long last, that being female was not enough. As Donna Haraway puts it again:

> White women, including EuroAmerican socialist feminists, discovered (i.e. were forced kicking and screaming to notice) the noninnocence of the category 'woman'. That consciousness changes the configuration of all previous categories; it denatures them as heat denatures a fragile protein.[21]

Yet if feminists have begun to discuss the use and misuse of the categories of woman/women, the concept of femininity has perhaps retained some of its innocence. While it has been deconstructed as a historically class-specific phenomenon, it is still rare in Britain to see an investigation into the racial meanings attached to being a white woman.

Theorizing can sometimes make me feel disconnected from political action. Then I remember one occasion, a meeting on feminism and racism called in response to the increase in racial attacks in London in 1986, which illustrated some of the problems in negotiating race, class and gender in politics. It was proposed that women at the meeting, who were white, take turns to sit with Bengali families on a particular housing estate threatened by persistent violent attacks. One woman said she felt uncomfortable in the presence of Bengali men, and declared that she did not intend to hide her feminism. The minutes to the meeting read:

> Women expressed the need to be up-front about feminist politics and not lose them 'for the sake of the larger struggle'; to give strength to each other when we are working in mixed organisations; and to recognise that men are on the receiving end of racism too, so that working with families involves coming into contact with them.

On the one hand I had sympathy with the reluctance many women expressed about working in mixed organizations with men; but I was naive perhaps in being surprised that some women felt so defensive at the prospect of dealing with black men, as though black men were not integral to the families that were being supported. No one questioned the assumption that Bengali men would be wary of or hostile to white feminists, because of their feminism. For all the awkwardness of the non-innocent categories, we are still left with social relations of race, class and gender that determine very real patterns of poverty, racial and sexual violence, discrimination and other forms of domination, and the ways in which people respond to them. So how does the act of deconstructing femininity actually affect how these relations are experienced?

In Part 1 I examined some of the ways in which comparisons between different kinds of femininity serve to highlight or even symbolize the supposed superiority of white, Western societies. This has been a theme throughout the book, as I frequently encountered nineteenth-century writers of different political persuasions who claimed that the position of women could be read as an index of civilization. Purdah, arranged marriages, the dowry system, were held up as examples of non-European, non-rational and even 'primitive' customs which marked out the societies that practised them as backward and needing to be civilized. The veil, and the degree to which women are obliged to cover their heads, continues to be one of the most potent symbols of cultural difference in the twentieth century. Women's bodies have become the site of cultural and political struggle that has implications far beyond the immediate practical use of the *hajib*, or headscarf. Both within European countries as well as in countries that are predominantly Muslim, women have been involved in battles over the conditions of its wearing which have been fraught with irony, contradiction and bitterness.[22] In 1990, the French government and the anti-racist movement were split over whether to allow schoolgirls the right to cover their heads. There was tension between the liberal anti-racist view that argued for cultural pluralism and support for minorities, and those who felt that the *hajib* was a symbol of fundamentalism which was counter to the secularism in French schools. The same year in Britain, two sisters, Fatima and Aisha Alvi, who attempted to wear their headscarves in secondary school, were banned for health and safety reasons. After a great deal of media attention the governors of the school reversed the decision, allowing the girls to wear them as long as they were in school colours and did not present a safety hazard.

For British feminists the veil presents something of a problem, theoretically at least, since the act of covering the head suggests submission to men. It poses the question: to what extent should women support other women's right to practise customs which appear to confirm their own subordination? The Rushdie Affair provided an opportunity for many people to voice their anxieties over the 'treatment of women' in Muslim communities in an attempt to highlight what they see as the real reason why their presence is unacceptable in a modern rational society. Fay Weldon, in her pamphlet, *Sacred Cows*, made a provocative statement on this subject as part of her feminist attack on multiculturalism.[23] For her the problem is 'the Muslim women in our midst, with their arranged marriages, their children in care, their high divorce rate: the wife-beatings, the penalties for incalcitrance: the unregulated work in Dickensian sweat-shops'. Although her rant was directed against the hypocrisy and cowardice of the middle classes, she reserved a special sort of venom for white feminists who, she claimed, found it 'easier to be seen on the side of the ethnic minorities, all in favour of the multicultural, too idle to sort out the religious from the racial, from the political: too frightened of being labelled as white racist, elitist, to interfere'. Black feminists, on the other hand, were 'too put-upon by the black brothers, who insist that any white interference is by definition racist, the imposing of white middle class standards upon ethnic working class people, to dare say no, no we are all sisters, our problems are all the same'.

To be able to say that 'our problems are all the same' because we are all women, and therefore sisters, sounds worthy of Frances Willard, and it is no coincidence that Weldon picked a nineteenth-century image to describe the oppression of Muslim women living in Britain. It is patently absurd and quite anachronistic, betraying a lack of imagination as to how complex social relations really are. However, she is right in her observations that some feminists have been wary of commenting on or interfering in what they see as a 'different culture', though whether that was through idleness or fear is another matter. Post-war feminist analysis of central theoretical questions such as the family and male violence, with a few exceptions, steered clear of cultural difference partly because racism, or lack of awareness of racism, made it too difficult to understand the social relations of 'different cultures'. It was mainly through the insistence of black women that the variety of women's lives in post-industrial Britain began to be acknowledged in the last decade.

Yet the question of cultural difference has remained a problem for feminism. It was constantly thrown up in the 1980s over the issue of arranged marriages and immigration laws, only to disappear into a cul-de-sac of unresolved contradictions. *Feminist Review*, for example, carried a series of articles in 1985–86 which tried to re-examine and debate socialist feminism and racism. One author, who discussed what she called the limits of cultural pluralism, began by stating that 'the call to respect cultural patterns uncritically' was problematic for feminists.[24] Whatever the merits of her particular argument, I personally have problems with the idea that there has ever been such a call. To claim this, in my view, is to misunderstand the nature of the relationship between black and white women and between race and gender. It is as if the only way white women can understand the demands that black women have been making for their support in fighting racism is to find problems in how they give that support, since it seems to involve respecting cultural practices that are distinctly unfeminist.

There is rarely a suggestion that white women have their own particular relationship to the idea of racial difference, a relationship which might give them a different but connected route to fighting racism, to providing support for black women, without compromising their feminist principles. As this book has demonstrated, the meanings of all the different ways of being female are constantly being referred to each other, so that women's qualities are always relative. White middle-class women are frequently seen in the dominant culture as representing a 'normal' type of femininity – although the boundaries of normality shift constantly – at the expense of other types of women, whether white working-class, non-European, black, Jewish, depending on the context. White women may appear to be 'liberated' compared to Asian women, while stereotypical ideas about the sexuality of Afro-Caribbean women might make them seem deviant and uncontrolled in comparison to white women. Thus different kinds of femininity can articulate racial and cultural difference, and in doing so help to secure domination by gender, race and class.

If it is accepted that definitions of womanhood and femininity are culturally constructed within the interlocking systems of domination that they also help to shape, then feminism actually needs to bring women together to take them apart. White and black women can unite not so much in favour of women being able to wear headscarves but against the combination of gender, class and race relations that forbids cultural differences and fears that the dominant culture will be 'swamped' by an Other one. Similarly, feminists can dissociate themselves from racist assumptions about predatory black men and vulnerable white women while continuing to campaign against violence from men in general. Just as black women have had to identify and oppose racist definitions of their identity as women in their struggles against racism and female subordination, so white women can potentially open up new avenues of political strategy and alliance by refusing racist definitions of white femininity.

Writing this book has confirmed my conviction that a historical perspective is needed to help break into the contemporary codes of race and gender, but I have arrived at a very different point from where I started. I look forward to a future in which an awareness of certain historical processes permits greater freedom and creativity in building new political coalitions and forcing an end to economic and social structures that exploit and oppress. Whereas when I began I was dubious about the prospects of a feminism that would be able to resolve some of the enormous problems and contradictions that women's politics had raised, now I feel greatly optimistic about the chances of developing networks and alliances that cut across race, class and gender in ways that might have seemed unthinkable in the

1970s or even the 1980s. That is not to say that post-war feminism is necessarily out-dated, but to emphasize the radically altered political and economic map of the world that we all face in the 1990s.

The arguments that I have made in all these essays rest on my conviction that political unity between women across race and class is potentially one of the greatest forces for change in the world, but that there is nothing about being a woman which necessarily guarantees that unity. If feminism is to survive the fragmentation of women's politics which has been happening as a result of realizing this lack of guarantees, then feminists need to acknowledge the inescapable diversity of femininity and womanhood without losing sight of the ways that we are all what Jane Flax refers to as 'prisoners of gender'. This means working out the dynamics of race, class and gender in every situation that demands a political response – adopting what some have called 'strategic identities' which allow opposition to one form of domination without being complicit in another. I recognize the dangers in over-simplifying what are infinitely complex and fractal patterns of social relations, constantly affected by the refinement of communication technologies and bio-technologies. As Sandra Harding says: ' "Something out there" is changing relations between races, classes and cultures as well as between genders – probably quite a few "somethings" – at a pace that outstrips our theorizing.'[25] Perhaps it is the very speed with which the changes are taking place that makes an awareness of history all the more urgent.

## Notes

1 From 'Aladdin, or Love Will Find a Way' by V. C. Clinton-Baddeley, London 1949, quoted in John Mackenzie, *Propaganda and Empire* (Manchester University Press, Manchester 1984, p. 57) as an example of the enduring nature of 'lively patriotic songs' in popular theatre.

2 In this Part I have used the words 'colonialism' and 'imperialism' almost interchangeably, except that the former refers more to systems and structures of domination in the colonies while the latter is used to describe the ideologies that sustained colonial rule. The adjective 'colonial' therefore refers to societies in the British Empire.

3 Helen Callaway, *Gender, Culture and Empire: European Women in Colonial Nigeria*, Macmillan, London 1987; Hilary Callan and Shirley Ardener eds, *Incorporated Wives*, Croom Helm, London/Sydney/Dover 1984.

4 Adrienne Rich, 'Disloyal to Civilisation', in *On Lies, Secrets and Silence*, W. W. Norton, New York/London 1979, p. 281.

5 See Patrick Brantlinger, *Rule of Darkness, British Imperialism, 1830–1914*, Cornell

University Press, Ithaca/London 1988; Robin Jared Lewis, 'The Literature of the Raj', in Robin W. Winks and James R. Rush, eds, *Asia in Western Fiction*, Manchester University Press, Manchester 1990.

6 I am thinking not just of the aviator hero, Biggles, or the books of Enid Nesbit. The heroine of *The Secret Garden* (Frances Hodgson Burnett), for example, is an English child born and brought up in India by an ayah. She was so traumatized by her colonial upbringing that she could only relate to the working-class people around her as if they were her Indian servants, and the story revolves round her transformation into a 'normal' English girl.

7 The book, *A Passage to India*, by E. M. Forster was first published in 1924. The film, directed by David Lean, was made in 1984.

8 For discussion of this extraordinary story, see Dick Hebdige, 'The Chronicles of Zero', *Emergency*, no. 4, 1986.

9 Jenny Sharpe, 'The Unspeakable Limits of Rape: Colonial Violence and Counter-Insurgency', *Genders*, no. 10, Spring 1991.

10 Sandra Harding, *The Science Question in Feminism*, Open University Press, Milton Keynes 1986, p. 164.

11 These questions are based on Sandra Harding's consideration of what she calls the 'curious coincidence of African and feminine world views' (*The Science Question in Feminism*, pp. 165–96). It proved too complicated to summarize her argument without doing injustice to it, and I can only recommend her book.

12 Jane Flax, *Thinking Fragments: Psychoanalysis, Feminism, & Postmodernism in the Contemporary West*, University of California Press, Berkeley, CA/Oxford 1990.

13 Donna Haraway, 'A Manifesto for Cyborgs: Science, Technology, and Socialist Feminism in the 1980s', in Linda J. Nicholson, ed., *Feminism/Postmodernism*, Routledge, New York/London 1990, pp. 193–4.

14 See, for example, Kathleen Barry, *Susan B. Anthony, A Biography*, New York University Press, New York/London 1988, pp. 185–6. In her account:

> Few have understood Anthony and Stanton's desperation and the isolation that resulted from the Republican and abolitionist opposition to them during the Train episode. Because they were committed to not prioritizing the rights of one group over another and because theirs was a special commitment to women, they refused to abandon the women's cause or subordinate it or themselves to the men who tried to dominate them. In doing so, they appeared to be taking a proslavery or antiblack position, thus prioritizing rights after all . . . In those painful moments of isolation, Anthony and Stanton learned that no political party or reform movement led by men could be their sustained natural ally, such as Republicans and abolitionists had been for black male slaves.

In *Women, Race and Class* (Random House, New York 1981, p. 76) Angela Y. Davis wrote:

> Whether the criticism of the Fourteenth and Fifteenth Amendments expressed by the leaders of the women's rights movement was justifiable or not is still being debated. But one thing seems clear: the defence of their own interests as white middle-class women – in a frequently egotistical and elitist fashion – exposed the tenuous and superficial nature of their relationship to the postwar campaign for Black equality . . . in articulating their opposition with arguments invoking the privileges of white supremacy, they revealed how defenceless they remained – even after years of involvement in progressive causes – to the pernicious ideological influence of racism.

15 *Marie-Claire*, February 1990.

16 'Icons of Our Age', *Guardian*, 18 April 1990.

17 Sue Cavanagh and Vron Ware, *At Women's Convenience: A Handbook on the Design of Women's Public Toilets*, Women's Design Service, London 1990, pp. 14–15.

18 In Nicholson, ed., pp. 196–7.

19 June Jordan, 'Report From the Bahamas', in *On Call*, South End Press, Boston 1985, p. 46.

20 Interview with Pratibha Parmar, *Spare Rib*, November 1987.

21 In Nicholson, ed., p. 199.

22 Ruth Mandel, 'Turkish Headscarves and the "Foreigner Problem" ', *New German Critique*, no. 46, Winter 1989.

23 Fay Weldon, *Sacred Cows*, Chatto & Windus, London 1989, pp. 35–6.

24 Sue Lees, 'Sex, Race and Culture: Feminism and the Limits of Cultural Pluralism', *Feminist Review*, no. 22, Spring 1986.

25 Harding, p. 244.

# Index